Insurance Redlining

GREGORY D. SQUIRES
Editor

Insurance Redlining

Disinvestment, Reinvestment, and the
Evolving Role of Financial Institutions

THE URBAN INSTITUTE PRESS
Washington, D.C.

Library of Congress Cataloging in Publication Data

Insurance Redlining: Disinvestment, Reinvestment, and the Evolving Role of Financial Institutions/Edited by Gregory D. Squires.

1. Homeowner's insurance—United States. 2. Discrimination in insurance—United States. I. Squires, Gregory D.

HG9986. 3. I57   1997   96-49249
368'. 096—dc 21   CIP

ISBN 0-87766-666-0 (paper, alk. paper)
ISBN 0-87766-665-2 (cloth, alk. paper)

Printed in the United States of America.

HG9986.3 .I57 1997

Insurance redlining :
disinvestment,

Distributed in North America by:
University Press of America
4720 Boston Way
Lanham, MD 20706

THE URBAN INSTITUTE is a nonprofit policy research and educational organization established in Washington, D.C., in 1968. Its staff investigates the social and economic problems confronting the nation and public and private means to alleviate them. The Institute disseminates significant findings of its research through the publications program of its Press. The goals of the Institute are to sharpen thinking about societal problems and efforts to solve them, improve government decisions and performance, and increase citizen awareness of important policy choices.

Through work that ranges from broad conceptual studies to administrative and technical assistance, Institute researchers contribute to the stock of knowledge available to guide decision making in the public interest.

Conclusions or opinions expressed in Institute publications are those of the authors and do not necessarily reflect the views of staff members, officers or trustees of the Institute, advisory groups, or any organizations that provide financial support to the Institute.

ACKNOWLEDGMENTS

I have often referred to the issue of insurance redlining as the ugly duckling of the fair housing movement. Over the years much has been learned about the sale and rental of homes, mortgage lending, appraisal practices, zoning ordinances, and other aspects of housing and housing-related services. Behavior and minds have been changed, generally for the better. But relatively little attention has been paid to the causes and consequences of insurance redlining. This is starting to change.

Much of the research, litigation, and other organizing activity related to insurance practices that has occurred, with increasing frequency in recent years, is chronicled in the pages of this book. While attention to insurance redlining concerns has intensified in recent years, this movement does have its pioneers.

Among those who have long raised questions about the insurance industry and challenges to traditional private practice and public policy are Bob Hunter, Howard Clark, and Gale Cincotta. Within the past few years organizers and volunteers with ACORN, NAACP, ACLU, and several other community-based organizations and law enforcement agencies have put insurance redlining at the center of fair housing and community reinvestment debates. Bill Tisdale, Sara Pratt, and Deepak Bhargava are among those who have turned these debates into significant actions. Many insurers have joined with these folks in collaborative efforts to eliminate the fact and effects of insurance redlining. Obviously, this book would not have been possible without their sacrifices.

I would also like to thank my many colleagues at the University of Wisconsin-Milwaukee and at HUD who have encouraged my work on this issue. My particular thanks goes to Peter Kaplan at HUD, who has worked with and supported me on several occasions going back to the late 1970s. The contributors to this book deserve great credit for their work, the significance of which extends far beyond author-ship of one chapter. Finally, I want to thank Felicity Skidmore, who encouraged me in this project from the start and who made this a much better book than otherwise would have been the case.

Gregory D. Squires

CONTENTS

List of Tables

FOREWORD

The Urban Institute has long been a part of the analytic community striving to disentangle the various forces affecting observed differences in access by race or ethnic group in America. Its major contribution has been development of techniques for measuring discrimination directly, which use pairs of testers—matched on all relevant characteristics except race—to apply for jobs, try to buy homes, and so on, and to record their experiences. The Institute has used paired testers to test for discrimination in housing and employment, and is now engaged in a similar project to test for discrimination in the market for home insurance.

This book concerns a particular form of discrimination in the home insurance area—redlining, the practice of marking certain neighborhoods for differential treatment by insurance agents because of the race/ethnic makeup of those neighborhoods. The contributing authors come from a variety of disciplines and bring a variety of perspectives to bear. Together they present the most current findings on a range of critical issues: why and how the federal Fair Housing Act applies to insurance; the distribution of insurance products and services and the significance of race in that pattern; industry practices that contribute, wittingly and unwittingly, to unequal access to insurance; enforcement efforts to ensure equitable access; and industry initiatives, frequently in collaboration with community groups, to alleviate the objective factors that raise the risk of loss in certain neighborhoods.

The Urban Institute Press has recently published a comprehensive review of current research and policy in the area of access to mortgage lending. The issue of insurance availability is an important part of the mortgage lending debate—not only as an issue of distributional justice, but as a crucial factor in city decay. As the President's National Advisory Panel put the case 30 years ago: "Insurance is essential to revitalize our cities. It is a cornerstone of credit. Without insurance

. . . new housing cannot be constructed, and existing housing cannot be repaired. New business cannot expand, or even survive."

This book provides a framework for the development of public policy, private industry practice, and community partnerships that can increase insurance availability in urban communities and promote the urban revitalization the nation so badly needs.

William Gorham
President

Chapter One

RACE, POLITICS, AND THE LAW: RECURRING THEMES IN THE INSURANCE REDLINING DEBATE

Gregory D. Squires

The insurance industry refrains from moral pronouncements about its customers. We measure risk as accurately as we can, applying experience and objective criteria refined for more than two centuries. We leave it to others to speak of discrimination and other such moral terms.
— National Association of Independent Insurers
(in Faulstich and Hall 1978)

Very honestly, I think you write too many blacks. . . . you got to sell good, solid premium paying white people.
— Sales manager for American Family Mutual Insurance Company, 1988 (from case files in *NAACP v. American Family Mutual Insurance Company* 1992)

Accusations of insurance redlining and racial discrimination by fair housing advocates, as well as investigations of industry practice by law enforcement officials, have occurred with increasing frequency in recent years. Activity has intensified on the part of state and federal regulators and legislatures, in the courts, and by various consumer groups. Insurers have responded with their own political initiatives in many of these same arenas. More research has been conducted, which means that more ammunition has been accumulated by the various contestants. And in many respects the stakes have risen higher in terms of the implications for the insurance industry, affected consumers, and urban communities generally. Yet the issues that are being debated have remained virtually unchanged for almost three decades.

Following the urban unrest of the 1960s, the President's National Advisory Panel on Insurance in Riot-Affected Areas (1968; henceforth, President's National Advisory Panel) issued a report detailing widespread redlining practices within the property/casualty insurance industry.[1] That report, known as the Hughes report, described explicit practices by the industry—practices that actually preceded the riots and that resulted in urban insurance availability problems in several cities. The Hughes panel also noted the risks many insurers confronted in responding to urban insurance needs.

During the late 1970s, the U.S. Congress considered legislative approaches to urban insurance availability problems, the U.S. Department of Housing and Urban Development (HUD) proposed regulations applying the Federal Fair Housing Act of 1968 to the property insurance industry, and a number of community-based organizations negotiated "reinvestment agreements" with insurers (Keenan 1979; Schachter 1979). Once again, problems confronting both residents seeking insurance and insurers seeking to provide it were documented.

In the 1990s, consumer groups charged the industry with redlining and unlawful discrimination (Association of Community Organizations for Reform Now 1993, 1994; Illinois Public Action Council 1993; Kincaid 1994). Insurers challenged these findings, and again asserted that urban communities posed unique risks (American Insurance Association 1993; National Association of Independent Insurers 1994a). Several states considered new rules limiting various underwriting and marketing practices. HUD once again considered but did not promulgate a Fair Housing regulation. And Congress debated but did not pass legislation that would have required insurers to disclose the geographic location of their policies, similar to the requirements placed on mortgage lenders by the Home Mortgage Disclosure Act.

Some fire did flare up amidst this smoke. In 1993 the California Insurance Commission settled a complaint against one insurer that included a $500,000 payment and commitments to change its marketing practices. In 1996 State Farm Insurance Companies settled a Fair Housing Act complaint with HUD, the National Fair Housing Alliance (NFHA), and the Toledo Fair Housing Center (TFHC), in which the insurer agreed to make several changes in its underwriting guidelines and to more effectively market its products in older, urban communities. More significantly, in 1995 the U.S. Department of Justice, the National Association for the Advancement of Colored People (NAACP), the American Civil Liberties Union (ACLU), and other community groups settled a fair housing complaint with the American Family Mutual Insurance Company, in which the insurer agreed to pay $14.5 million to encourage homeownership in the central city of Milwaukee and to implement dramatic changes in the company's underwriting, marketing, and employment practices. (See chapters 8 and 9 for analyses of this case.)

A constant throughout these years and these struggles has been the basic parameters of the redlining debate. Industry critics charge insurers with discriminating unfairly against older, urban communities, particularly those with high concentrations of minority residents. Insurers respond that they underwrite and price consumers objectively on the basis of the differing potential for losses that various groups present. Racial minorities, they acknowledge, unfortunately happen to reside in areas that pose greater levels of risk. From this one fundamental area of disagreement, several other disputes arise over underwriting, marketing, and other industry practices, the legal obligations of various actors, and ultimately who is responsible for the causes and consequences of industry actions. In fact, a subtext of the insurance redlining controversy is the contemporary debate surrounding "the underclass" in urban America.

This book examines the issues that have framed almost 30 years of debate over insurance redlining. If the fundamental issues have remained unchanged, the knowledge base that participants have brought to the debate has expanded significantly, particularly within the past few years. The chapters in this volume present the most current findings on the most critical issues. Consequently, they provide a framework for the development of public policy, private industry practice, and partnerships with community-based organizations that can ameliorate insurance availability and discrimination problems currently confronting urban communities.

One of the first questions that arises, however, is that of why the rather arcane matter of property insurance matters. In fact, access to affordable insurance is vital for virtually any aspect of urban development or any effort to ensure equal opportunity for residents of the nation's metropolitan areas.

WHY INSURANCE REDLINING?

Access to affordable property insurance is essential for homeownership, business and commercial development, and any urban redevelopment initiative. If insurance is not available, or is only available on unfavorable terms and conditions, efforts to achieve fair housing, to nurture economic opportunity, or even to secure the basic rights of citizenship are undermined.

The property/casualty insurance industry is big business, one that significantly affects the development of metropolitan areas and residents' quality of life. The industry controlled assets totaling $704.6 billion at the end of 1994. The 3,300 companies that write property/casualty insurance, along with thousands of affiliated agencies and service organizations, employ approximately 1 million people (Insurance Information Institute 1996). Property/casualty insurance is a global industry that is regulated at the state level, to the extent that regulation exists in the industry. There is virtually no federal regulation of insurance. Unlike the mortgage lending industry, which is subject to a range of federal regulatory agencies (e.g., the Federal Reserve Board, the Federal Deposit Insurance Corporation, the Office of Thrift Supervision, the Comptroller of the Currency), no federal agency exercises ongoing oversight of the insurance industry, including the property/casualty segment.

Yet, property insurance is increasingly essential in today's economy and society. Its critical role in urban redevelopment has long been widely recognized (Badain 1980; Yaspan 1970). The need to ensure the availability of adequate insurance is not simply a moral or social welfare concern. As State Farm Insurance Companies' associate general counsel, Leo Jordan, stated, "(1) there is an urban insurance availability problem which is contributing to and aggravating the overall urban problem; and (2) regardless of whether out of social or moral obligation or enlightened self-interest, insurers must develop an efficient response" (1978: 6). The problem has not disappeared. As the Massachusetts attorney general, Scott Harshbarger, recently concluded, "It is apparent that the major problem is that insurance companies have, by and large, abandoned inner city areas" (1995: 23).

In an often-quoted statement that bears repeating, the President's National Advisory Panel captured the nature of insurance when it stated almost 30 years ago:

> Insurance is essential to revitalize our cities. It is a cornerstone of credit. Without insurance, banks and other financial institutions will not—and cannot—make loans. New housing cannot be constructed, and existing housing cannot be repaired. New business cannot expand, or even survive.
>
> Without insurance, buildings are left to deteriorate; services, goods and jobs diminish. Efforts to rebuild our nation's inner cities cannot move forward. Communities without insurance are communities without hope. (1968: 1)

Inseparable from the broader issues of community development are the questions of fair housing and fair access to financial services. The fact that insurance is more difficult to obtain in older, urban communities, particularly those with large concentrations of nonwhite residents, is widely recognized, though the reasons for such disparities are heatedly disputed, as discussed later in this chapter. The general pattern of uneven access to property insurance exacerbates segregation of urban housing markets and concentration of poverty particularly in minority neighborhoods (Jackson 1985; Massey and Denton 1993). Where the full range of financial services is unavailable, or is available only on unfavorable terms, fair access to housing is denied and the benefits associated with homeownership (including the capital accumulation that generally results from the largest investment most families make) are scaled back (Oliver and Shapiro 1995; Yinger 1995).

Consequently, a focal point of much recent debate has been the 1968 Federal Fair Housing Act. Its effectiveness as a tool for remedying these problems and the fundamental jurisdictional question of whether insurance is even covered by the act are topics of vigorous debate. (This matter is detailed in chapter 2.) These general concerns have generated ongoing disputes over several industry practices and public policy responses.

PARAMETERS OF THE DEBATE

The fundamental dispute in the redlining debate has been over the extent to which subjective bias or objective analysis has shaped industry practice. Critics charge the industry with operating on the basis of subjective stereotypes regarding urban communities, particularly those with high concentrations of minority residents, resulting in a denial of service or provision of service on unequal terms in these markets. Insurers respond that they measure risk as accurately as they can and that any uneven provision of services reflects varying exposure to the possibility of compensable losses (i.e., loss costs) in metropolitan areas. Although all parties to the debate have marshaled evidence over the years, the fundamental contours of this discussion have remained unaltered. Confounding matters is the reality that both sets of considerations may well be operating. The challenge is to sort out the extent to which various perceptions and practices result in availability and affordability problems, and to develop appropriate remedies.

There is clear anecdotal evidence of industry practices reflecting adverse perceptions and calling for unfavorable treatment of urban communities and racial minorities, sometimes explicitly and at other times through recognized code words for race.[2] The Hughes panel observed that insurers frequently based decisions on their perceptions of the neighborhood where a property was located, regardless of the merits of the particular risk. According to one underwriting manual cited by the panel, "A good way to keep this information available and up to date is by the use of a red line around the questionable areas on territorial maps centrally located in the Underwriting Division for ease of reference by all Underwriting personnel" (President's National Advisory Panel 1968: 6).

In a 1958 report to its subscribers entitled "Report on Negro Areas of Chicago," the National Inspection Company noted the "encroachment of Negroes" and observed that "the Puerto Ricans, Mexicans, Japanese and 'Hillbillies' have worked into some colored areas, particularly on the fringe of the cheaper or poorer districts and, in some cases, are in the same category with the lower class Negroes." This report concluded:

> It is difficult to draw a definite line between the acceptable and the undesirable colored or cheap mixed white areas; the near west side (Madison Street) and near north side (Clark Street) still attract the derelict or floating elements with "honky tonk," mercantiles and flop houses. Any liability in the areas described should be carefully scrutinized and, in case of Negro dwellings, usually only the better maintained, owner occupied risks are considered acceptable for profitable underwriting."

In 1977 the chief actuary of the New York Department of Insurance stated: "Take Harlem, for example. They don't need any insurance because they don't have anything of value to insure" (in Keenan 1979: 9). In 1988 some American Family Mutual Insurance Company agents were instructed in writing to "*quit writing* all those *blacks* [emphasis in original]" (Michael Shannon, of American Family, in a note to agent Rueben Ziehlsdorf). And, reminiscent of code words long used for exclusionary purposes, a 1993 Nationwide Mutual Insurance Company underwriting manual stated that an "applicant must be a person of integrity and financial stability who takes pride in his property."

Such practices have caused many to question the objectivity of industry underwriting and marketing practices, including some insurance commissioners. In 1977 the Michigan insurance commissioner observed that "many of the underwriting 'rules' are not rules at all, but are a conglomeration of myths, notions, perceptions, and beliefs. They are often subjective, not based upon scientific, empirical fact" (Jones 1977: 10). In 1994 the Texas commissioner told the U.S. Senate Committee on Banking, Housing, and Urban Affairs that "we still find insurance companies making underwriting decisions based on all kinds of factors that have nothing to do with a statistically measured or measurable probability of risk" (Hunter 1994: 1).

Statistical evidence has also accumulated of significant racial disparities between the types and levels of service provided older, urban areas, particularly those with large minority populations, and predominantly white areas (Midwestern Regional Advisory Committees to the U.S. Commission on Civil Rights 1979; Squires and Velez 1987). In the past few years paired testing of specific insurers (whereby insurance "shoppers" are matched on all characteristics except their race or the racial composition of the neighborhood of the home they are trying to insure) has revealed differences in the availability of insurance and types of products available, along with requirements and terms and conditions of available policies that are clearly associated with the racial composition of neighborhoods, the race of the applicant, or both. (See chapter 5 for a review of recent testing evidence by the National Fair Housing Alliance.)[3]

Insurers and many industry regulators recognize these gaps and frequently acknowledge that underwriting is as much an art as a science. But they attribute these findings to the uneven distribution of risk in metropolitan areas. The Hughes report repeatedly referred to the challenges facing insurers in "blighted" areas (President's National Advisory Panel 1968).

Yet, particularly since the advent of the FAIR Plan[4] in 1968, insurers have asserted that basic availability problems have generally been solved, and that well over 90 percent of homeowners—black and white, in virtually all areas—have coverage (American Insurance Association 1993; Illinois Department of Insurance 1994). To the extent that prices or other terms and conditions vary, these are attributable to higher crime and fire rates, an aging housing stock, declining public services (including fire and police protection and building code enforcement), and other factors that increase the likelihood of loss (National Association of Independent Insurers 1994a).

Clearly, this debate lends itself to empirical analysis. The stumbling block has been the unavailability of public information on loss costs. In recent years, some states have begun to collect data on such costs by rating territories, and the National Association of Insurance Commissioners (NAIC) has begun to analyze this information. Statistical analysis of these data (discussed in chapter 3) indicates that even after taking loss costs into consideration, availability and cost of insurance remain statistically significantly associated with the racial composition of neighborhoods.

The general "race versus risk" discussion has given rise to contentious debate over several related industry practices and public policy initiatives. The most controversial topic is whether the Fair Housing Act even applies to the property insurance industry.

McCarran-Ferguson Act and Federal Fair Housing Act

The insurance industry has repeatedly asserted that the Fair Housing Act does not apply to the insurance industry. Fair housing advocates claim the act does cover discriminatory insurance practices. The consensus of case law to date rejects the industry's arguments and asserts that the act does apply, but future legal and political developments could change the terms of this jurisdictional debate.

Four principal arguments are offered to support the industry's contention. First, the industry points to the McCarran-Ferguson Act, passed in 1945, which provides for state regulation of the industry. This act exempts state insurance laws from federal law unless the federal statute specifically addresses insurance. Where state insurance laws and federal laws conflict, state laws will prevail because of the exemption provided by McCarran-Ferguson. Second, it is argued that Congress has considered amending the Fair Housing Act to include insurance but has not done so; therefore, the intent of Congress is to exempt the industry from the act. Third, industry advocates point to the FAIR Plan as the appropriate federal response to these problems. Fourth, they assert that state laws already prohibit discrimination, thus obviating a need for federal regulation in this area, which would be unduly burdensome for the industry. These arguments have been made repeatedly in congressional hearings, legal briefs, speeches, monographs, and other settings for almost 30 years.

Fair housing advocates reject each of these positions. They point to sections of the Fair Housing Act itself as providing proof that it applies to insurance. Under the Fair Housing Act it is unlawful to "otherwise make unavailable or deny a dwelling to any person because of race" or other prohibited classifications (42 U.S.C. Section 3604 [a]) or to "discriminate against any person . . . in the provision of services or facilities in connection therewith" (42 U.S.C. Section 3604 [b]). Because insurance is required to qualify for a mortgage loan, and because homeownership depends on access to mortgage financing, it is argued that enjoyment of the full rights provided by the Fair Housing Act requires nondiscrimination in the provision of property insurance. HUD made this explicit when it enacted regulations implementing the Fair Housing Amendments Act of 1988, defining as prohibited conduct "refusing to provide . . . property or hazard insurance for dwellings or providing such services or insurance differently because of race, color, religion, sex, handicap, familial status, or national origin" (24 C.F.R. Section 100.70 [d][4]).

Fair housing advocates also point to the case of the *NAACP v. American Family Mutual Insurance Company* (978 F.2d 287, 299 [7th Cir. 1992]), in which the court concluded there are several reasons why Congress may not have expressly included insurance in the act, yet intended it to apply to insurance in any case. The court observed, for instance, that members may have assumed that insurance applied and saw no need to take further action, or that simply the press of other business could have precluded its explicit inclusion.

The FAIR Plan, it is furthermore argued, was enacted for purposes other than those of the Fair Housing Act. Although fair housing advocates recognize some overlap, they claim that the problems of insurance availability and affordability in urban areas are simply not the same as issues of unlawful discrimination due to race and other protected classes.

According to this position, although there are state laws that address discrimination, they do not provide the same protection as the Fair Housing Act. Most states do not provide the same coverage or procedural rights (e.g., private right of action in the federal courts, investigation by the federal government of discrimination complaints, and representation by the government in court) or the same range of remedies (e.g., civil penalties and punitive damages). Consequently, it is argued, the Fair Housing Act complements rather than contradicts state law and, therefore, the McCarran-Ferguson Act does not bar application of the Fair Housing Act.

To date, the courts have rejected the industry's positions and have ruled that the Fair Housing Act applies to property insurance. In several district court cases (e.g., *Dunn v. Midwestern Indemnity Co.*, 472 F. Supp. 1106 [S.D. Ohio 1979]; *McDiarmid v. Economy Fire & Casualty Co.*, 604 F. Supp. 105 [S.D. Ohio 1984]; and *Strange v. Nationwide Mutual Insurance Company*, No. 93-6585 [E.D. Pa. 9-22-94]) and two circuit court cases (*NAACP v. American Family Mutual Insurance Company*, 978 F.2d 287 [7th Cir. 1992] *cert. denied*, 113 S. Ct.

2335 [1993], and *Nationwide Mutual Insurance Company v. Cisneros,* 52 F.3d 1351 [6th Cir. May 1, 1995] *cert. denied,* 116 S. Ct. 973 [1996]), application of the Fair Housing Act has been reaffirmed.

In 1984 the Fourth Circuit Court ruled to the contrary (in *Mackey v. Nationwide Insurance Companies,* 724 F.2d 419 [4th Cir. 1984]). Subsequent to this decision, however, HUD issued its ruling explicitly applying the Fair Housing Act to insurance. Pointing to this rule, in 1992 the Seventh Circuit Court concluded in the *American Family* case that "events have bypassed Mackey," and found that the act did apply. In *Nationwide v. Cisneros,* the Sixth Circuit Court observed: "We conclude that HUD's interpretation of the Act is consistent with goals of the Act and a reasonable interpretation of the statute. . . . we hold that the McCarran-Ferguson Act does not preclude HUD's interpretation of the Act." In both of these cases, the defendants filed petitions for review by the U.S. Supreme Court and the Court rejected the appeals.

Having lost this battle in the courts, industry lobbyists managed to insert language in the House of Representatives' version of HUD's 1996 appropriations bill that would prohibit the agency from spending funds on any insurance-related activity; however, this language was removed by the House-Senate Conference Committee. This action does not clarify the agency's jurisdiction under the Fair Housing Act, but it does reflect the industry's concern and clout when it comes to civil rights law enforcement. A Supreme Court decision or legislative action by Congress could change the law. But currently the case law clearly indicates that discrimination in the provision of property insurance violates the Federal Fair Housing Act.

Underwriting and Pricing Standards and Practices

Several common underwriting practices have long been debated, including the selective utilization of certain practices as well as the impact of other practices even if uniformly applied to all applicants and insureds. In other words, both disparate-treatment and disparate-impact issues are subject to dispute.

Among the most longstanding and widely challenged practices are the use of maximum age and minimum value requirements (i.e., refusing to insure homes or varying the terms and conditions for homes that are older than or valued below selected thresholds); the so-called moral hazard (when insurers refuse to provide full replacement coverage for homes where the market value is appreciably below replacement value for fear of creating an incentive for arson); utilizing subjective criteria (e.g., "pride of ownership"); underwriting on the basis of neighborhood or geographic location; and utilizing criteria that appear unrelated to the risk of the insured or the property (e.g., occupation, marital status, life-style, and, in recent years, credit rating). (See chapter 6 for a comprehensive analysis of the disparate impact of underwriting practices frequently used by leading insurers today.)

As indicated earlier, race (of neighborhoods and individual applicants) has historically been explicitly utilized as an underwriting and pricing factor. If the most egregious forms of discrimination have been reduced, clearly they have not disappeared. Equally, if not more, problematic is the effect of many guidelines currently in wide use. In Texas, for example, 90 percent of the insurance market is served by companies that have underwriting restrictions based on age or value of homes (Kincaid 1994). Such rules clearly have an adverse impact on racial minorities. The effects of common thresholds illustrate the point. Many insurers have restrictions for homes built prior to 1950 or valued at less than $50,000. Nationwide, 40 percent of black households, compared to just under 30 percent of white households, reside in homes built prior to 1950. And black households are more than twice as likely as white households (47 percent compared to 23 percent, respectively), to live in homes valued at below $50,000.

Insurers respond that risks are measured objectively and decisions are based on objective evaluation of the potential for loss. Underwriting guidelines and rating systems, therefore, reflect different levels of risk posed by different groups. According to the insurers, to avoid unfair subsidization of bad risks by good risks, to encourage homeowners to maintain their homes and thus avoid losses, and to maintain the overall efficiency of market-based insurance delivery systems that currently meet the needs of well over 90 percent of the market, such decisions should be left to the discretion of private insurers and the forces of open competition (National Association of Independent Insurers 1994b).

The disparate-impact standard of discrimination is particularly problematic for many insurers. Again, they acknowledge the uneven provision of insurance services in urban communities, with racial minorities often adversely affected. But this they attribute to risk, not race; therefore, they reject efforts to eradicate or modify many traditional underwriting standards and pricing practices. Under the Fair Housing Act, a policy or practice that has an adverse disparate impact on minority communities does not violate the law if such an action is required for safe and efficient operation of the business and there is no less-discriminatory alternative that could serve the same business objectives. This raises the question of the extent to which many of these traditional industry practices can in fact be justified in terms of objective assessment of risk and loss costs.

Underwriting guidelines are not generally available to the public. Nor are the loss data that putatively support underwriting and pricing decisions. Public disclosure of such information is currently being debated, but resolution of this matter remains uncertain.

Agent Location and Marketing of Insurance

Most homeowners' insurance policies are sold through agents, either exclusive agents representing only one company or independent agents who represent several insurers. Recent studies have documented a growing concentration of agents in suburban communities and a declining representation within urban areas (Illinois Public Action Council 1993; Squires, Velez, and Taeuber 1991). A common feature of most public hearings in recent years is a map prepared by a consumer or fair housing advocacy group illustrating a classic doughnut pattern where several agents are found in the suburban ring but few are located within the central city. A related issue is the difficulty several minority agents have in securing contracts to represent major insurers, particularly if their book of business tends to be in central-city areas.

Again, this is not a new issue. The Hughes report also acknowledged the small number of agents serving urban communities, and pointed to assumed problems of writing profitable business in central cities, the availability of more lucrative business in other parts of metropolitan areas, and the closer scrutiny that companies gave to applications from central city areas (President's National Advisory Panel 1968). Insurers frequently point to the relative attractiveness of different communities, in terms of profitability of available business, as the primary factor accounting for location of agents. They maintain that the cost of soliciting and serving customers increases with the distance of the risk from the agent's office, but they also note that since most business is conducted over the telephone, insurance is available even in neighborhoods where agents are not located. The difficulty that some minority agents have in securing company contracts is generally attributed to agents' relatively small books of business, which do not meet the minimum threshold requirements of major insurers.

Agents tend to locate, and companies tend to market, in areas where they plan to do business. Regardless of the cause, this pattern of agent location restricts the choice of insurance products in many urban communities. As with the distribution of insurance policies, the proffered explanations for agent location patterns lend themselves to empirical investigation. Whereas data on racial composition, income, and age of property at the neighborhood level have long been available to the public, loss costs have not been released. In recent years, however, some insurance commissioners have obtained such data. The Missouri Department of Insurance has begun to collect this information and, as discussed in chapter 4, researchers are finding that racial composition and income of neighborhoods, but *not* the recent history of losses in those neighborhoods, appear to account for the uneven distribution of agents.

Terms, Conditions, Services, and Eligibility Requirements

As the Hughes report indicated, insurers have long scrutinized applications from urban communities more closely than others. Advocacy groups have asserted that urban properties are more frequently inspected, are less likely to be bound by an agent over the telephone, and are generally examined more carefully than other applications. In cases where such applications are approved, they maintain that policies cost more, provide less coverage, require higher deductibles, and generally constitute an inferior product.

Perhaps the most serious accusation is the unequal service that policyholders receive after the policy is purchased, particularly when they file a claim. According to a former adjuster for a major national insurer, black claimants routinely receive smaller settlements and their claims are more vigorously challenged than those filed by whites; and Hispanics are even more mistreated than blacks (Saadi 1987).

Insurers attribute variations in the terms and conditions of insurance to fluctuations in the costs associated with various communities and policyholders. It is argued, for example, that older homes generally pose greater risks than newer homes. Older homes must be inspected more frequently, therefore, to determine their insurability. If insurers could not inspect older homes on a selective basis, but were required to inspect either every home or none, the result would be even less business in urban communities. It would be prohibitively expensive to inspect every home; therefore, an insurer's only choice would be to pull out of older, urban areas completely (National Association of Independent Insurers 1994d). Disparate treatment in claims settlements is, at worst, an anecdotal occurrence that violates standard industry practice according to insurers and their trade associations. Again, the issues are framed in terms of "race versus risk," with the critical loss-cost data unavailable for empirical verification of the various contentions.

The first systematic investigation of claims settlements was launched following Hurricane Andrew in south Florida. The findings (discussed in chapter 7) reinforce charges of bias, particularly against Hispanic residents.

Law Enforcement or Voluntary Initiatives

Another ongoing controversy pertains to the appropriate roles for law enforcement as well as for voluntary initiatives on the part of the industry, including collaborative efforts with regulators and community organizations. (This issue is separate from the debate over application of the Fair Housing Act discussed earlier.) Related to this discussion are the costs of insurance-related problems (and their appropriate allocation) as well as determining the responsible parties.

Fair housing and consumer advocacy groups have long called for more vigorous enforcement of the law (including state unfair trade practices acts, unfair discrimination prohibitions of state insurance codes, state civil rights statutes, and the Fair Housing Act), tighter regulation of rates, restrictions on the use of selected underwriting guidelines, fuller disclosure of industry practices, mandated appointment of more minority agents and more agents in urban communities, reinvestment commitments covering underwriting and investment activity of insurers, and related activities. Such proposals are based, in part, on the essential nature of property insurance and the many social costs to individuals and communities denied such financial services.

Insurers respond that unfair discrimination provisions of state insurance laws are being aggressively enforced. Tighter rate regulation would discourage lenders from pursuing business in urban areas precisely at a time when more insurers should be competing for this business. Restricting underwriting flexibility would result in good risks subsidizing bad risks, thus reducing the efficiency of the insurance industry. Fuller disclosure, it is argued, will simply lead to more unfounded charges that will be costly for the industry to respond to (although some insurers and trade associations would accept some minimal disclosure of policies at the zip code level). Appointment of more minority agents, and more urban agents, is recognized as a desirable objective, and the industry contends it is taking steps in this direction, including developing mentoring programs in urban markets. Regulation of investments for fair housing and community development purposes is considered beyond the pale by most insurers, agents, trade associations, and state insurance commissioners. From their perspective, insurers, by writing and seeking out business in urban communities, and purchasing municipal bonds along with related investments, are generally meeting their reinvestment responsibilities.

The industry continues to recognize urban insurance problems, and its representatives point to several voluntary initiatives already in place. Companies are working with community organizations in various crime-watch, fire prevention, and other risk management programs to attack what insurers see as the root cause of these problems, the higher losses and greater exposure to risk in older, urban communities. In addition, many insurers are investing in such organizations as Neighborhood Housing Services, Habitat for Humanity, and other entities working to increase homeownership in distressed communities. No doubt many of these initiatives have been launched to forestall enforcement activity. In any case, they constitute an important part of the current debate over what should be done to address discrimination and related urban insurance issues. (See chapter 10 for an analysis of voluntary industry initiatives.)

Not surprisingly, perceptions of what should be done are shaped by beliefs regarding underlying causes. The fact that insurance services are provided unevenly throughout metropolitan areas, often in ways associated with race, is not subject to much debate, although causes certainly are. Frequent anecdotal occurrences of discrimination are evident, but the pervasiveness of systematic unlawful discrimination remains a contentious issue. If loss costs account for these disparities, as the industry contends, it has jealously guarded the information that would permit empirical verification. As indicated previously and as will be discussed in subsequent chapters, where loss-cost information has been accessible, the best available research indicates that even after taking losses into consideration, racial effects persist.

Equally persistent is the industry's assertion that risk, and not race, accounts for these patterns and practices. Yet, in the spirit of negative stereotyping that for decades explicitly shaped the housing industry's appraisal and underwriting practices (Jackson 1985; Massey and Denton 1993), and in the jargon of many contemporary proponents of an emerging underclass, the industry also resorts to a style of victim-blaming in efforts to account for these problems. One trade association recently pointed to "a lack of education, the presence of unsupervised children, the instability of family units, and poorly maintained heating systems as among the reasons for the fire hazard in some communities" (National Association of Independent Insurers 1994d: 4). Unlawful discrimination is not acknowledged in this statement as even among many factors contributing to these problems. And although no evidence is presented linking loss costs to "family values," responsibility is clearly assigned to defects in the behavior of inner city families.

ORGANIZATION OF THIS VOLUME

Recent political developments and social science research have begun to clarify some of these longstanding debates. In so doing, at least the outlines of a framework for public policy and private industry activity for ameliorating discrimination and related urban insurance problems have begun to emerge. Each of the chapters following elucidates what has been learned regarding the most critical and controversial debates. Some chapters address issues on which a small literature has developed, whereas others address virtually uncharted territory.

Chapter 2 reviews the fundamental "rules," that is, why and how the Federal Fair Housing Act applies to insurance. Chapters 3 and 4 provide an overview of the distribution of insurance products and services and the significance of race in that pattern. Chapter 4 also explores, along with chapters 5, 6, and 7, substantive practices of the property/casualty insurance industry that create these patterns. Chapters 8 and 9 examine enforcement efforts, brought primarily under the authority of the Fair Housing Act, to eliminate redlining and discrimination. The concluding chapter 10 examines voluntary initiatives on the part of the industry, frequently in collaboration with community groups, to address redlining and urban insurance availability issues.

INSURANCE REDLINING: WHAT WE KNOW
AND WHY WE KNOW IT

The most disputed political issue in the redlining debate is the question of whether the Fair Housing Act applies to insurance. As indicated earlier, and as Stephen M. Dane delineates in chapter 2, this question has been answered in the affirmative. The case law to date establishes that discriminatory property insurance practices are prohibited under this statute. A U.S. Supreme Court ruling to the contrary, or legislation by Congress amending the act to explicitly exclude insurance, could fuel the jurisdictional debate once again. Such action in either arena could generate a counter-action in the other. So, for example, if the Supreme Court should address this issue, whichever side lost might seek relief through Congress. Similarly, if Congress should amend the act, such legislation could be challenged in court. Dane has litigated several cases involving financial institutions and has written widely on this topic. As he concludes, if this debate is not over, as the law currently stands, insurance practices are covered by the Fair Housing Act.

The critical, substantive issue has long been whether current industry practices and the uneven distribution of services in metropolitan areas can be accounted for by factors associated with risk, or whether subjective bias resulting in racial disparities in the market constitutes a contributing factor. The best available research indicates that risk alone cannot account for these patterns in urban communities. Recent research by staff members of the National Association of Insurance Commissioners (NAIC) constitutes the first serious investigation that formally takes into consideration loss costs. In chapter 3, Robert W. Klein, an economist at Georgia State University and former director of research for the NAIC, reports the results of NAIC's research, which reveals that even after controlling for loss costs, the availability and cost of insurance remain significantly associated with the racial composition of neighborhood. As Klein observes, several factors in addition to unlawful discrimination may explain these patterns, but his findings constitute strong evidence that risk alone does not account for these racial disparities.

A related, longstanding debate has concerned the causes and consequences of where agents locate their offices. Again, this is an issue that has suffered from an absence of data on the central issue: loss costs. The Missouri Department of Insurance recently collected this information and has begun such research. Jay D. Schultz, an economist formerly with the department, reports in chapter 4 that loss costs cannot account for the distribution of agents in the St. Louis metropolitan area. Schultz does find, however, that after controlling for loss costs and several other demographic variables, racial composition remains significantly associated with the number of agents in a neighborhood.

As indicated earlier, at least anecdotal instances of overt discrimination are widely acknowledged to occur. But there is evidence that discrimination due to the racial composition of a community or the race of an applicant is not simply an occasional event. The National Fair Housing Alliance (NFHA) recently conducted paired testing in nine cities. In over half (between 30 and 40 tests were conducted in each city), the alliance found that business was eagerly pursued from white applicants or residents of predominantly white neighborhoods, whereas African Americans and Hispanics or residents of minority areas were not offered insurance, were offered an inferior product or a higher price for the same product, or were otherwise discouraged from pursuing a policy. Chapter 5, by Shanna L. Smith and Cathy Cloud, NFHA's executive director and assistant director, respectively, reviews the evidence provided by these tests.

Widespread racial disparities persist in the impact of many common underwriting guidelines. Even where no racial animus is intended, such rules violate the Fair Housing Act unless they can be justified as a business necessity and no less-discriminatory alternative would serve the business purpose. If the pervasiveness of explicitly discriminatory underwriting guidelines has faded, the racial effects of frequently utilized rules persist. The impact on families and communities, of course, matters little if the discriminatory practices are intentional or unintentional. D. J. Powers, former general counsel for the Texas Department of Insurance, assesses in chapter 6 the widespread adverse effects of underwriting guidelines commonly used today by leading insurers nationwide.

These problems do not end with the purchase of an insurance policy. Racial disparities persist in the servicing of policyholders after they have paid their premiums. In the first systematic investigation of claims practices, Tom Baker and Karen McElrath (associate professors of law and sociology, respectively, at the University of Miami) report in chapter 7 that claims adjustors provided quicker and more comprehensive responses to whites than Hispanics in the wake of Hurricane Andrew.

Victimized communities have begun to respond. As mentioned earlier, the most successful effort was launched by the NAACP, the ACLU, and several local organizations in Milwaukee, along with the assistance of the Justice Department, culminating in 1995 in a $14.5 million settlement with the American Family Mutual Insurance Company. These funds were earmarked for victims of the company's prior discriminatory practices and for residents of Milwaukee's central city to encourage homeownership. American Family also agreed to eliminate specific underwriting guidelines, including maximum age and minimum value requirements, that had adversely affected Milwaukee's African American community. The company furthermore agreed to appoint more agents in the central city, to increase minority employment, to take specific advertising and marketing initiatives to reach central city residents, and to increase its market share in these neighborhoods. This case clearly demonstrates the value of effective community organizing and aggressive law enforcement. William Lynch, the lead attorney for the plaintiffs, describes in chapter 8 the origins of the case, the legal strategies employed, and the significance of the outcome for insurance consumers in urban America.

The Justice Department played an essential role in the *American Family* case and, perhaps more crucially, confirmed the importance of effective federal law enforcement in addressing insurance discrimination problems in the future. In chapter 9, Richard J. Ritter, a former Justice Department attorney, details the department's role in that case, as well as the role that law enforcement can play in the wake of *American Family.*

Yet, it is clear that enforcement alone is not sufficient. Resources of law enforcement agencies simply do not permit a case-by-case approach on a broad enough scale. And as political winds change, the willingness to use the tools of law enforcement may diminish. Ideally, selective law enforcement initiatives will generate voluntary activities on the part of the industry. Apparently this has already begun to occur. Several insurers are working with community groups to develop crime-watch and other safety programs that increase the insurability of urban properties; to educate the industry on business opportunities currently being missed in many areas; to recruit and appoint more minority agents and more agents in urban communities; and to take other innovative steps to eliminate discrimination and urban insurance problems. George Knight, executive director of the Neighborhood Reinvestment Corporation, describes the contributions of these voluntary approaches in chapter 10.

Much has been learned to inform the insurance redlining debate and to suggest directions for future policy. If the fundamental objective is to increase the availability of affordable property insurance on an equitable basis, part of the strategy must be to significantly reduce those factors that contribute to loss. More educated consumers and homeowners, more effective fire protection and crime prevention, and stricter enforcement of building codes are vital.

These actions alone, however, will not eliminate racial disparities or reduce discrimination that persists in the market. Industry perceptions and practices must change as well. There is still a need to overcome negative racial stereotyping that long permeated financial institutions. Underwriting and pricing of insurance should reflect more accurately actual risk, rather than inaccurate perceptions of the linkage between race and risk. A range of marketing practices must be altered, including the location of agents and the appointment of agents, to reach currently underserved markets. And services to policyholders must be provided on an equitable basis.

These outcomes will not occur without continued struggle and conflict. Critical research needs remain, but they require disclosure of information, including geographically coded application and policy counts and underwriting guidelines, that is not readily available. No doubt more lawsuits and administrative complaints will be filed. A more detailed regulation clarifying how the Fair Housing Act applies to insurance would provide guidance to insurers, regulators, and consumers, thus mitigating some of this conflict. HUD has considered promulgating such a rule but has yet to do so. (A proposed model regulation is presented in the appendix to this book.) These actions, it is hoped, will lead to more collaborative efforts among industry and consumer groups.

Valuable lessons have emerged for the insurance industry, regulators, and consumers on how the specific problems of insurance discrimination and redlining can be addressed. Perceptions and perspectives of broader urban policy matters clearly influence the ideas various parties bring to these particular debates. At the same time, lessons from the insurance debate can inform broader discussions of urban policy and race relations.

INSURANCE AND THE URBAN QUESTION

Urban policy has reemerged as at least part of the public policy agenda, though clearly not the priority item it was 30 years ago. Much of the current discussion among policymakers, social scientists, journalists, and others has focused on the so-called underclass. Whether the particular issue is welfare reform, civil rights, economic development, or urban policy generally, the discussion often focuses on the values and culture of poor people themselves, particularly inner-city residents and most especially residents of color in these areas. Left out of these discussions is the historical and social context in which such attributes emerge. Recent developments in the insurance redlining debate constitute part of a healthy antidote to the direction of this larger debate over urban policy.

The conservative assault comes from a range of scholars, journalists, and others, including Charles Murray, George Gilder, William Bennett, Lawrence Mead, Shelby Steele, Thomas Sowell, Linda Chavez, and Glen Loury, to name only a few. The basic tenets of this philosophy are the following: (1) poverty, inequality, and emerging "underclass" behavior reflect defects in the values and culture of the poor; (2) most problematic values include a disrespect for honest work and a "live for today" mentality manifested in dependence on welfare, higher crime rates, teenage pregnancy, and out-of-wedlock births, all of which lead to a breakup of the traditional family; (3) well-intended government programs nurture dependence and stifle entrepreneurial attributes vital for economic success; and (4) only by forcing people to take care of themselves will these problems be effectively addressed.

Sowell clearly articulated the problematic behavioral traits when he concluded, "One of the most important causes of differences in income and employment is the way people work—some diligently, carefully, persistently, cooperatively, and without requiring much supervision or warnings about absenteeism, tardiness, or drinking, and others requiring much such concern (1984: 47). Mead concurred: "There is a culture of poverty that discourages work, but the poor will work more regularly if government enforces the work norm" (1992: 24). The solution, according to Murray, is simple: "Scrapping the entire federal welfare and income-support structure for working-aged persons, including AFDC, Medicaid, Food Stamps, Unemployment Insurance, Worker's Compensation, subsidized housing, disability insurance and the rest. It would leave the working-aged person with no recourse whatsoever except the job market, family members, friends, and public or private locally funded services" (1984: 227–28).

But this vision ignores the context in which such attributes emerge and behaviors occur. The fact of poverty itself, disinvestment and deindustrialization of urban communities, persistent discrimination, and the collapse of public institutions ranging from schools to police departments are just some of those forces often ignored in the conservative critique. The reality of urban poverty and the well-known problems confronting many declining urban communities are not subject to significant dispute. It is the causes and possible solutions of these all-too-familiar urban ills that are contested. As Stephen Steinberg has stated:

> The question is not whether such facts exist or whether they should be
> discussed, but rather how they should be *interpreted*: whether these
> observations are accepted at face value, or whether they are placed

within a larger historical and social context; whether as social scientists we indulge in gratuitous moral judgements, or whether we *explain*
the behavior that violates prevailing codes of morality; that is, whether
we label this behavior as antisocial and treat it as self-explaining, or
whether we establish the *linkages* between the behavior we can observe
and the more distant and less visible social forces that are ultimately
responsible for the production and reproduction of the ghetto and all
its notorious ills [emphasis in original]. (1995: 6)

As Michael Katz (1989, 1995) has pointed out, the emerging consensus on poverty reflects ingrained beliefs about the poor, the nature
of poverty, the role of welfare, and what to do about these matters
generally. What has long been missing in this conception, and particularly in its more recent formulations, is a recognition of power. As
Katz concluded, the discussion "slipped easily, unreflectively, into a
language of family, race, and culture rather than inequality, power,
and exploitation" (1989: 237).

One perhaps small but still significant piece of the historical and
social context of urban development has been the behavior of financial
institutions. Again, the explicit utilization of race historically in the
appraisal and underwriting of property by financial institutions (including property insurers), along with other housing-related industries, and the persistence of disparate treatment and disparate impact
in connection with the provision of housing and related financial
services constitute critical pieces of the context in which the dynamics of poverty play out.

Even if we leave aside the issue of unlawful discrimination, uneven
access to capital and related financial services, including property
insurance, leads to the uneven development of metropolitan areas.
Such practices undermine the economic development and quality of
life in the urban core of many cities, fueling racial inequality in those
areas. Where inner cities are distressed, the social and economic
health of entire metropolitan areas is threatened (Cisneros 1993;
Persky et al. 1991). To the extent that such practices are unlawful,
these inequalities are exacerbated and are potentially even more in-
cendiary.

The property insurance industry, in other words, constitutes one
component of the political economy of urban America. It is part of
the structural context, one with an explicitly racist history in many
respects and one that exhibits persistent patterns of racial disparities
today, which must be addressed if the behavioral problems that have
been identified are to be altered. Structural problems, in other words,
require structural solutions.To some extent, of course, the challenge

of urban policy generally and the role of the property insurance itself are interactive. It is true that safer streets, more-educated and wealthier homeowners, and better-maintained homes will increase the availability and reduce the price of insurance in many urban areas. But public policy and private action specific to insurance need not await the resolution of other social problems. In fact, changes in the provision of property insurance are essential to the achievement of these broader objectives. Ameliorating insurance redlining and discrimination must be part of the broader package of urban policy.

As the subsequent chapters illustrate, the narrow issue of insurance redlining itself requires structural solutions (e.g., changes in underwriting guidelines, different patterns of agent location, retraining of insurance professionals, education of insurance consumers, new relationships between the industry and consumers). Although there is no blueprint for policymakers, regulators, insurers, consumers, or others to follow, the outlines of effective strategies are emerging. It is not a tidy process, and there is no technological quick fix. Indeed, developing responses to insurance redlining constitutes a contentious political process often involving conflicting parties with varying degrees of power. Lawsuits, fair housing complaints, legislative and regulatory actions, and negotiated partnerships involving industry and consumer groups typically compose the landscape. This effort, in other words, differs little from the processes that play out in any significant struggle to achieve meaningful social change.

The lessons reported in this volume certainly do not represent the final word on these issues. But they offer guidance, based on at least preliminary successes, for resolving over three decades of debate and materially addressing this particular form of financial disinvestment. To seek and implement solutions to the problems of insurance redlining and discrimination is to pursue a bumpy road. But at least there are more signposts to guide the way.

Notes

1. The term *insurance redlining* is frequently used in the literature to refer to discrimination against neighborhoods and individuals. That is, insurers can redline (i.e., refuse to insure or to vary the terms of insurance because of some neighborhood characteristic, such as its racial composition, unrelated to risk), and they can discriminate against an individual owing to a factor also unrelated to risk, such as an individual's race or ethnicity. Technically, *redlining* refers to the geographic level, whereas

discrimination refers to the individual level. Throughout the "redlining" debates, and for the purposes of this book, the term *redlining* is often used to refer to both types of behavior. Where discrimination at the geographic or individual level is discussed specifically, the terms *redlining* and *discrimination* are used as appropriate. But in much of this volume *redlining* refers to the broader phenomenon.

2. Unless noted otherwise, information in this section is taken from responses to notices of proposed rulemaking issued by HUD in 1980 and 1994 as well as from several hearings, including those held by the U.S. Senate Judiciary Subcommittee on Citizens and Shareholders Rights and Remedies (1978), the House Banking, Housing, and Finance Subcommittee on Consumer Credit and Insurance (1993), the Senate Committee on Banking, Housing, and Urban Affairs, as well as Commerce (1994), and HUD (1994).

3. As this book went to press, the Urban Institute was completing a paired-testing study for HUD, but the results were not available to the general public. This study examined the experiences of shoppers who posed as first-time homebuyers seeking a price quote for property insurance. Testing occurred in two cities: Phoenix and New York. In Phoenix, testing examined Hispanic/white differences, whereas in New York, testing examined black/white differences.

4. The FAIR (Fair Access to Insurance Requirements) Plan is a publicly administered pool operating in 31 states and the District of Columbia to which insurers refer applicants who do not qualify for regular or "voluntary market" policies. All companies writing insurance in those states share in the costs associated with these policies. Initially, the FAIR Plan was designed to provide federal "riot reinsurance." When implemented, its objective was to encourage insurers to accept applicants whose property represented an acceptable risk, except for the exposure to civil disobedience; the federal government would reinsure the companies for losses resulting from future unrest as an incentive to encourage them to provide policies in urban communities. The federal government no longer is involved, but insurers still pool the costs associated with these policyholders.

References

American Insurance Association. 1993. *Availability and Use of Homeowners Insurance in the Urban Core of Major American Cities*. Washington, D.C.: Author.

Association of Community Organizations for Reform Now. 1993. *Allstate: The Good Hands People?* Washington, D.C.: Author.

──────. 1994. *A Policy of Discrimination? Homeowners Insurance Redlining in 14 Cities*. Washington, D.C.: Author.

Badain, David. 1980. "Insurance Redlining and the Future of the Urban Core." *Columbia Journal of Law and Social Problems* 16: 1–83.

Cisneros, Henry G., ed. 1993. *Interwoven Destinies: Cities and the Nation*. New York: W. W. Norton & Co.

Faulstich, James R., and C. Robert Hall. 1978. "Statement before the Subcommittee on Citizens and Shareholders Rights and Remedies." U.S. Senate Judiciary Committee, 95th Cong., 2d Sess., January 18.

Federal Register. 1980. 45(38): 12265–12266. February 25.

————. 1994. 59(157): 41995–41997. August 16.

Harshbarger, Scott. 1995. *A Special Report on Redlining in the Homeowners Insurance Market.* Boston: Attorney General of the Commonwealth of Massachusetts.

Hunter, Robert. 1994. "Insurance Redlining." Testimony before the Committee on Banking, Housing, and Urban Affairs, U.S. Senate, 103rd Cong., 2d Sess., May 11.

Illinois Department of Insurance. 1994. *Status of Homeowners Insurance in Illinois.* Springfield: Author.

Illinois Public Action Council. 1993. *An Analysis of Zip Code Distribution of State Farm and Allstate Agents and Policies in Chicago.* Chicago: Author.

Insurance Information Institute. 1996. *The Fact Book 1996: Property/Casualty Insurance Facts.* New York: Author.

Jackson, Kenneth T. 1985. *Crabgrass Frontier: The Suburbanization of the United States.* New York: Oxford University Press.

Jones, Thomas C. 1977. *Essential Insurance in Michigan: An Avoidable Crisis.* Lansing: Michigan Department of Commerce, Insurance Bureau.

Jordan, Leo. 1978. Speech delivered to the American Insurance Association, New York, May 23.

Katz, Michael B. 1989. *The Undeserving Poor: From the War on Poverty to the War on Welfare.* New York: Pantheon Books.

————. 1995. *Improving Poor People: The Welfare State, the "Underclass," and Urban Schools as History.* Princeton: Princeton University Press.

Keenan, Gerald M. 1979. *Insurance Redlining: Profits vs. Policyholders.* Chicago: National Training and Information Center.

Kincaid, Mark L. 1994. *Insurance Redlining in Texas: A Preliminary Report.* Austin: Office of the Public Insurance Counsel.

Massey, Douglas S., and Nancy Denton. 1993. *American Apartheid: Segregation and the Making of the Underclass.* Cambridge, Mass.: Harvard University Press.

Mead, Lawrence M. 1992. *The New Politics of Poverty.* New York: Basic Books.

Midwestern Regional Advisory Committees to the U.S. Commission on Civil Rights. 1979. *Insurance Redlining: Fact not Fiction.* Washington, D.C.: U.S. Government Printing Office.

Murray, Charles. 1984. *Losing Ground: American Social Policy, 1950–1980.* New York: Basic Books.

National Association of Independent Insurers. 1994a. *An Analysis of Crime and Fire Statistics, Dwelling Characteristics, and Homeowners Insurance Losses for Selected Urban Areas.* Washington, D.C.: Author.

————. 1994b. *A Review of Possible Measures Identified by the NAIC to Address Urban Insurance Problems.* Washington, D.C.: Author.

————. 1994c. "Statement of the National Association of Independent Insurers at the Public Meeting of the Office of Fair Housing and Equal Opportunity, U.S. Department of Housing and Urban Development." Chicago, August 18.

————. 1994d. *Urban Property Insurance: The Issues, the Realities, and Some Observations on Future Actions*. Washington, D.C.: Author.

Oliver, Melvin L., and Thomas M. Shapiro. 1995. *Black Wealth/White Wealth: A New Perspective on Racial Inequality*. New York: Routledge.

Persky, Joseph, Elliott Sclar, and Wim Wiewel. 1991. *Does America Need Cities? An Urban Investment Strategy for National Prosperity*. Washington, D.C.: Economic Policy Institute.

President's National Advisory Panel on Insurance in Riot-Affected Areas. 1968. *Meeting the Insurance Crisis of Our Cities*. Washington, D.C.: U.S. Government Printing Office.

Saadi, Michele. 1987. *Claim It Yourself: The Accident Victim's Guide to Personal Injury Claims*. New York: Pharos Books.

Schachter, Rob. 1979. *Insurance Redlining! Organizing to Win!* Chicago: National Training and Information Center.

Sowell, Thomas. 1984. *Civil Rights: Rhetoric or Reality?* New York: William Morrow & Company.

Squires, Gregory D., and William Velez. 1987. "Insurance Redlining and the Transformation of an Urban Metropolis." *Urban Affairs Quarterly* 23(1): 63–83.

Squires, Gregory D., William Velez, and Karl E. Taeuber. 1991. "Insurance Redlining, Agency Location, and the Process of Urban Disinvestment." *Urban Affairs Quarterly* 26(4): 567–88.

Steinberg, Stephen. 1995. *Turning Back: The Retreat from Racial Justice in American Thought and Policy*. Boston: Beacon Press.

Yaspan, Robert. 1970. "Property Insurance and the American Ghetto: A Study in Social Irresponsibility." *Southern California Law Review* 44: 218–74.

Yinger, John. 1995. *Closed Doors, Opportunities Lost: The Continuing Costs of Housing Discrimination*. New York: Russell Sage Foundation.

Chapter Two

APPLICATION OF THE FEDERAL FAIR HOUSING ACT TO HOMEOWNERS INSURANCE

Stephen M. Dane

The Federal Fair Housing Act was enacted in 1968 "to provide . . . for fair housing throughout the United States" (42 U.S.C. § 3601 [1988]). One of the most far-reaching civil rights statutes ever passed by Congress, it was drafted to be "as broad as Congress could have made it" (*United States v. Youritan Construction Company*, 370 F. Supp. 643, 648 [N.D. Cal. 1973]). The courts have consistently interpreted the act expansively to encompass housing-related practices and forms of housing-related discrimination not directly mentioned in it.[1]

For almost three decades since passage of the Fair Housing Act, fair housing advocates and the insurance industry have disagreed on whether Congress intended the act to apply to homeowners insurers. Several courts have addressed the issue, and all but one have reached the same conclusion; namely, that homeowners insurers are indeed subject to the nondiscrimination prohibitions contained in the act. Nevertheless, the industry still clings to the hope that it may conduct its business without fear of repercussion under the act. Until the Supreme Court rules definitively on the question or Congress expresses its intent more clearly, the uncertainty will persist and the arguments will continue.

Tangled up with the question of whether the Fair Housing Act as written applies to homeowners insurance is the issue of whether, as a matter of sound policy, it should. Regardless of which way the Supreme Court construes the language of the act (if it comes to that), the losing side will no doubt lobby Congress to amend the act to conform to its wishes. Several other chapters of this book discuss the broader policy and social implications of homeowners insurance discrimination and redlining. This chapter addresses some of the legal policy implications of homeowners insurance coverage under the Fair Housing Act.

SCOPE OF COVERAGE OF FEDERAL FAIR HOUSING ACT

Express Language of the Act

The insurance industry is quick to point out that the Federal Fair Housing Act makes no mention of homeowners insurance. Such insurance is mentioned neither in the definitional section of the act (§ 802) nor in the prohibitory sections (§§ 804, 805, 806). If the concept of homeowners insurance is never even mentioned in the act, how can one claim that the act is intended to cover homeowners insurance?

Fair housing advocates, however, point out that the Fair Housing Act uses broad, general language, both in the definitional section and in the prohibitory sections, that was intended by Congress to be flexible enough to cover all housing-related transactions. It would have been unreasonable for Congress to attempt to provide a laundry list of all possible housing-related transactions covered by the act, and it chose not to do so. This act, like many other civil rights statutes, intentionally uses open-ended, all-inclusive language to attack a problem—discrimination in housing markets—that occurs in countless different forms.

For example, discrimination by apartment managers and landlords is without question prohibited by the act, but the terms *apartment*, *landlord*, and *manager* are nowhere mentioned. Discrimination by banks and savings institutions in making available home mortgage loans is without question encompassed within the act, but neither banks nor savings institutions are expressly mentioned. Thus, say fair housing advocates, applying the Fair Housing Act to insurance companies is no different than applying the act to any other participant in housing-related transactions that are also not mentioned in the act.

The insurance industry is not convinced. The prohibitory sections of the act focus on types of housing-related *transactions*, rather than on the specific identity of transaction participants. Thus, for example, it is illegal under the act "to refuse to sell," "to refuse to rent," "to refuse to negotiate for the sale or rental" of housing (42 U.S.C. §3604(a)). It is unlawful "to make, print, or publish" any discriminatory statement or advertisement in connection with the sale or rental of dwellings (42 U.S.C. § 3604(c)), and it is illegal to discriminate in "the making or purchasing of loans" (42 U.S.C. § 3605(b)(1)). Yet the act does *not* explicitly state, for example, that it is illegal "to refuse to insure," "to refuse to negotiate for insurance," or "to discriminate in the terms and conditions of insurance." This certainly must be compelling evidence, the industry says, that the *insurance transaction* was not intended by Congress to be included.

But fair housing advocates have a rejoinder to these comments as well. The prohibitory sections of the act contain other, broader language than that highlighted by the insurance industry. For example, under § 805, it is unlawful to discriminate in any real estate-related transactions that involve "the making or purchasing of loans *or providing other financial assistance for . . . constructing . . . or repairing . . . a dwelling. . . .* [emphasis added]." This language makes clear that Congress intended to prohibit discrimination in financial transactions other than loans. One cannot simply ignore the phrase "other financial assistance." The purpose of homeowners insurance, advocates point out, is to provide money to the insured ("financial assistance") for the "repair" or "construction" of a dwelling that has been damaged or totally destroyed by a covered peril. The statutory requirements are plainly met. Congress intentionally used broad, all-inclusive language throughout the entire Fair Housing Act. It was entirely consistent, therefore, for Congress to do so in the financial services section, and it used language that is broad enough to include homeowners insurance.

Fair housing advocates also cite other provisions of the act that could apply to the insurance transaction. For example, § 804(a) makes it illegal to "otherwise make unavailable or deny" a dwelling on a prohibited basis, such as race. Because the purchase of satisfactory homeowners insurance is a precondition to obtaining mortgage financing, which in turn is necessary to purchase a dwelling, the failure to obtain such insurance will make the mortgage loan unavailable, which in turn makes the dwelling unavailable. By this logical progression, the failure to obtain adequate homeowners insurance makes "unavailable" or "denies" housing to otherwise qualified applicants. This rationale has been embraced by the courts (e.g., in *Nationwide Mutual Insurance Company v. Cisneros* [henceforth, *Nationwide v. Cisneros*], 52 F.3d 1351, 1359–60 [6th Cir. 1995], *cert. denied*, 116 S. Ct. 973 [1996]; *NAACP v. American Family Mutual Insurance Company* [henceforth, *NAACP v. American Family*], 978 F.2d 287, 298, 300–01 [7th Cir. 1992], *cert. denied*, 113 S. Ct. 2335 [1993]; *Dunn v. Midwestern Indemnity Co.* [henceforth, *Dunn v. Midwestern*], 472 F. Supp. 1106, 1109 [S.D. Ohio 1979]). In addition, § 804(b) of the act prohibits discrimination "in the provision of services or facilities in connection" with the sale or rental of dwellings. In its regulations, HUD considers homeowners insurance to be a "service" that relates to the sale or rental of dwellings (24 C.F.R. § 100.70[d][4]).

Finally, fair housing advocates observe that the Fair Housing Act has consistently been construed broadly to prohibit many practices not directly mentioned in it. For example, the courts have found exclusionary zoning practices (*United States v. City of Parma*, 661 F.2d 562 [6th Cir. 1981], *cert. denied*, 456 U.S. 926 [1982]); racial steering (*Zuch v. Hussey*, 394 F. Supp. 1029 [E.D. Mich. 1975], *aff'd*, 547 F.2d 1168 [6th Cir. 1977]); discriminatory loan foreclosure procedures (*Harper v. Union Savings Association*, 429 F. Supp. 1254 [N.D. Ohio 1977]); mortgage redlining (*Laufman v. Oakley Building & Loan Company*, 408 F. Supp. 489 [S.D. Ohio 1976]); appraisal practices (*United States v. Association of Independent Real Estate Appraisers*, 442 F. Supp. 1972 [N.D. Ill. 1977]); and the registration of deeds containing racially restrictive covenants (*Mayers v. Ridley*, 465 F.2d 630 [D.C. Cir. 1972]) to be violations of the act, even though none of these transactions are expressly mentioned in it.[2] It would be anomalous in light of these expansive interpretations of the act for the courts to exclude homeowners insurance transactions from the reach of the statute.

Legislative History

Courts struggling to interpret an ambiguous statute often look to the law's legislative history to glean congressional intent. Unfortunately, the Fair Housing Act's legislative history on the question of homeowners insurance is unenlightening.

The industry points out, first, that several attempts were made in the early 1980s to amend the Fair Housing Act to expressly include insurance, but that those efforts were unsuccessful. It also observes that when the Fair Housing Act eventually was successfully amended in 1988, Congress chose not to mention insurance. Indeed, an early version of amended § 805 made specific reference to "insurance," but that reference was later *removed* before the final bill became law.

With respect to unsuccessful efforts to amend the act to expressly mention insurance, fair housing advocates contend that it is not rational to glean "legislative intent" from failed efforts that occurred in Congresses that did not enact the original act. The Congress of the early 1980s was not the one that passed the initial Fair Housing Act in 1968 or that passed the Fair Housing Amendments Act in 1988. Moreover, there could have been several reasons why those attempts failed, all unrelated to the issue of whether insurance should be expressly mentioned or not. Maybe the efforts failed because Congress believed the act already covered insurance transactions—at least one court had so held by 1980 (*Dunn v. Midwestern* 1979). Maybe the efforts failed because there were other proposed amendments to the act, unrelated to insurance, that were unacceptable. The Seventh Circuit Court of Appeals in the *NAACP v. American Family* (1992) case agreed that it would be improper to decipher any legislative intent on this specific issue by analyzing legislative attempts that could have failed for countless other reasons:

> Proposed legislation can fail for many reasons. Some Members of Congress may oppose the proposal on the merits; others may think it unnecessary and therefore not worth the political capital needed to write the "clarification" into the statute over opposition; still others may be indifferent, or seek to use the bill as a vehicle for some unrelated change. Congress may run out of time, as a noncontroversial bill sits in a queue while a contentious proposal is debated. No surprise, therefore, that the Supreme Court repeatedly reminds us that unsuccessful proposals to amend a law, in the years following its passage, carry no significance. (*NAACP v. American Family*, 978 F.2d 287, 299 [7th Cir. 1992]; see also *Nationwide v. Cisneros*, 52 F.3d 1351, 1358–59 [6th Cir. 1995])

With respect to the legislative history of the 1988 amendments, fair housing advocates demand a more careful reading of the committee report that produced the final bill. The House Committee on the Judiciary, which reported the final bill, made a total of 11 changes to the original bill without any officially recorded discussion (*U.S. Code & Cong. Admin. News* 1988). In explaining these changes, the committee used such words as "excludes," "clarifies," "creates," "allows," and similar descriptive verbs. With respect to the change regarding insurance, the committee did *not* "exclude" insurance from coverage like it did other types of transactions. Instead, the committee indicated that it had simply "removed reference" to insurance. Fair housing advocates suggest that the committee's "removal" of any reference to insurance could have been because the committee concluded that any specific reference to insurance was unnecessary in light of the more inclusive term "other financial assistance," which is broad enough to include it. Why should Congress pick one form of financial assistance—insurance—and name it specifically, while not naming other forms of financial assistance, such as grants, gifts, donations, scholarships, credit cards, rebates, and the like? Congress knew how to "exclude" matters otherwise within the scope of the Fair Housing Act's coverage, as it did for drug addicts (§ 3602[h][3]), transvestites (§ 3602: note), religious organizations (§ 3607[a]), housing for older persons (§ 3607[b]), and certain housing transactions

(§ 3603[b]). It could have done so for insurance companies or insurance transactions if it wanted to exclude them from the act's otherwise broad, all-inclusive language. It chose not to.

Federal Court and HUD Interpretations

Several courts have addressed the reach of the Fair Housing Act to homeowners insurers, and have almost uniformly ruled in favor of coverage. In *Dunn v. Midwestern* (1979) and *McDiarmid v. Economy Fire & Casualty Co.* (604 F. Supp. 105 [S.D. Ohio 1984]), two separate judges of the United States District Court for the Southern District of Ohio recognized the causal connection between homeowners insurance and mortgage financing, as well as the necessity of financing as a precondition to adequate housing. "Since insurance is a precondition of adequate housing, a discriminatory denial of insurance would prevent a person economically able to do so from buying a house" (*Dunn v. Midwestern*, 472 F. Supp. at 1109). The United States District Courts for the Eastern District of Pennsylvania and the Western District of Missouri have ruled the same way (in *Strange v. Nationwide Mutual Insurance Company*, 867 F. Supp. 1209 [E.D. Pa. 1994] and *Canady v. Allstate Insurance Co.*).

Two federal appellate courts have also decided that the prohibitions of the Fair Housing Act apply to homeowners insurers. In *NAACP v. American Family* (1992) and again in *United Farm Bureau Mutual Insurance Company, Inc. v. Metropolitan Human Relations Commission* (24 F.3d 1008 [7th Cir. 1994]), the U.S. Court of Appeals for the Seventh Circuit held that §804 of the act applies to discriminatory denials of homeowners insurance, as well as to discriminatory insurance pricing. The Sixth Circuit followed suit in *Nationwide v. Cisneros* (1995).

Moreover, in its interpretive regulations promulgated under the authority of the Fair Housing Act, HUD has clearly stated its position that insurance is one of those "services and facilities" that are prerequisites to obtaining dwellings. In a final rule promulgated January 23, 1989, HUD declared:

> (b) It shall be unlawful, because of race . . . to engage in any conduct relating to the provision of housing or of services and facilities in connection therewith that otherwise makes unavailable or denies dwellings to persons. . . .

(d) Prohibited activities relating to dwellings under paragraph (b) of this section include, but are not limited to: . . . .
(4) Refusing to provide . . . property or hazard insurance for dwellings or providing . . . insurance differently because of race. (24 C.F.R. § 100.70[b][d]).

The specific example of insurance was used by HUD "in order to indicate that the refusal to provide, or the provision of different . . . property or hazard insurance for dwellings because of race . . . can constitute a violation of 'the otherwise make unavailable or deny' provisions in the Act" (54 Fed. Reg. 3240 [Jan. 23, 1989]). HUD's new regulations are consistent with the position it took over a decade ago on the issue: "Insurance redlining, by denying or impeding [insurance] coverage, makes mortgage money unavailable, rendering dwellings 'unavailable' as effectively as the denial of financial assistance on other grounds" (memorandum of General Counsel of Housing and Urban Development to Chester McGuire, Assistant Secretary for Equal Opportunity, August 15, 1978, quoted in *Dunn v. Midwestern*, 472 F. Supp. at 1109). The interpretation given to the statute by HUD is to be given "great weight" by the courts (*NAACP v. American Family*, 978 F.2d at 300).

The sole contrary decision is that of *Mackey v. Nationwide Insurance Companies* ([henceforth, *Mackey v. Nationwide*], 724 F.2d 419 [4th Cir. 1984]). The U.S. Court of Appeals for the Fourth Circuit ruled in *Mackey* that the Fair Housing Act was not intended to cover the business of insurance. The court drew this conclusion because there is no mention of insurance in the statute or in its legislative history, and because several bills introduced in later sessions of Congress to include such a reference had been defeated.

The *Mackey* rationale on this issue has been criticized by commentators, explicitly rejected by several other federal courts, and superseded by HUD's interpretative regulations, which were promulgated after and with full knowledge of the decision in *Mackey*. *Mackey*'s reasoning has also been seriously eroded in light of the Fair Housing Amendments Act of 1988, in which Congress made a number of changes to the Fair Housing Act. Perhaps implicitly acknowledging these new developments after *Mackey* was decided, the U.S. Supreme Court has twice refused to grant certiorari to resolve the issue despite the alleged "conflict" between the circuits.

Congress certainly could have expressed its intent more clearly, not just in the language of the act itself but also in its legislative history. As the record now stands, HUD and the courts generally agree that the act's language encompasses insurance transactions and that the act's legislative history does not indicate otherwise.

THE MCCARRAN-FERGUSON ACT

There is an additional reason, according to the insurance industry, why the Fair Housing Act cannot be construed to cover insurance transactions. This argument rests on an interpretation of the McCarran-Ferguson Act of 1945, which provides:

> No Act of Congress shall be construed to invalidate, impair, or supersede any law enacted by any State for the purpose of regulating the business of insurance, or which imposes a fee or tax upon such business, unless such Act specifically relates to the business of insurance. . . . (15 U.S.C. §1012[b]).

The insurance industry contends that this language precludes any court from interpreting the Fair Housing Act to apply to the business of insurance.

The McCarran-Ferguson Act was passed by Congress in response to a Supreme Court decision holding that the business of insurance was "interstate commerce" within the meaning of the Commerce Clause of the U.S. Constitution (*United States v. South-Eastern Underwriters Association*, 322 U.S. 533 [1944]). This decision was perceived as a threat to the states' ability to regulate insurance transactions, for it called into question the constitutionality of *any* state regulation or taxation of insurance. The purpose of the McCarran-Ferguson Act was to ensure "that silence on the part of Congress shall not be construed to impose any barrier to the regulation or taxation of such business by the several states" (15 U.S.C. § 1011). The act operates to ensure that the states remain free to regulate insurance companies without fear of a Commerce Clause attack, and permits the states to continue to regulate and tax the business of insurance companies, in spite of the Commerce Clause (*Group Life & Health Insurance Company v. Royal Drug Company*, 440 U.S. 205, 218, n. 18 [1967]).

Fair housing advocates do not discern any legitimate issue here. First, they observe that the McCarran-Ferguson Act is implicated only when the interpretation of some federal law will threaten "to invalidate, impair, or supersede" a state law regulating the business of insurance. The insurance industry has never been able to identify any state law that would be invalidated, impaired, or superseded should the Fair Housing Act be interpreted to include homeowners insurance transactions. To the contrary, racial discrimination by homeowners insurers is probably prohibited by most state laws in one form or another, so there would be consistency with, not impairment of, state law.

Second, advocates point out that the Fair Housing Act was passed as a valid exercise of congressional power under the Thirteenth Amendment (*Williams v. Mathews Company*, 499 F.2d 819 [8th Cir. 1974]), not the Commerce Clause, and so the concerns underlying the passage of the McCarran-Ferguson Act are not present. In the absence of an attempt to subvert or avoid some state law on the grounds that Congress has preempted the requirements of that law through the exercise of its powers under the Commerce Clause, the McCarran-Ferguson Act is simply not relevant.

On this issue the courts have uniformly rejected the industry's position. All of the federal courts that have discussed the McCarran-Ferguson Act in this context have held that the McCarran-Ferguson Act has no bearing on the scope of the Fair Housing Act's coverage (*Nationwide v. Cisneros* 1995; *NAACP v. American Family* 1992; *Mackey v. Nationwide* 1984). The McCarran-Ferguson Act defense to the application of the Fair Housing Act to insurers therefore appears dead.

FAIR PLANS

Fair Access to Insurance Requirements (FAIR) Plans were enacted by many states in response to the federal Urban Property Protection and Reinsurance Act (UPPRA, PL 90-448, 82 Stat. 476, Title XI of the Housing and Urban Development Act of 1968). A special federal commission that was convened after the riots of the 1960s concluded that many inner-city areas lacked adequate property insurance coverage, and that reinsurance was not available for losses caused by civil disorders. The federal government therefore established a riot reinsurance program to protect against abnormally high property insurance losses resulting from riots and other civil disturbance. To obtain the benefits of federal riot reinsurance, however, a state was required to enact a FAIR Plan containing certain mandatory provisions required by UPPRA. The act was designed to encourage and assist the various state insurance authorities and the property insurance industry to develop and carry out statewide programs which will make necessary property insurance coverage against the fire, crime, and other perils more readily available for residential, business, and other properties meeting reasonable underwriting standards. (PL 90-448, § 1102, 12 V.S.C.A. § 1749bbb nts.)

Several insurance companies take the position that the enactment of UPPRA and the establishment of FAIR Plans constitute the congressional "solution" to the problem of urban redlining and that an expansive interpretation of the Fair Housing Act will usurp this solution. They contend that the enactment of UPPRA and FAIR Plans demonstrate a legislative acknowledgment that location is a legitimate risk factor and that location can therefore be used by the insurance industry to set standards, underwriting policies, and insurability guidelines. They argue that allowing claims to be asserted under the Fair Housing Act will impose a different distribution of risks than that intended by FAIR Plans. This approach would be inconsistent with Congress's solution to the redlining problem and would conflict with the intended functioning of the FAIR Plans. In particular, disparate-impact suits will destroy the allocation of risks among insurers established by the FAIR Plans.

Fair housing advocates assert that this is a tortured reading of UPPRA, FAIR Plans, and the legislative intent behind them. FAIR Plans typically say nothing about race discrimination, discriminatory impact, or civil rights. FAIR Plans do not sanction, condone, or approve the behavior and practices of the conventional insurance market in urban areas that resulted in the problems addressed by the Fair Housing Act. UPPRA was an emergency response to what Congress considered an extraordinary situation that was leading to the decay of urban areas. It draws no distinctions between areas, locations, or neighborhoods within urban areas or between how they should be treated. The act's purpose was clearly to increase the availability of insurance to urban areas generally and to provide federal reinsurance for riot insurance coverage. Moreover, most FAIR Plans contemplate the eventual elimination of their existence. In other words, Congress intended that, over time, the private homeowners insurance market would provide adequate insurance in all urban areas.

On this issue the courts, again, have rejected industry claims. In both *Dunn v. Midwestern* (1979) and *Nationwide v. Cisneros* (1995), the courts rejected the insurers' arguments that the existence of UPPRA or FAIR Plans had any bearing on the scope of coverage of the Fair Housing Act. "We agree that the purposes of the two acts are different and that the enactment of UPPRA does not shed light on Congress' intent regarding the application of the Fair Housing Act to insurance" (*Nationwide v. Cisneros*, 52 F.3d, at 1358).

DISPARATE-IMPACT ANALYSIS

A final argument put forth by the insurance industry as to why the Fair Housing Act cannot be interpreted to apply to the business of homeowners insurance or, at the least, why it cannot apply to insurance transactions to the same extent it may apply to other housing-related transactions rests upon the concept of disparate-impact liability.

There is a strong consensus among the federal courts that the Fair Housing Act prevents not only intentional discriminatory housing practices but also those practices that have a disparate impact on groups protected by the act, even if unintentionally so (see, generally, R. Schwemm, *Housing Discrimination Law and Litigation*, at 10-20 to 10-24, in Schwemm 1994). Every federal appellate court to squarely address the issue has so held, as have several lower courts. Moreover, when Congress amended the Fair Housing Act in 1988, it expressly approved of these disparate-impact holdings (134 Cong. Rec. S12449 [1988] [Statement of Sen. Kennedy]). Federal agencies charged with enforcement of the act against mortgage lenders (such as the U.S. Department of Justice, the Comptroller of the Currency, the Board of Governors of the Federal Reserve System, and other financial regulatory agencies) have recognized the appropriateness of using disparate-impact analysis.

To make a prima facie case of liability under a disparate-impact theory, a plaintiff must show that the practice at issue has a disproportionate impact on members of a protected class. Once a prima facie case of disparate impact has been shown, the burden shifts to the defendant to prove a business necessity sufficiently compelling to justify the challenged practice. Even if such a business necessity is proven, the challenged practice will be found illegal under the Fair Housing Act if a less-restrictive alternative is available to the defendant that achieves the same business purpose. Conversely, even if minorities and other protected groups are disproportionately affected by certain business practices, there will be no liability under the Fair Housing Act if those practices are necessary to operate the business and no alternatives with a lesser impact are available.

The insurance industry contends that exposing insurers to liability under the Fair Housing Act through the use of a disparate-impact analysis interferes with the nature of risk-spreading that is fundamental to the insurance underwriting and pricing processes. Insurers believe that disparate-impact analysis will force otherwise low risks to artificially subsidize high risks, thus resulting in "unfair discrimination" between separate classes of risks.

For example, insurers typically use aggregate-loss experience to establish appropriate premium rates. Because losses are generally higher in urban areas than in suburban communities, homeowners insurance rates should be higher for cities than for suburbs. Yet because a high proportion of minorities live in urban areas as distinct from suburban areas, there is arguably a "disparate impact" on minority communities in the form of higher prices. The higher prices have nothing to do with race or racial composition, the insurers argue, so why should they be exposed to liability under the Fair Housing Act simply because of the accidental circumstance of where minorities tend to live?

Fair housing advocates respond by pointing out that liability cannot be visited upon an insurer under the Fair Housing Act by a showing of disparate impact alone. Rather, only practices that are *unjustified* by a business need may be found illegal. If, in fact, the industry can demonstrate that a practice having a disparate impact is justified by a legitimate business necessity, and that no less-restrictive alternatives are available to satisfy the same business need, there can be no liability under the Fair Housing Act.

To use the insurers' example, if an insurance company can demonstrate through statistics that higher prices charged in urban areas are the result of higher losses in those areas, and if there is no alternative to the pricing mechanism that could achieve the same purpose consistent with sound insurance principles, then it would not be a violation of the Fair Housing Act for the company to price its products in that way, even if a higher proportion of the minority community in that metropolitan area ended up paying higher premiums than the nonminority community.

Thus, fair housing advocates say, for those business practices that can be shown to have a disparate impact on minorities or other protected categories of persons, the industry need only justify those practices with sound, empirical data. That does not seem to be an onerous requirement, and the industry will not violate the act in those circumstances. Under a disparate-impact analysis, only those insurers who engage in practices for which there is no legitimate empirical basis are at risk.

POLICY REASONS FOR AND AGAINST COVERAGE UNDER FAIR HOUSING ACT

Regardless of what Congress may have written or intended in connection with the applicability of the Federal Fair Housing Act to property insurance, ultimately it may have to revisit the issue and decide definitively whether to include or exclude property insurance transactions from the act's coverage. A discussion of the numerous possible policy implications pro and con is beyond the scope of this chapter; these are addressed elsewhere in this book. Nevertheless, some legal aspects to the policy debate deserve consideration here.

First is the issue of *federal/state relations and the proper role of the national government in our federal system of regulation.* On the one hand, the federal government has historically taken a hands-off approach to the insurance industry and has avoided intense regulation of that industry in deference to state regulation. It should not, the industry contends, make an exception for homeowners insurance. On the other hand, the federal government has also historically been the champion and protector of civil rights, not just in housing but in all segments of the economy, including employment, banking, education, public accommodations, and others, all of which are *also* regulated in one way or another by the several states. Fair housing advocates suggest that the federal government's longstanding predominance in the field of civil rights is more important than its deference to the states on insurance regulation. Moreover, advocates observe that the federal government *has* chosen to preempt state regulation of insurance in certain significant areas, such as employee benefits and product liability insurance.[3] If it has been willing to do so in some areas, it should consider doing so in the civil rights context for homeowners insurance.

Second, there is the natural tendency to lean toward *consistency and comprehensiveness* in this field of law. Fair housing advocates point out that the Fair Housing Act prohibits discrimination in virtually every type of housing-related transaction, including the rental of property, the sale of property, the financing of property, the foreclosure of property, evictions, zoning, municipal services relating to housing, and others. Excluding only one of the many housing-related transactions that are otherwise covered by the act—the insuring of property—makes no rational sense.

Moreover, regardless of the type of transaction involved, those who are protected by the Fair Housing Act can enforce their right to be free of discrimination using the same standards and guidelines that are applicable to all other housing-related transactions. Yet if the home-owners insurance transaction is excluded from the act, there is a substantial risk that different rules and standards will be applied, which themselves will vary on a state-by-state basis. This kind of inconsistency and non-uniformity in the law should be avoided.

The industry will no doubt argue in response that the insuring of property *is* so uniquely different from any other housing-related transaction that treating it differently as a matter of legal policy makes perfect sense. In contrast to the relatively simple economics involved in the decisions to sell or rent property, the marketing, underwriting, and pricing of insurance involves complexities that no ordinary jury, judge, or civil rights law enforcement agency could hope to understand. It is not appropriate, therefore, to lump the insurance transaction together with all other housing-related transactions.

Interrelated with these considerations are those concerning *what remedies should be available to victims of discrimination.* Setting aside for a moment the "disparate-impact" issue discussed previously, and assuming that there is agreement on both sides that intentional race discrimination is, or should be, unlawful, what kinds of remedies, if any, should be made available to victims of intentional racial discrimination by insurers?

Under the Federal Fair Housing Act a full panoply of remedies is available, including non-economic compensatory damages for emotional distress, humiliation, and the loss of civil rights; economic losses, such as higher premiums or a loss caused by inadequate coverage; and affirmative remedies like injunctions and specific performance. In contrast, most state unfair insurance practices laws do not provide for these remedies and are generally limited to sanctions, fines, and civil penalties imposed on the offending insurance company by the state insurance commissioner. State insurance laws can typically be enforced only administratively by the state Department of Insurance, where investigations must be conducted by department staff and hearings are before administrative officers. These state laws generally do *not* provide for a private cause of action, any rights of intervention or participation by victims, or discovery by victims (see, generally, *NAACP v. American Family*, 978 F.2d at 301). In other words, the applicant or homeowner actually discriminated against has very little, if any, access under traditional state enforcement to the full spectrum of remedies available under federal civil rights laws.

These concerns all relate intimately to the proper administration of justice in our society. They cannot be ignored if and when Congress ever revisits this important issue.

CONCLUSION

The weight of legal authority to date clearly supports the proposition that the Federal Fair Housing Act applies to homeowners insurance. The Department of Housing and Urban Development, the Department of Justice, and almost all of the courts to address the issue have come to this conclusion. The Supreme Court has consistently refused to review these decisions. Nevertheless, the arguments for and against coverage under the Fair Housing Act of the homeowners insurance transaction will no doubt continue. As more and more lawsuits are brought against insurance companies, more courts will make rulings on these contentions and perhaps, some day, a clear consensus will be reached. If not, either the Supreme Court—or, in the end, Congress—must resolve this issue once and for all.

Notes

1. The Federal Fair Housing Act originally prohibited discrimination in housing-related transactions on the bases of race, color, religion, and national origin, but was later amended to prohibit discrimination in housing-related transactions on the bases of sex, handicap, and familial status. The term "familial status" relates generally to the presence of children in the household.

2. Discriminatory appraisal practices were explicitly added to the act by the 1988 Fair Housing Amendments Act (42 U.S.C. § 3605).

3. The Employee Retirement Income Security Act (29 U.S.C. § 1001 *et seq.*) preempts state laws that conflict with it. The Liability Risk Retention Act (15 U.S.C. § 3901 *et seq.*) preempts state laws that prohibit insurance companies from participating in risk-retention pools relating to product liability claims.

References

Schwemm, Robert G. 1994. *Housing Discrimination Law and Litigation*. New York: Clark-Boardman.

U.S. Code & Cong. Admin. News. 1988: 2,174–5.

Chapter Three

AVAILABILITY AND AFFORDABILITY PROBLEMS IN URBAN HOMEOWNERS INSURANCE MARKETS

Robert W. Klein

Problems with the availability and affordability of property insurance in urban communities and allegations of industry redlining practices have received considerable political attention and generated extensive policy debate since the mid-1960s. The importance of property insurance for homeownership makes insurance availability and affordability a critical economic issue for many inner-city areas. Urban insurance problems are strongly rooted in the severe economic and social ills afflicting the urban core. Diminished access to insurance contributes to the economic difficulties of urban communities, which drive insurers even farther away. Insurers contend that there are risk-related reasons for the disparities in rates and coverages available, but such explanations have not satisfied urban residents and government officials (Duncan 1995). The fact that underserved areas tend to have high-minority populations leads to charges of racial as well as geographic discrimination.

Urban insurance problems could be caused by a number of factors, including risk conditions, low income, costly information and other barriers to entry, regulatory constraints, and unfairly discriminatory industry practices. In addition, certain industry underwriting and marketing practices that are not intended to discriminate racially or geographically may still have a negative impact on urban communities because of the communities' particular economic and demographic characteristics. The term *redlining* is defined here as unfair discrimination (i.e., discrimination that is not based on differences in cost or risk) against a particular geographic area. Hence, by this definition, redlining is only one of a number of possible contributors to urban insurance problems.

The complexity of urban insurance problems and the difficulties inherent in changing market practices have hampered public and private attempts to make property insurance more available and less

expensive for urban homeowners. Substantial efforts to alleviate urban insurance problems have occurred at the state level, where insurance is principally regulated, but federal agencies also have sought to
police industry practices and have intervened in other ways to influence the availability of property insurance. The Los Angeles riots in
May 1992 refocused national attention on urban maladies, including
the cost and availability of insurance. This prompted the National
Association of Insurance Commissioners (NAIC) and a number of
states to launch investigations and to take further steps to address
urban insurance problems. At the same time, the U.S. Department of
Housing and Urban Development and the U.S. Department of Justice
have stepped up antidiscrimination enforcement actions against insurers under the Federal Fair Housing Act.

The relative roles of state and federal governments in regulating
property insurance practices is an important issue in the overall policy debate about how to address urban insurance problems. Can federal regulation complement state efforts to improve urban market conditions? The answer to this question depends, in part, upon the nature
and principal causes of urban insurance problems and the remedies
available to state and federal agencies. The more these problems are
driven by unfairly discriminatory practices, the stronger the case for
toughening state regulation and federal regulatory enforcement efforts,
if the states are unwilling or possess insufficient resources to ade-
quately prosecute illegal industry behavior. On the other hand, if
urban insurance availability and affordability conditions are influenced primarily by the risk of loss and other economic factors, the
need to implement a broader array of measures that address these
underlying causes becomes clearer. Many of these measures could be
most effectively implemented through private and public efforts at the
state and local levels, although the federal government has a role here
as well.

This chapter seeks to illuminate this policy debate by drawing a
picture of the availability and affordability of homeowners insurance
in urban communities based on information gleaned from the NAIC's
recent investigation. Of particular interest are differences in the cost
and availability of insurance within metropolitan areas that are revealed by zip code insurance data compiled by the NAIC and the
Missouri Department of Insurance. The study adds to previous research by analyzing urban insurance problems in a number of cities
across the nation and exploring the link between these problems and
the racial composition of neighborhoods, while controlling for the
effects of various other factors, including variables related to the risk

of loss. Although this research does not definitively answer all the questions about the causes of urban insurance problems, it provides insights that should help guide public policy toward solutions that are likely to have greater success than previous efforts.

The next section of this chapter reviews the economics of urban insurance markets and the conditions under which market failures might occur. This is followed by an empirical analysis of urban insurance market structure and performance, including a multiple regression analysis of the availability of and price of homeowners insurance in urban neighborhoods that isolates the effects of various determinants of market conditions. The chapter concludes with a discussion of the policy implications of this research for public and private remedies to alleviate urban insurance problems.

MARKET PROBLEMS AND POTENTIAL MARKET FAILURES IN URBAN INSURANCE MARKETS

In theory, a competitive market should supply an optimal amount of insurance at a price just sufficient for insurers to cover their costs, including a competitive rate of return on the capital they have invested (Scherer and Ross 1990). At this price, the quantity of insurance that insurers are willing to sell will equal the quantity of insurance that consumers are willing to buy. If expected loss costs vary among homes, the market will supply coverage at prices that will vary for homes commensurate with their expected costs (i.e., "actuarially fair" prices) (Harrington and Doerpinghaus 1993). Economic self-interest will motivate insurers to set accurate cost-based prices (Harrington and Niehaus 1992). If an insurer sets a price below the expected cost for a group of similar risks, it will lose money. If an insurer sets a price above the expected costs for a group, it will lose that group to competitors who will undercut its price. This does not mean that every home will necessarily have insurance, but it does imply that every homeowner with an insurable risk exposure who is willing and able to pay an actuarially fair premium based on his or her exposure should be able to obtain insurance.

With the exception of insurer and consumer information, most economists believe that personal lines insurance markets (i.e., private passenger automobile, homeowners, and dwelling fire insurance) generally satisfy the conditions necessary for workable competition

(Klein 1989, 1994b). In excess of 500 insurers (groups) sold home-owners insurance countrywide in 1993, and market concentration at the state and national level is moderate compared to standard bench-marks used by economists (Klein 1994b). The estimated average rate of return on net worth for homeowners insurance has been negative since 1988, in part because of high catastrophe losses, so insurers are clearly not earning excessive profits from this line on the whole (NAIC 1995).

However, high information costs for both insurers and insureds could impair insurance market efficiency. Considerable literature has dealt with the implications of imperfect and asymmetric infor-mation for market structure and the supply of insurance for differ-ent risks (Varian 1992). This literature suggests that insurers will seek to establish risk categorization schemes that allow approxi-mately actuarially fair prices, but that are costly, and asymmetric information may result in excessive classification and suboptimal market outcomes. Other violations of the conditions necessary for efficient markets could contribute to urban insurance problems (Klein 1994a).

Urban insurance concerns are concentrated in three basic areas: (1) the availability of needed or desired insurance coverage; (2) the cost or affordability of insurance coverage; and (3) the quality of service provided by insurers and agents.[1] These problems could be caused by market failures or other economic factors, or both. Economists use the term *market failure* to encompass circumstances in which violations of the basic assumptions underlying competitive markets result in less than optimal outcomes.

Market failures could occur in urban markets for various reasons. Some of these may involve unfair discrimination and others do not. The risk characteristics of urban core neighborhoods could raise high informational barriers and other barriers to market entry, for example. Presumably, homes in older neighborhoods vary more in terms of quality and risk than homes in newer neighborhoods. Lack of detailed information about risk conditions in inner-city neighborhoods and the need to perform costly inspections of older structures could cause some insurers to avoid writing insurance, to underwrite more selec-tively, or to require a "risk premium" to write in these areas.[2] Some insurers have expressed willingness to enter an urban area with a degree of uncertainty about risk conditions so long as they were con-fident that they could subsequently raise their rates or withdraw from the area, if necessary. However, insurers may fear that regulators will constrain their efforts to make such adjustments, effectively locking them into a money-losing situation.[3]

Some insurance company personnel and agents may have an irrational prejudice toward minorities or people who live in poor and high-minority areas (i.e., they might believe that minorities or people who live in poor and high-minority areas are more likely to have claims) and therefore may avoid selling insurance to such individuals or may charge them a higher price (Squires and Velez 1988). Irrational or prejudicial cultural views may have a greater chance of influencing business decisions when lack of "hard data" necessarily increases reliance on subjective judgment. It has been noted that few insurance personnel in decision-making positions live in or have personal experience with inner-city areas.

Moral hazard and adverse selection are other potential sources of insurance market failure (Varian 1992). Purchasing insurance causes insureds to have diminished incentives to prevent losses. Insurers seek to counteract moral hazard by controlling which properties they insure and requiring insureds to share losses through deductibles, copayments, and policy limits. This is not a situation confined to urban markets, but it could be more severe in areas where the replacement cost of homes can considerably exceed their market value. Some properties may simply not be insurable at all if the risk of loss is very high or impossible to calculate, or if the insured would have little incentive to prevent loss. Adverse selection also could be a problem for insurers with lax underwriting standards who could attract an increasing and excessive concentration of high-risk insureds that would outstrip the insurers' ability to raise premiums to match the higher risk of loss.

Other barriers to market entry or exit and regulatory restrictions on prices, products, and market practices could reduce the supply of insurance in urban markets. Differences between areas in the quality of housing stock and other risk-related factors will cause variation in the availability and cost of insurance, although this would not constitute a market failure per se. Inner-city neighborhoods suffer from higher fire and crime rates, which necessarily cause premiums to be higher and restrict the availability of full coverage to high-risk properties (National Association of Independent Insurers [NAII] 1994).

Some insurers and agents are disinclined to market insurance in areas subject to high losses or where income and property values are low. Because agent commissions are typically fixed as a percentage of the policy premium (e.g., 10 to 15 percent), the amount of commission an agent receives increases with amount of insurance purchased and premiums paid. Consequently, agents may target their sales activities toward areas with higher-value homes that carry more insurance and offer higher commissions. Also, agents may perceive more opportunities to sell other policies (e.g., general liability coverage, auto insurance, and life insurance) to higher-income individuals from which they will earn additional commissions. Insurers also appear to be attracted to high-income communities where they may perceive better opportunities and greater profits in selling various types of policies with high amounts of coverage.

Circumstances on the demand side also can result in market failures and other market problems. Costly information can limit consumers' effectiveness in shopping for the best insurance prices and products to fit their needs. Costly search can result in excessive prices and suboptimal purchase decisions by consumers, a problem of particular concern in insurance (Joskow 1973; Varian 1992). If search is particularly costly for inner-city consumers and there are other barriers to market entry, it could result in excessive insurance prices in these areas. The lack of agents in inner-city areas could increase search costs for consumers (Squires, Velez, and Taeuber 1991; see also Schultz, chapter 4, this volume). Inner-city consumers also may lack sufficient income to purchase the insurance that they need, which could be a particularly acute problem for low-income households residing in high-cost areas. In addition, homeowners may choose not to purchase insurance if their financial losses will be paid by other parties through defaulting on home loans and receiving tax deductions or government financial assistance for uninsured losses.

From an economic perspective, the presence of market failures stemming from arbitrary restrictions on the supply of insurance to certain groups of individuals or from other causes of urban insurance problems are difficult to ascertain simply by comparing the amount of insurance purchased or prices paid between different communities. The price, quantity, and quality of insurance purchased are jointly determined by demand and supply conditions. This makes it problematic to sort out the presence and impact of unfairly discriminatory practices and other potential causes of market difficulties from the full set of variables affecting supply and demand.[4] Hence, in studying insurance market conditions in urban areas, great caution must be exercised in drawing inferences from statistical patterns that may or may not be caused by discriminatory practices or other market failures.

STRUCTURE AND PERFORMANCE OF URBAN INSURANCE MARKETS

Urban versus Nonurban Disparities

Workable competition at a national and state level does not guarantee optimal performance in urban markets if there are structural impediments to competition in urban markets. The top panel of table 3.1 compares information on insurance prices, costs, and availability in 33 cities versus nonurban areas for the years 1989–91. The average premium entries indicate what homeowners typically pay for property insurance. The other variables provide comparative information on the cost of claims, which should be the principal factor influencing the level of premiums. The loss ratio shows the claims payments or benefits that insureds receive in relation to the premiums they pay and is a relative measure of fairness and efficiency in insurance pricing. The higher the loss ratio, the less insureds pay in premiums relative to the benefits they receive. If loss ratios differ significantly between different areas, it would indicate that pricing is inefficient or unfair for areas with lower loss ratios.[5]

Separate figures are shown for dwelling fire policies, which typically cover the structure but not its contents against fire; limited-coverage policies (HO-1 and HO-8 policy forms), which cover both a structure and its contents but typically limit the perils covered and pay only the market value of a property if it is less than the cost of its replacement; and broad-coverage policies (HO-2, HO-3, and HO-5 policy forms), which cover a larger set of perils as well as replacement cost. Broad-coverage policies provide the most desirable form of coverage, price considerations aside.

These figures confirm the common view that urban residents pay more for insurance than homeowners in nonurban areas for every type of coverage. The greatest disparity in pricing was for limited-coverage policies where urban insureds pay $353 a year on average, 69 percent higher than what their nonurban counterparts pay (see table 3.1). Urban residents paid an average of $386 for broad coverage, which was 31.7 percent higher than the nonurban premium. Premiums per

Table 3.1 HOMEOWNERS INSURANCE COSTS AND AVAILABILITY: URBAN VERSUS NONURBAN AREAS, (33 CITIES)

a. Costs

	1989–91 Annual Average		
	Dwelling Fire (Percentage increase over nonurban areas)	Limited-Coverage Homeowners (Percentage increase over nonurban areas)	Broad-Coverage Homeowners (Percentage increase over nonurban areas)
Average premium (dollars)	185.81 (7.9)	352.95 (69.0)	385.73 (31.7)
Average premium per $1,000 (dollars)	N.A.	5.33 (34.3)	4.67 (26.2)
Average loss cost (dollars)	140.70 (60.8)	233.02 (73.2)	329.66 (57.0)
Frequency of claims (per 100 insured homes)	2.47 (0.4)	7.54 (24.8)	10.40 (14.3)
Average severity (dollars)	5,704 (60.2)	3,089 (38.7)	3,170 (37.3)
Loss ratio (percentage)	75.7 (49.0)	66.0 (2.5)	85.5 (19.2)

b. Availability

	1991			
	Cities	Nonurban Areas	Total State	Percentage Availability over Nonurban Areas
FAIR Plan (percentage)[a]	7.6	1.2	2.2	633.3
Limited-coverage policies (percentage)[b]	23.2	13.3	14.6	174.4

Sources: AAIS, ISO, NAII, NISS, and NAIC.

N.A. = not applicable.

a. FAIR Plan exposures/total exposures for states with FAIR Plan.

b. Dwelling fire, HO-1, and HO-8 exposures/dwelling fire, HO-1, HO-2, HO-3, HO-5, and HO-8 exposures.

$1,000 of insurance coverage also are significantly higher in the cities, although not by as much for the average premium per home. The smaller differences for premiums per $1,000 may be due to the fact that city policies, on the whole, carry higher amounts of insurance.[6]

At the same time, the data indicate that disparities in loss costs are even greater between urban areas and nonurban areas than the differences in premiums. Average loss costs were 73.2 percent and 57 percent higher for limited-coverage and broad-coverage policies, respectively, in the cities than in nonurban areas (see table 3.1). City/nonurban cost disparities appear to be more attributable to differences in the average cost or severity of a claim than in the relative number or frequency of claims.

Because the differences in loss costs are greater than the differences in premiums, the loss ratios for cities are higher than the loss ratios for other areas (see table 3.1). Hence, these data do not indicate that urban areas are being charged excessive premiums in relation to their loss costs. Indeed, the data suggest that urban homeowners overall are receiving a relative bargain in what they pay for insurance given what they receive in claims payments.

The lower panel of table 3.1 provides some indication of the relative availability of insurance, as measured by the proportion of total homes insured through the Fair Access to Insurance Requirements (FAIR) Plan and the proportion of limited-coverage policies sold. FAIR Plans are "residual market" facilities where homeowners must obtain coverage if they cannot find an insurer who will sell them coverage voluntarily. Typically, FAIR Plan coverage is more limited and can cost relatively more than purchasing coverage through the voluntary market.[7] Consequently, it is not generally perceived as a desirable source of coverage. The only exception would be situations where FAIR Plan rates are suppressed below voluntary market rates for some insureds (Duncan 1995). The proportions of FAIR Plan and limited-coverage policies are the best statistical indicators of insurance availability we have, but they can be misleading. Some consumers may prefer to purchase these policies if they are cheaper than their alternatives.

These data confirm the concerns expressed by many regulators and consumer advocates that cities have a significantly higher proportion of FAIR Plan and limited-coverage policies than nonurban areas. Indeed, the average FAIR Plan market share in cities, 7.6 percent, was more than six times that in other areas (see table 3.1). Limited-coverage policies comprised 23.2 percent of the market in cities compared to 13.3 percent for nonurban areas. These patterns tend to support consumer allegations of the lower availability of voluntary market and broad coverage in urban areas. These patterns could be caused by a number of factors, including a higher risk of loss in urban areas and inadequate FAIR Plan rates in some states, as well as discriminatory insurance practices or other market failures. Lack of availability of voluntary and broad-coverage policies is still a concern, even if the premiums that urban insureds pay for the policies they do purchase are commensurate with the claims payments they receive.

Differences within Metropolitan Areas: Descriptive Statistics

Although the preceding data do not suggest that urban insurance premiums are excessive relative to nonurban premiums, it is possible that market performance varies across different cities and areas within cities. Insurance prices could be excessive in some inner-city neighborhoods but not in other urban neighborhoods because of conditions unique to these inner-city areas. The availability of property insurance also is alleged to be more restricted in the core areas of cities than in other urban neighborhoods. To assess market structure and performance at a more refined geographic level, zip code data on insurance premiums and insured homes for calendar year 1992 were compiled through a special data call coordinated by the NAIC. This data set includes 1,333 zip codes in 33 metropolitan areas in 20 states and encompasses most of the largest metropolitan statistical areas (see Klein 1994a).

As shown in tables 3.2 to 3.4, cross-tabulations of availability and average premium measures across zip codes grouped by median household income and the percentage of nonwhite persons reveal fairly consistent patterns.[8] The FAIR Plan market share is positively related to minority concentration and negatively related to household income. For example, FAIR Plan policies account for only 2.9 percent of the total insured homes in low-minority, low-income zip codes, but 18.2 percent of exposures in high-minority, low-income zip codes. The FAIR Plan market share falls to 0.6 percent for low-minority, high-income zip codes (table 3.2). The proportion of dwelling fire and limited-coverage homeowners policies also is positively related to minority concentration and negatively related to median income. The estimated percentage of insured homes declines with minority concentration and increases with income.[9] The average premium tends to increase (although not consistently) with median income, but the ratio of the average premium to the mean house value decreases with median income. This may be partially or totally attributable to the fact that mean house value also increases with median income.

Average premiums also tend to increase with minority concentration, although this pattern does not hold true in all cases. For broad-coverage policies in low-income zip codes, the average premium increases from $5.53 per $1,000 of mean house value in low-minority zip codes to $7.21 per $1,000 in high-minority zip codes (see table 3.4). Similarly, the average premium per $1,000 for limited-coverage homeowners policies increases from $4.86 per $1,000 for low-minority, low-income zip codes to $7.09 per $1,000 for high-minority, low-income zip codes (table 3.3).

These data are consistent with complaints about high insurance prices and the diminished supply of insurance in the inner city. Higher premiums are particularly burdensome for low-income households. Higher prices, in turn, could negatively affect the amount of insurance coverage purchased in poor neighborhoods. However, these data do not necessarily demonstrate that insureds in the inner city are subject to discrimination or are being overcharged for the insurance protection they are receiving. Various factors related to higher loss costs (besides income) could be positively correlated with minority concentration and could explain some or all of these differences in average premiums and the residual market share.

Additional insight into the fairness and efficiency of insurance pricing comes from data for the state of Missouri, the only state that has compiled comprehensive loss as well as premium information by zip code over a long time period. Tables 3.5 and 3.6 compare aggregate values (i.e., weighted means) for several standard measures of costs, average premiums, loss ratios, and availability across urban Missouri zip codes, grouped by the percentage of minority (nonwhite) persons for the period 1989–94. These zip codes were divided into four categories: low minority (0–3 percent), marginally integrated (4–10 percent), highly integrated (11–50 percent) and predominantly minority (51 percent plus).

Table 3.5 compares aggregate values for homeowners' average loss costs and the severity of claims per $1,000 of insurance coverage and the number of claims per 100 insured homes across the different zip code groups. This comparison also is disaggregated by the type of coverage.[10] Average loss costs tend to increase with minority concentration for both limited and broad coverage in Missouri, although this pattern is not consistent across all comparisons. For example, the aggregate average loss cost for limited coverage increases from $4.31 per $1,000 in low-minority areas to $5.75 in predominantly minority

Table 3.2 HOMEOWNERS INSURANCE MARKET PENETRATION BY COVERAGE (MEAN VALUES): 1992 DATA

	Dwelling Fire Market Share[a]		HO-1/HO-8 Market Share[c]		FAIR Plan Market Share[d]		Percentage of Insured Structures[e]	
	Value	Value/State[b]	Value	Value/State[b]	Value	Value/State[b]	Value	Value/State[b]
High-Income Zip Codes								
High-minority zip codes	11.0%	1.37	1.4%	0.89	4.7%	2.16	70.6%	0.96
Medium-minority zip codes	6.2%	0.77	1.2%	0.51	0.8%	0.74	78.8%	1.08
Low-minority zip codes	4.1%	0.55	0.8%	0.51	0.6%	0.68	81.5%	1.12
All zip codes	5.1%	0.67	1.0%	0.54	0.9%	0.78	80.0%	1.10
Medium-Income Zip Codes								
High-minority zip codes	11.0%	1.41	3.4%	1.72	2.8%	2.66	71.4%	0.98
Medium-minority zip codes	8.2%	1.05	1.7%	0.93	1.9%	1.31	73.5%	1.00
Low-minority zip codes	5.3%	0.68	1.4%	0.90	1.2%	2.03	78.5%	1.08
All zip codes	7.2%	0.94	1.9%	1.06	1.7%	1.90	75.5%	1.03

Low-Income Zip Codes

High-minority zip codes	25.9%	3.20	5.2%	2.73	18.2%	8.33	57.6%	0.80
Medium-minority zip codes	13.8%	1.68	3.5%	1.92	4.8%	2.59	64.9%	0.87
Low-minority zip codes	12.2%	1.31	3.7%	1.93	2.9%	1.06	75.3%	1.00
All zip codes	20.9%	2.60	4.5%	2.43	12.7%	6.05	61.2%	0.84

All Zip Codes

High-minority zip codes	20.1%	2.64	4.3%	2.35	12.4%	6.53	61.9%	0.86
Medium-minority zip codes	8.7%	1.13	2.0%	1.06	2.2%	1.47	72.3%	0.99
Low-minority zip codes	4.9%	0.65	1.2%	0.77	0.9%	1.29	79.9%	1.09
All zip codes	9.6%	2.14	2.1%	1.30	3.9%	2.78	72.7%	1.00

Sources: NAIC; plus 1990 Census of Population and Housing (Detailed Population Characteristics).
a. Dwelling fire exposures/total owners forms exposures.
b. Zip code value/statewide value.
c. Forms HO-1 and HO-8 exposures/total owners forms exposures.
d. FAIR Plan exposures/total exposures.
e. Dwelling fire plus homeowners forms exposures/estimated occupied residential one- to four-unit structures.

Table 3.3 LIMITED-COVERAGE AND DWELLING FIRE POLICIES AVERAGE PREMIUMS (MEAN VALUES); 1992 DATA

| | Homeowners Forms 1 and 8 | | | | Dwelling Fire | | | |
| | Average Premium[a] | | Average Premium/Mean Housing Value ($1,000) | | Average Premium[a] | | Average Premium/Mean Housing Value ($1,000) | |
	Value	Value/State[b]	Value	Value/State[b]	Value	Value/State[b]	Value	Value/State[b]
High-Income Zip Codes								
High-minority zip codes	$725.39	1.69	$3.60	1.19	$250.02	0.99	$1.29	0.81
Medium-minority zip codes	$512.91	1.47	$2.68	0.91	$272.58	1.13	$1.33	0.73
Low-minority zip codes	$386.62	1.23	$2.67	0.72	$245.08	1.21	$1.63	0.71
All zip codes	$443.48	1.33	$2.74	0.80	$254.09	1.18	$1.49	0.72
Medium-Income Zip Codes								
High-minority zip codes	$519.92	1.40	$4.06	1.36	$269.20	1.02	$1.93	1.02
Medium-minority zip codes	$583.82	1.39	$5.58	1.31	$242.33	1.12	$2.26	1.06
Low-minority zip codes	$397.17	1.10	$4.92	1.06	$199.69	1.09	$2.46	1.03
All zip codes	$480.99	1.25	$4.96	1.19	$226.62	1.09	$2.26	1.04
Low-Income Zip Codes								
High-minority zip codes	$458.74	1.41	$7.09	2.41	$217.13	0.98	$3.23	1.67
Medium-minority zip codes	$357.11	1.11	$5.90	1.66	$207.39	1.05	$3.33	1.53
Low-minority zip codes	$248.54	1.02	$4.86	1.41	$177.46	1.08	$3.44	1.48
All zip codes	$413.40	1.30	$6.62	2.12	$211.13	1.01	$3.27	1.61
All Zip Codes								
High-minority zip codes	$491.34	1.43	$5.52	2.08	$232.15	0.99	$2.48	1.45
Medium-minority zip codes	$498.26	1.34	$4.14	1.28	$243.91	1.10	$1.88	1.06
Low-minority zip codes	$383.52	1.16	$3.44	0.90	$221.42	1.15	$1.93	0.90
All zip codes	$448.45	1.29	$4.15	1.34	$231.33	1.09	$2.04	1.10

Sources: NAIC; 1990 Census of Population and Housing (Detailed Population Characteristics).
a. Premiums written/house years written.
b. Zip code value/statewide value.

Table 3.4 BROAD-COVERAGE AND TENANTS POLICIES AVERAGE PREMIUMS (MEAN VALUES): 1992 DATA

| | Homeowners Forms 2, 3, and 5 | | | | Homeowners Forms 4 and 6 | | | |
| | Average Premium[a] | | Average Premium/Mean Housing Value ($1,000) | | Average Premium[a] | | Average Premium/Mean Housing Value ($1,000) | |
	Value	Value/State[b]	Value	Value/State[b]	Value	Value/State[b]	Value	Value/State[b]
High-Income Zip Codes								
High-minority zip codes	$685.47	1.62	$3.49	1.03	$195.25	1.11	$1.01	0.79
Medium-minority zip codes	$746.81	1.76	$3.67	1.04	$226.31	1.20	$1.11	0.77
Low-minority zip codes	$529.23	1.47	$3.53	0.80	$192.17	1.19	$1.28	0.69
All zip codes	$607.20	1.57	$3.58	0.89	$203.21	1.19	$1.20	0.72
Medium-Income Zip Codes								
High-minority zip codes	$559.70	1.30	$4.02	1.20	$172.01	0.93	$1.23	0.96
Medium-minority zip codes	$441.29	1.16	$4.13	1.06	$164.67	0.96	$1.54	0.91
Low-minority zip codes	$323.99	1.00	$4.00	0.94	$147.12	0.99	$1.82	0.95
All zip codes	$405.24	1.11	$4.05	1.03	$157.44	0.97	$1.52	0.94
Low-Income Zip Codes								
High-minority zip codes	$483.30	1.26	$7.21	2.18	$170.90	0.99	$2.55	1.76
Medium-minority zip codes	$366.23	1.05	$5.88	1.53	$162.70	1.01	$2.61	1.50
Low-minority zip codes	$285.63	0.94	$5.53	1.30	$143.42	0.98	$2.78	1.37
All zip codes	$433.76	1.18	$6.74	1.92	$166.32	0.99	$2.58	1.65
All Zip Codes								
High-minority zip codes	$515.30	1.30	$5.53	1.87	$172.86	0.98	$1.85	1.50
Medium-minority zip codes	$524.75	1.33	$4.11	1.18	$185.14	1.05	$1.45	1.02
Low-minority zip codes	$425.67	1.24	$3.73	0.89	$169.76	1.09	$1.49	0.84
All zip codes	$481.24	1.28	$4.28	1.25	$175.43	1.05	$1.56	1.08

Sources: NAIC; 1990 Census of Population and Housing (Detailed Population Characteristics).
a. Premiums written/house years written.
b. Zip code value/statewide value.

Table 3.5 MISSOURI HOMEOWNERS INSURANCE COSTS AND MINORITY CONCENTRATION: 1989–94

Limited Coverage
(per $1,000 in Coverage)

Minority Concentration	Average Loss Cost			Frequency of Claims[a]			Severity		
	Mean	Aggregate	Standard Deviation	Mean	Aggregate	Standard Deviation	Mean	Aggregate	Standard Deviation
51 percent plus	5.43	5.75	1.92	0.22	0.24	0.07	55.53	59.41	23.40
11–50 percent	4.99	4.79	6.01	0.17	0.20	0.08	59.34	54.26	51.48
4–10 percent	4.09	4.34	3.57	0.23	0.23	0.16	42.61	46.58	30.50
0–3 percent	6.10	4.31	9.21	0.31	0.22	0.27	52.80	45.73	73.70
All zip codes	5.21	4.83	6.80	0.26	0.22	0.21	50.47	51.69	55.32

Broad Coverage
(per $1,000 in Coverage)

Minority Concentration	Average Loss Cost			Frequency of Claims[a]			Severity		
	Mean	Aggregate	Standard Deviation	Mean	Aggregate	Standard Deviation	Mean	Aggregate	Standard Deviation
51 percent plus	3.74	3.37	1.07	0.17	0.16	0.02	30.00	28.55	7.13
11–50 percent	2.97	2.58	1.31	0.15	0.14	0.04	25.48	23.74	7.75
4–10 percent	3.04	2.55	1.24	0.16	0.14	0.05	24.46	21.15	8.51
0–3 percent	3.59	2.92	1.88	0.16	0.14	0.05	27.84	23.11	10.96
All zip codes	3.34	2.74	1.57	0.16	0.14	0.05	26.58	22.80	9.60

Sources: Missouri Department of Insurance; NAIC.
a. Per 100 insured homes.

Table 3.6 MISSOURI HOMEOWNERS PREMIUMS AND LOSS RATIOS BY MINORITY CONCENTRATION: 1989–94

Limited Coverage

Minority Concentration	Average Premium per $1,000			Paid Loss Ratio		
	Mean	Aggregate	Standard Deviation	Mean	Aggregate	Standard Deviation
51 percent plus	8.79	9.04	1.87	0.65	0.64	0.29
11–50 percent	6.69	7.04	1.77	0.69	0.68	0.68
4–10 percent	6.68	6.88	1.67	0.60	0.63	0.49
0–3 percent	7.30	6.87	2.21	0.83	0.63	1.03
All zip codes	7.16	7.54	2.03	0.71	0.64	0.78
		Broad Coverage				
51 percent plus	5.06	4.76	0.63	0.73	0.71	0.15
11–50 percent	4.12	3.83	0.69	0.71	0.67	0.25
4–10 percent	4.15	3.78	0.69	0.73	0.67	0.27
0–3 percent	4.37	3.81	0.74	0.81	0.77	0.38
All zip codes	4.33	3.87	0.75	0.76	0.71	0.32

Sources: Missouri Department of Insurance; NAIC.

areas. The aggregate average loss cost for broad coverage increases from $2.92 in low-minority zip codes to $3.37 in predominantly minority areas.[11] Other variables such as home values that are correlated with minority concentration also could affect these comparisons. As with the national urban/nonurban comparisons, the differences in loss costs across urban Missouri zip codes appear to be more attributable to differences in the severity of loss per claim than to the frequency of claims.[12]

Table 3.6 compares average premiums per $1,000 of insurance coverage and paid loss ratios (paid losses divided by written premiums) across Missouri urban zip codes.[13] The average premium for limited and broad coverages tends to increase with minority concentration, as do loss costs. For limited coverage policies, the aggregate premium per $1,000 increases from $6.87 for low-minority areas to $9.04 for predominantly minority areas. For broad-coverage policies, the aggregrate premium increases from $3.81 for low-minority areas to $4.76 for predominantly minority areas.

The paid loss ratio for limited coverage tends to increase marginally with minority concentration, reflecting the fact that the differences in loss costs across urban neighborhoods are greater than the differences in premiums. This also is consistent with the national urban/nonurban comparisons discussed above. The pattern for broad-coverage loss ratios is less clear. The highest loss ratio, 77 percent, was in zip codes with the fewest minorities (table 3.6). The loss ratio drops for zip codes with more minority residents, although the loss ratio in predominantly minority neighborhoods (71 percent) was higher than in integrated neighborhoods (67 percent).

These results make it difficult to offer any broad characterization of the relationship between loss ratios and minority concentration. It is not apparent that homeowners in minority areas generally pay higher premiums than other homeowners in relation to the claims payments they receive.[14] In addition, the considerable variation in loss ratios across zip codes, which is likely caused by random variation in loss experience, undermines the confidence that these patterns in loss ratios are necessarily indicative of underlying structural differences in these markets. The possible influence of other variables besides race, as well as the volatility of loss costs at the zip code level, leaves the question of the fairness of insurance pricing in the inner city still open.

Differences within Metropolitan Areas: Regression Analysis

To control for some of the other variables affecting the supply of insurance, multiple regression analysis was used to examine the relationship between the availability of homeowners insurance and housing characteristics, economic conditions, and demographic composition in urban neighborhoods across the country. Availability and price measures were regressed on different explanatory variables to determine how income levels and the racial composition of an area affect market conditions, independent of other factors. This analysis contributes to previous research by incorporating explicit loss-cost information and other explanatory variables in a multivariate model of availability and average premiums in urban areas.

This analysis focused on 25 metropolitan statistical areas (MSAs) (some MSAs contain more than one community or rating territory) in the 13 largest states for which territory-level loss data were obtained (see Klein 1995a). A total of 1,185 zip codes are contained in this data set. Three primary sources of data were used for this analysis: (1) zip code insurance data; (2) statistical data on earned premiums, incurred losses, and insured homes compiled by statistical agents at a territory level; and (3) the 1990 Census of Population and Housing. Several other supplemental data sources were tapped and are discussed in upcoming paragraphs. Variable descriptions, data sources, and descriptive statistics for this analysis are summarized in appendix table 3A.1. Unless otherwise indicated, all variables are disaggregated at a zip code level.

The variable used to measure the availability of voluntary market homeowners coverage was the percentage of total insured homes written through the FAIR Plan. If insurers are more reluctant to insure or their underwriting criteria tend to exclude properties in inner-city neighborhoods or areas where minorities tend to live, then a higher proportion of policies will be sold through the FAIR Plan (for all homeowners' policy forms) in these areas. However, the FAIR Plan market share is not a sure indicator of the supply of voluntary market coverage, since it also could be affected by greater demand for FAIR Plan coverage if such coverage is less expensive than voluntary coverage for some homes.

Two measures of average premiums were used to evaluate whether the insurance prices that homeowners pay are higher if they live in a neighborhood with more minority residents: the average premium per insured home for limited-coverage homeowners policies and the average premium per insured home for broad-coverage homeowners policies. The average premium is a crude price measure because it does not reflect differences in the exposure to loss and differences in policy provisions such as deductibles, limits, and supplemental coverages. Median house value is included in the average premium equations as an explanatory variable to control for the amount of insurance.

The principal loss-cost measures used were the rating territory-level average loss costs per insured home for limited-coverage and broad-coverage policies, respectively. The average loss cost is equal to incurred losses divided by the number of insured homes.[15] The territory combined loss ratio (incurred losses divided by earned premiums) for all homeowners' coverages also was included as an explanatory variable in the FAIR Plan market-share equation.[16] These variables were compiled on a calendar/accident year basis and averaged over the calendar/accident years 1989–91 to reduce volatility.[17] These data were disaggregated by the standard rating territories utilized by the Insurance Services Office (ISO).[18]

The average loss cost was used to control for the impact of claims costs on premiums and to better isolate the effect of race on insurance pricing. The average loss cost is expected to have a positive effect on the average premium. The variation among territory average loss costs should account for at least a portion of the variation among zip code average loss costs. The degree to which zip code average loss costs differ from territory average loss costs is unknown. It is presumed that the standard rating territories comprise areas with similar risk characteristics. However, some companies no longer use these territories for rating purposes, and the ISO is reevaluating its territories using zip code loss data and other information that it has begun to compile. The territory loss ratio was used to control for the effect of rate adequacy and profitability on insurers' willingness to supply coverage voluntarily.

To control for the residual variation in zip code loss costs not explained by territory loss costs, several other zip code level explanatory variables were included that could affect losses and average premiums:

- The median age of single-family homes, which is expected to have a positive effect on the average premium and a negative effect on availability. Older homes are perceived to have a higher risk of fire loss, and many insurers will not write coverage on structures above a certain age (e.g., 40 years).
- The median market value of single-family houses, which should have a positive impact on price as well as availability. Higher-value homes are expected to carry higher amounts of insurance and more extensive coverage, both of which require higher premiums. Insurers also may find it more attractive to write higher-value homes, and some insurers refuse to write coverage on homes below a certain value (e.g., $50,000).

- The percentage of occupied housing units heated with either fuel oil, kerosene, or wood. These types of heating systems are associated with a higher risk of fire loss, and some insurers require a higher premium for or refuse to write homes with these types of heating systems. Riskier heating systems are expected to be positively associated with the average premium and negatively associated with the FAIR Plan market share.
- The number of persons per square mile, included to account for a portion of the variation in expected losses across zip codes. It presumes that more densely populated areas tend to have higher fire and crime rates. If that is true, population density should have a positive effect on price and a negative effect on availability. However, greater density could yield administrative efficiencies for insurers and agents, which could lower expenses and have the opposite effects on price and availability. Hence, the overall effect of population density on price is ambiguous.

Other explanatory variables attempt to measure "neighborhood stability," which also may affect the risk of loss and insurers' prices and willingness to provide coverage. The percentage of owner-occupied housing units should have a positive effect on availability if insurers perceive that neighborhoods with a high proportion of owner-occupied units are likely to be more stable and, hence, to have lower risk. The relationship between owner-occupied homes and the average premium also should be negative if insurers perceive such neighborhoods to be less risky. A higher percentage of vacant dwellings is presumed to increase the risk of loss due to fire, vandalism, and theft. Vacancy rates are expected to have a negative effect on availability and a positive effect on the average premium.

Several variables were used to test the effects of economic and demographic factors on availability and price. The first is median household income, which should be positively related to availability if insurers perceive high-income homeowners and neighborhoods to be more desirable. The expected sign for income in the average premium equations is ambiguous, however. Higher income may increase the demand for insurance, which could have a positive effect on the market price. But insurers also may charge an additional risk premium to low-income policyholders or policyholders living in low-income neighborhoods.[19]

The demographic variable of particular interest in this analysis is the percentage of nonwhite persons. If insurers discriminate against minority consumers or consumers living in high-minority neighborhoods, then minority population should be negatively correlated with availability and positively related to the average premium. Unfortunately, the lack of good controls for loss costs at a zip code level in these equations still leaves the potential for biased estimates of the coefficient for minority population. If high-minority neighborhoods tend to have higher fire and property crime rates than other zip codes within the same territory, some of the effect of higher fire and crime rates will be incorrectly attributed to minority concentration. On the other hand, if high-minority neighborhoods tend to have lower fire and crime rates, then the effect of minority concentration will be underestimated. An alternative specification of this variable, the percentage of nonwhite and white Hispanic persons, was also tested.

Since minority population is highly correlated with other socioeconomic variables such as unemployment and female-headed households, any effect attributed to minority concentration may, in fact, be partly or wholly caused by these other variables or vice versa. The reality may be that insurers do not differentiate between neighborhoods on the basis of racial composition per se, but, rather, distinguish between what they perceive to be "high-risk" and "low-risk" neighborhoods based on a number of characteristics that could include or be highly correlated with race.

Another demographic variable tested was the percentage of non–English-speaking households. Non–English-speaking households may have greater difficulty in shopping for insurance because they have higher information costs and/or face greater discrimination by insurers. If that is the case, then non–English-speaking households should be positively associated with average premiums and the FAIR Plan market share.

State dummy variables were added to control for the impact of state-specific factors on the availability and price of insurance in a zip code. The availability and price of insurance in a given zip code may be affected by such state-specific factors as regulation, other state laws, entry and exit barriers, and other variables not easily measured with available data. The inclusion of state dummy variables isolates the effects of factors specific to a zip code from the effects of factors attributable to the state in which a zip code is located.

Alternatively, explicit dummy variables for state prior approval rate regulation and for the existence of a state antiredlining law were substituted for state-effects dummy variables in another formulation of this model to assess how regulation affects market conditions. Some states that require prior approval of insurance regulations before they go into effect tend to restrict rate differences between areas, whereas states without such requirements tend to let the market set prices (Klein 1995c). Rate regulation is expected to lower insurance premiums and increase the size of the FAIR Plan. Insurers have alleged that some regulators have suppressed insurance prices in urban areas, which could cause insurers to tighten their underwriting and reduce supply, resulting in a higher FAIR Plan market share. Suppression of FAIR Plan rates below costs also could increase the size of the FAIR Plan. FAIR Plan rates must be approved by regulators in both prior approval and competitive rating states, but prior approval jurisdictions may tend to regulate FAIR Plan rates more stringently because of regulators' more active role in influencing market conditions in these jurisdictions.

The expected effects of antiredlining laws on prices and availability are ambiguous. These laws can take a number of forms, ranging from specific restrictions on excluding insurance applications for certain property or homeowners' characteristics to prohibitions on refusing to write insurance in certain geographic areas or pricing these areas higher than others. An antiredlining law could restrict insurers' underwriting selection, pricing, or both practices with different effects on average premiums and the FAIR Plan market share, depending on regulators' objectives.

These also are somewhat crude measures of regulatory policy because a great deal depends on how regulators implement prior approval and antiredlining statutes, which is not reflected in these variables. Depending on the regulation and how it is enforced, insurers may find ways to circumvent or respond to the regulation, leading to a different effect than regulators intend.

The model used for estimating the FAIR Plan market-share equation is described by equation 3.1.

$$FAIRPCT = \sigma_0 + \sigma_1 C + \sigma_2 D + \sigma_3 S + u_i, \qquad (3.1)$$

where C = a vector of cost-related variables (AGE, VALUE, HEAT, OWN, VAC, LRC or ALL or ALB, POPDENS);

D = a vector of demographic variables (INC, MIN or BLKHSP, NOENG);

S = a vector of state-effects dummy variables (or RATE and NORED); and

u_i = a disturbance term.

The basic model used for estimating the average premium equations is described by equation 3.2.

$$AP = \alpha_0 + \alpha_1 C + \alpha_2 D + \alpha_3 S + \epsilon_i, \qquad (3.2)$$

where AP = the average premium (either APL or APB); and
  ϵ_i = a disturbance term.

One possible drawback to this formulation is the failure to explicitly model demand and supply functions for urban markets. The preceding equations represent a composite of both and, hence, the interpretation of the coefficients for some independent variables is complicated.

Ordinary least squares (OLS) regression was used to estimate the parameters of these equations. Screens were applied to mitigate the effects of anomalous data and outliers. Observations were omitted for zip codes with less than 100 policies in force. The regressions for the average premium equations also excluded outlier values of the dependent variable falling within the 1st and 99th percentiles.

Table 3.7 presents the multiple regression results for the FAIR Plan market-share equation.[20] These results suggest that vacancy rates, owner-occupied homes, population density, non–English-speaking households, and minority concentration all tend to increase the relative size of the FAIR Plan in a zip code. The coefficient for income was significantly negative in most specifications, indicating that low-income areas have greater FAIR Plan penetration.

The significantly positive coefficients for both specifications of the minority concentration variable indicate that homeowners in neighborhoods with high proportions of minorities are less likely to acquire insurance through the voluntary market, all else equal. The magnitude of the coefficient for minority concentration indicates that a 10 percentage point increase in the proportion of minorities is associated with a 2 percentage point increase in the FAIR Plan market share. This could reflect greater difficulty in obtaining voluntary market coverage and/or the effect of other factors (e.g., steering by agents, costly information, subsidized residual market rates, etc.) that might cause more consumers in minority communities to purchase insurance from the FAIR Plan. These results are consistent with the allegation that some insurers seek to avoid writing coverage in inner-city areas, which could make voluntary coverage more difficult to obtain. This result is particularly important because it occurs even after controlling for the risk of loss. Interestingly, the average loss cost for the rating territory in which a zip code resides was not statistically significant. However, the fact that the controls for zip code loss costs are imperfect leaves the possibility that a higher risk is at least part, if not all, of the reason why inner-city homeowners find it more difficult to obtain insurance.

Table 3.7 REGRESSION ANALYSIS OF FAIR PLAN MARKET-SHARE ORDINARY
LEAST SQUARES ESTIMATION: 1992 DATA

Independent	Dependent Variable: FAIRPCT			
Variable	(1)	(2)	(3)	(4)
INTERCEPT	−4.7876	−4.8647	−.4444	−3.099
	(1.390)	(1.405)	(.177)	(1.212)
AGE	−6.9508 E4	−.0118	.1598***	.0022
	(.022)	(.371)	(5.184)	(.072)
VALUE	−6.4365 E6	−5.3886 E6	−2.8099 E5***	−1.3871 E5**
	(.955)	(.793)	(3.992)	(2.067)
OWN	.0930***	.0944***	.0854***	.0688***
	(3.517)	(3.555)	(3.140)	(2.747)
VAC	.1939***	.2035***	.2329***	.2474***
	(3.637)	(3.807)	(3.955)	(4.451)
HEAT	.0421	.0415	−.0349	.0533
	(1.192)	(1.170)	(1.191)	(1.566)
INC	−2.0550 E4***	−2.1472 E4***	−1.3970 E5	−1.3842 E4***
	(3.921)	(4.088)	(.263)	(2.847)
MIN	.1833***		.1929***	.2053***
	(13.584)		(13.398)	(15.455)
BLKHISP		.1869***		
		(13.287)		
NOENG	.0705**	.1446***	.0779**	.0612**
	(2.150)	(4.227)	(2.554)	(2.035)
POPDENS	6.1810 E5*	6.7926 E5**	1.0916 E4***	8.0821 E5***
	(1.947)	(2.135)	(3.347)	(2.775)
LRC	.0395	.0398	−.0022**	
	(1.316)	(1.323)	(2.257)	
ALL				−3.1668 E4
				(.951)
RATE			−3.8680***	
			(3.551)	
NORED			−9.9908***	
			(7.313)	
State effects	Yes	Yes	No	Yes
Adjusted R^2	.4677	.4641	.3399	.4914
F-statistic	41.574***	40.987***	45.540***	48.759***
DW statistic	.95	.68	.55	2.02

Note: T-statistics are in parentheses.
*** = 1 percent significance; ** = 5 percent significance; * = 10 percent significance
for two-tailed tests.

The effects of older homes and their market value are less clear. The age of homes has a significantly positive effect on FAIR Plan penetration only when explicit regulatory variables are substituted for state effects. Higher-valued homes reduce the residual market share only when explicit regulatory variables or the territory average loss cost are used as explanatory variables. It is possible that the effects of the age and value of homes are confounded with the effects of other state-specific variables, which makes it difficult to isolate their independent effects on availability.

Surprisingly, owner-occupied homes also had a positive effect on residual market penetration, which is the opposite of what was expected. One possible explanation is that homeowners will be more likely to purchase insurance through the FAIR Plan if they are rejected by the voluntary market, whereas renters may be more likely to go without insurance. Such an occurrence would affect this analysis because the FAIR Plan market share includes both owner's-forms and tenant's-forms coverages. Yet, many FAIR Plans do not offer tenants coverage.

The role of insurer profitability, as measured by the loss ratio, also is unclear. The territory loss ratio was significantly negative (when explicit controls for regulation were included), which is contrary to what would be expected. Conventional economic theory suggests that higher loss ratios will discourage, rather than encourage, insurers from offering voluntary coverage. There is no obvious explanation for this result other than the possibility that what is actually being observed is the FAIR Plan decreasing loss ratios in some states by charging higher premiums than the voluntary market.

The evidence that antiredlining regulations lower FAIR Plan penetration is not surprising, but the negative effect of rate regulation is. One possible explanation is that rate regulation suppresses voluntary market rates more than FAIR Plan rates as suggested here, leading consumers to increase their efforts to seek voluntary market coverage (including coverage with nonstandard insurers that tend to offer more limited coverage at higher prices than other insurers) despite insurers' greater reluctance to write them. Regulators also may be more likely to impose restrictions on insurers' ability to reject applicants in jurisdictions with tighter rate regulation.

There also is some evidence that a higher concentration of minorities increases insurance prices, after controlling for other factors. Table 3.8 shows the regression results for the limited-coverage average premium equations. All of the independent variables for the limited-coverage average premium equation that were statistically significant

Table 3.3 REGRESSION ANALYSIS OF LIMITED-COVERAGE AVERAGE PREMIUM ORDINARY LEAST SQUARES ESTIMATION: 1992 DATA

Independent	Dependent Variable: APL		
Variable	(1)	(2)	(3)
INTERCEPT	158.4549***	155.6424***	200.3588***
	(3.811)	(3.732)	(5.073)
AGE	.3321	.2599	1.3103***
	(.670)	(.524)	(2.687)
VALUE	1.4453 E4	1.5574 E4	3.6129 E4***
	(1.248)	(1.340)	(3.178)
OWN	−1.5723***	−1.5586***	−1.3301***
	(3.662)	(3.628)	(2.980)
VAC	−.1044	−.0277	.7625
	(.119)	(.032)	(.881)
HEAT	.3724	.3814	1.1210**
	(.626)	(.641)	(2.554)
INC	.0025***	.0025***	.0025***
	(2.981)	(2.935)	(2.836)
MIN	1.2207***		1.4507***
	(5.833)		(6.845)
BLKHISP		1.2754***	
		(5.865)	
NOENG	.8827*	1.4141***	2.1935***
	(1.700)	(2.612)	(4.631)
POPDENS	.0026***	.0026***	.0017***
	(4.238)	(4.220)	(2.715)
ALL	.0493*	.0516*	.1065***
	(1.835)	(1.919)	(3.837)
RATE			−112.0896***
			(6.716)
NORED			−45.8914**
			(2.228)
State effects	Yes	Yes	No
Adjusted R^2	.5628	.5629	.5029
F-statistic	58.745***	58.783***	84.203***
DW statistic	1.81	2.05	2.00

Note: T-statistics are in parentheses.
*** = 1 percent significance; ** = 5 percent significance; * = 10 percent significance for two-tailed tests.

had coefficients consistent with their expected signs. A higher percentage of owner-occupied homes tends to reduce the average premium. The average premium increases with household income, suggesting that the demand-side effect of income on price is greater than any supply-side effect related to unfair discrimination against low-income areas that might be present. Greater population density also appears to increase prices, as do average loss costs.

The presence of more minorities and of non–English-speaking residents also are associated with higher insurance prices.[21] In terms of magnitude, a 1 percentage point increase in the percentage of minorities was associated with a $1.20 to $1.40 increase in the average premium. These results tend to support concerns about higher insurance premiums in areas where minorities are concentrated and the presence of discrimination against these areas. However, the lack of an explicit zip code level loss-cost measure still raises the possibility that part or all of the effect attributed to minority concentration is actually due to higher losses in minority neighborhoods. These results also suggest that higher search costs for non–English-speaking households or other factors associated with their presence in urban communities tend to result in higher average premiums for limited coverage.

In addition, the data suggest that the presence of older and more valuable homes and riskier heating systems raise prices for limited coverage, but the coefficients for these variables were statistically significant only when controls for state effects were not included. Using controls for state effects may mask the impact of these cost-related variables on premiums, as already discussed. The analysis indicates that rate and antiredlining regulation lower limited-coverage premiums.

The results for the broad-coverage average premium equation, shown in table 3.9, were similar to the results for the limited-coverage average premium equation in table 3.8. The analysis indicates that the age and value of housing, vacancy rates, income, the territory average loss cost, and minority concentration all had significantly positive effects on the average premium for broad-coverage policies. A 1 percentage point increase in the percentage of minorities was associated with a $.65 to $.97 increase in the average premium. A greater percentage of owner-occupied housing units also lowered premiums, as expected. The data provide only weak evidence that riskier heating systems increase broad-coverage insurance prices when controls for state effects are included.

This analysis also suggests that non–English-speaking households lower broad-coverage premiums, contrary to what was expected. There is no clear intuition for this result. It is possible that non–English-speaking households have lower demand for broad coverage, which tends to decrease the average premium.

Regulation does not appear to make a significant difference for broad-coverage premiums, contrary to what was found for limited-

Table 3.9 REGRESSION ANALYSIS OF BROAD-COVERAGE AVERAGE PREMIUM ORDINARY LEAST SQUARES ESTIMATION: 1992 DATA

Independent Variable	Dependent Variable: APB		
	(1)	(2)	(3)
INTERCEPT	−168.2535***	−172.5449***	−196.7862***
	(3.160)	(3.234)	(4.147)
AGE	2.9281***	2.8613***	3.6399***
	(4.588)	(4.481)	(6.042)
VALUE	.0018***	.0018***	.0017***
	(12.985)	(13.039)	(13.073)
OWN	−.9544*	−.9230*	−1.0427**
	(1.799)	(1.739)	(1.981)
VAC	3.5216***	3.5586***	2.3670**
	(3.254)	(3.292)	(2.280)
HEAT	1.1825*	1.1768*	.4983
	(1.671)	(1.664)	(.966)
INC	.0020*	.0019*	.0022**
	(1.896)	(1.879)	(2.153)
MIN	.9687***		.6521**
	(3.582)		(2.494)
BLKHISP		1.0516***	
		(3.744)	
NOENG	−1.7746***	−1.3346**	−2.3336***
	(2.707)	(1.957)	(4.103)
POPDENS	−2.8910 E4	−2.7303 E4	−5.0899 E4
	(.392)	(.371)	(.702)
ALB	.9991***	.9991***	1.0571***
	(17.102)	(17.112)	(19.351)
RATE			−4.0316
			(.203)
NORED			44.7933*
			(1.869)
State effects	Yes	Yes	No
Adjusted R^2	.7347	.7350	.7258
F-statistic	128.890***	129.096***	225.172***
DW statistic	1.86	1.91	1.87

Note: T-statistics are in parentheses.
*** = 1 percent significance; ** = 5 percent significance; * = 10 percent significance for two-tailed tests.

coverage policies. This may reflect a tendency on the part of regulators to allow more flexibility in the pricing of broad coverage than for limited coverage. Regulators may feel a greater responsibility to control the price of limited coverage, which is deemed to be more essential than broad coverage. In addition, insurers could be allowed to charge higher rates for broad coverage to compensate for restrictions on their ability to refuse applications for broad coverage.

Although these results support concerns about high urban insurance prices and could reflect discriminatory pricing or other market failures present in minority neighborhoods, the limitations on the controls for differences in the risk of loss and the results of other studies leave unresolved the significant question as to whether inner-city homeowners pay excessive insurance prices.[22] A recent study by Klein (1996) using multiple regression analysis and the refined data set for Missouri urban homeowners insurance markets did not find a significant relationship between neighborhood racial concentration and loss ratios.[23] However, it should be pointed out that the volatility in zip code loss data for this study qualifies these findings to some extent. Hence, while the bulk of evidence supports the conclusion that the supply of homeowners insurance to the inner-city is restricted, it is still not certain that inner-city residents pay premiums that are too high for the insurance payments they receive.

CONCLUSIONS AND POLICY IMPLICATIONS

Summary of Empirical Results

To date, considerable evidence has been presented that residents of poor and minority neighborhoods in our nation's cities have diminished access to property insurance coverage and pay more for it than residents of other areas. This study further documents the magnitude and widespread nature of these disparities. The sale of voluntary market coverage and the extent of insurance coverage is lower in cities and even lower yet within high-minority, low-income areas. Average premiums also tend to be higher in cities and even higher yet within high-minority, low-income neighborhoods. Problems with the availability and cost of insurance undermine the economic viability of urban communities and their ability to rebuild.

This chapter identifies some of the factors that contribute to urban insurance problems by presenting a multivariate analysis of homeowners' average premiums and residual market penetration in urban areas. These factors include homeownership, vacancy rates, and population density. The proportion of minorities living in a neighborhood also is strongly associated with both higher insurance prices and more limited coverage. Most important, the indicated relationship

~~between race and~~ the availability of insurance persists, even imperfectly controlling for the risk of loss. Conversely, median income and house values decrease the proportion of FAIR Plan policies. There also is some evidence that stricter regulation of rates and of underwriting tends to lower FAIR Plan penetration and premiums for limited-coverage policies, but not broad-coverage insurance.

As expected, territory average loss costs were found to have a significant and positive effect on zip code average premiums in urban areas. However, the effect of minority concentration on average premiums remained significantly positive even when controlling, to the extent possible, for risk-related factors. The regression results also indicate that the age and value of housing, vacancy rates, riskier heating systems, income, non–English-speaking households, and population density increase average premiums for limited-coverage and/or broad-coverage homeowners policies. The percentage of owner-occupied homes, on the other hand, tends to lower average premiums.

However, the research to date remains inconclusive as to whether inner-city residents pay too much in premiums for the claims payments they receive. The data from this study suggest that this may be the case, but the controls for loss costs are incomplete, and more recent studies did not find that loss ratios are lower for minority neighborhoods than for nonminority neighborhoods. Assessing the fairness of insurance pricing for different neighborhoods is inherently difficult with the data readily available.

Regardless, other studies (Klein 1995b; Squires et al. 1991; Schultz, chapter 4, this volume) indicate there are fewer agents and low-price insurers in inner-city areas, which could have a negative effect on competition and market performance. Restricted entry by insurers and inefficient pricing in these areas could decrease the availability of insurance and possibly increase its relative cost for some inner-city homeowners, depending on their risk characteristics and the coverage they purchase. However, increasing entry and refining insurance pricing also could result in higher prices for some insureds while lowering prices for other insureds in the inner city, making it difficult to predict the overall effect on average premiums and loss ratios.

These results lend significant support to the view that the causes of urban insurance availability problems are not confined to a higher risk of loss in urban areas, even though the results do not offer a definitive picture of all the contributors to these problems. The statistical data presented here, combined with the reams of anecdotal testimony and other empirical evidence that have been compiled, suggest that market barriers, including a lack of information and industry perceptions, as well as higher-risk factors, have impeded urban residents' ability to obtain low-cost property insurance. Indeed, a number of insurers have acknowledged that they have neglected economic opportunities to market a full array of products in inner-city areas. At the same time, it is fairly clear that higher losses and various other factors also add significantly to insurance availability and affordability problems in urban communities.

The complexity of the forces that drive urban insurance conditions complicates the task of crafting appropriate remedies. These empirical results suggest that a broad array of policy measures, not just regulation, will be necessary to lower the cost of and increase access to property insurance in the urban core.

Policy Implications

The challenge facing policymakers and regulators is to determine and implement measures that improve, rather than worsen, conditions in urban insurance markets. Policy measures aimed strictly at reducing risk will not fully resolve urban insurance problems unless they also correct insurers' perceptions of urban markets. There is no dispute over the need to eradicate practices that are blatantly discriminatory. However, very few actions fall into this category, leaving a range of industry behaviors where the incidence of discrimination is difficult for authorities to isolate and prosecute. Other measures targeted toward increasing entry and competition could ultimately be more effective in improving the performance of urban markets.

At the same time, even the complete elimination of unfairly discriminatory practices in the presence of full competition will not guarantee low insurance prices and the availability of coverage for all properties in urban areas. The high risk of loss in the inner city means that some properties will still be uninsurable through conventional means. If policymakers are to fully alleviate urban insurance problems, they will have to attack the underlying causes of higher loss costs or develop approaches to subsidizing urban insurance premiums that fairly distribute the burden of these subsidies and minimize any perverse incentives that subsidization may create.

With respect to regulatory and legal sanctions, current state insurance laws prohibit discrimination in rates and in underwriting selection against certain risks or geographic areas that does not have an underlying actuarial or economic justification. This leaves insurers fairly wide latitude in determining who they will provide coverage to and under what terms, so long as they can rationalize their decisions to regulators. However, imposing more arbitrary restrictions on insurers' underwriting and pricing practices, implemented by state and/or federal authorities, could also prove difficult to enforce as well as self-defeating in terms of improving market conditions. Insurers may find ways to circumvent rating and underwriting restrictions by finding new factors that could serve as surrogates for the characteristics they seek to avoid. Regulators could be sucked into a deepening morass in attempting to micromanage insurers' market decisions with increasingly complex regulations. Availability problems will be worsened if insurers are able to reject insureds for whom they cannot charge an adequate premium. Forcing cross-subsidies through the rating structure also will distort consumers' decisions in terms of the amount of insurance purchased and their efforts to reduce risk.

In addition, the federal government's efforts to regulate property insurance raises difficult policy questions, legal issues aside. Although federal agencies have achieved considerable success in attacking discriminatory business practices in employment, lending, and housing, insurance presents unique considerations that make the application of disparate-impact standards problematic (Duncan 1995). The economic factors underlying insurance pricing and underwriting decisions are more complex than the variables affecting business decisions in other industries. Insurers' pricing systems use a number of variables to reflect the expected cost of insuring a given property and evaluating these variables, and their relative weights require considerable analysis and judgment. In addition, insurance, unlike banking, is regulated principally by the states, which increases the potential conflicts between state and federal standards if these standards or their legal interpretation varies between state and federal authorities. Federal prosecution of clear instances of racial discrimination in insurance could support state regulation, but broad federal regulation of insurance practices could undermine state public policy and efforts to improve urban insurance market conditions. This argument is valid even acknowledging recent court settlements with large insurers (e.g., American Family Mutual Insurance Company, State Farm Insurance Companies) to increase their marketing efforts to underserved communities. Legal settlements will not have a broad, long-lasting, positive effect on the supply of insurance unless insurers sincerely believe that increasing their marketing efforts to urban areas will increase their profits. Regulatory pressure on banks does appear to have improved their perceptions of the profitability of making inner-city loans, but it is questionable whether the same results would be achieved by imposing similar federal legal sanctions on insurers. The ultimate success of federal insurance regulation could depend greatly on the scope of this regulation and its coordination with state efforts.

States have the primary role in insurance regulation. They have a much wider array of policy tools than the federal government, including measures that could increase entry and competition in urban markets. State strategies could encompass easing the regulation of pricing, underwriting, and policy design as well as improving the information available to both insurers and consumers.[24] These measures can be woven into an overall strategy that considers the specific market and regulatory environment in each urban area. Federal regulation, by its nature, would be more uniform across the country.

A promising set of initiatives involves enhancing insurers' and producers' understanding of urban markets and facilitating consumers' ability to shop for and purchase insurance under the best possible terms. The Illinois Department of Insurance has developed a pathbreaking program to educate insurance company underwriters and marketing personnel on economic opportunities in the inner city. Company educational programs will be bolstered by efforts underway to make pooled industry data on premiums and losses at a zip code level available to all insurers. Research on the causes of urban property losses, both those related to geography and those that are not, could further help insurers to improve the efficiency and fairness of their pricing systems and underwriting criteria.[25]

A second program in Illinois counsels homeowners on how to purchase property insurance. A number of other states are beefing up their insurance consumer education and information efforts, which could benefit urban residents. Other states are using the Illinois program as a model and/or expanding access to insurance market information through special publications, consumer counseling programs, the media, and telephone and computer on-line information systems. Various distribution points such as community organizations and public libraries are being utilized to try to maximize the dissemination of information to underserved groups.

Some states are implementing market assistance plans (MAPs), which are more focused, voluntary efforts to match consumers seeking coverage with insurers willing to provide it. Urban MAPs, typically coordinated by local community organizations operating under national umbrella groups such as Neighborhood Housing Services (NHS), help insurers overcome their lack of familiarity with risk conditions and insurance needs in inner-city neighborhoods. The programs also efficiently counsel and screen consumers, reducing insurers' uncertainty and risk, and enhancing consumers' incentives and ability to improve the insurability of their properties (Doherty and Tennyson 1996). Public pressure as well growing awareness of untapped economic opportunities have motivated a number of insurers to actively participate in urban MAPs. If these programs succeed in significantly increasing entry into urban markets, these markets could sustain long-term improvements in the form of lowered prices and increased access to insurance.

The best overall strategy may be the one recommended by the NAIC, which encourages use of voluntary, competition-enhancing measures, coupled with the threat of more coercive regulatory measures if the private market fails to respond to voluntary measures. The NAIC believes that some degree of continued public monitoring is necessary to ensure that voluntary efforts are successful and sustained. This will help to motivate insurers who would otherwise engage in discrimination or fail to pursue legitimate economic opportunities to serve the inner city. Regulators also need to rigorously enforce existing unfair discrimination statutes to the maximum extent possible, which could require additional resources in some states.

The success of competition-enhancing efforts will still leave some urban properties uninsurable by the private market. Consequently, it will be necessary to maintain some form of residual market mechanism so long as insurers can refuse to write some risks. The current FAIR Plans could be made less punitive by expanding the coverages they provide and refining their pricing structures so that low-risk properties are not forced to subsidize high-risk properties. Regulators have to be careful, however, not to heavily subsidize residual market coverage overall, or they will accelerate the residual market's growth and ultimately cause the voluntary market to implode. Establishing "keep out" and "take out" incentives for insurers can help to minimize the size of the residual market.

Government-sponsored insurers and urban insurance cooperatives are other approaches that have been proposed to cover inner-city risks rejected by the voluntary market. Their specialization toward urban risks could offer certain economic efficiencies that would benefit inner-city communities.[26] However, such insurers are subject to adverse selection problems unless they also can reject some risks and/or charge them cost-based premiums. Consequently, they cannot fully replace residual market mechanisms.

The issue of public subsidies may ultimately prove to be unavoidable if inner-city residents are to have the same opportunities to buy insurance as people in other communities. Such subsidies could take the form of monetary payments to low-income homeowners living in high-cost areas or the insurers who insure them. Unfortunately, subsidies of this kind can encourage overpurchase of insurance as well as diminish incentives to prevent losses. The mechanism used to fund the subsidy (e.g., premium surcharges, taxes, etc.) will affect related economic activities. Hence, subsidies, depending on how they are structured, could worsen economic efficiency and/or equity. The political prospects for explicit subsidies to urban insureds are also dim. Subsidies in the form of greater economic aid to urban communities to improve housing conditions and police and fire protection might prove to be more politically feasible and economically efficient in terms of diminishing the root causes of higher property insurance costs. This is an area where federal expenditures could yield more long-term benefits than in the regulation of insurance practices.

Local, state, and federal government efforts to improve urban insurance markets should be properly integrated in a comprehensive strategy to avoid unnecessary conflicts as well as gaps. Further research should help to better delineate the causes of urban insurance problems and their relative contributions to these problems. The measures implemented to address these problems could be evaluated to determine what works and what does not. This research, in turn, should provide further guidance to regulators and policymakers on how to prioritize and coordinate remedial efforts.

APPENDIX

Table 3A.1 VARIABLE DESCRIPTIONS

Variable	Mean (Std. Dev.)	Definition and Source
APL	384.03 (220.15)	Average premium for homeowners' forms 1 and 8 (special data call)
APB	493.33 (383.69)	Average premium for homeowners' forms 2, 3, and 5 (special data call)
FAIRPCT	5.38 (12.89)	Percentage of homeowners' exposures in FAIR Plan (special data call)
AGE	36.43 (12.41)	Median age of housing units (U.S. Census)
VALUE	114,218.10 (90,834.86)	Median value of owner-occupied housing units (U.S. Census)
OWN	52.37 (24.22)	Percentage of owner-occupied housing units (U.S. Census)

Table 3A.1 VARIABLE DESCRIPTIONS (continued)

Variable	Mean (Std. Dev.)	Definition and Source
VAC	7.77 (7.28)	Percentage of housing units that were vacant (U.S. Census)
HEAT	14.40 (18.26)	Percentage of occupied housing units heated using fuel oil, kerosene, or wood (U.S. Census)
INC	31,635.94 (13,596.30)	Median household income (U.S. Census)
MIN	30.78 (30.92)	Nonwhite population percentage (U.S. Census)
BLKHISP	26.52 (29.86)	Percentage of population who are black or of Hispanic origin (U.S. Census)
NOENG	17.98 (15.11)	Percentage of households in which English is not the primary language spoken (U.S. Census)
ALL	281.77 (336.55)	Territory pure premium (1989–91 annual average) for homeowners' forms 1 and 8 (statistical agents)
ALB	296.05 (201.04)	Territory pure premium (1989–91 annual average) for homeowners' forms 2, 3, and 5 (statistical agents)
LRC	68.60 (12.97)	Territory combined loss ratio (1989–91 annual average) for all homeowners' forms (statistical agents)
POPDEN	10,983.16 (16,515.19)	Population density per square mile (U.S. Census and University of Missouri-Columbia)
RATE	.17 (.38)	Equals 1 for states with prior approval filing laws; 0 for all other states (NAIC)
NORED	.87 (.34)	Equals 1 for states with antiredlining law; 0 for all other states (NAIC)

Notes

1. See Klein (1994a) for an extensive review of this literature.

2. Kunreuther (1996) discusses the concept of a "risk premium" in insurers' pricing structures to account for greater uncertainty about expected insurance losses.

3. This statement is based on several conversations between the author and personnel from different insurance companies.

4. This problem also plagues measurement of discrimination in labor, housing, and lending markets; see Galster (1993) for a discussion.

5. This assumes that in areas with relatively high loss ratios, insurers still charge adequate insurance rates and earn a fair rate of return.

6. Premiums would be expected to increase less than proportionately with the amount of insurance because of the effect of certain fixed policy expenses and partial losses.

7. FAIR Plan coverage also can cost less than comparable coverage in the voluntary market if regulators suppress FAIR Plan rates below costs. The fairness of FAIR Plan rates can vary among different insureds, in that low-risk properties may pay too much and high-risk properties pay too little because of inefficiencies in the FAIR Plan rate structure.

8. Zip codes were divided into the following categories: low income ($0–$13,000), medium income ($13,001–$18,000), and high-income ($18,001 +); and low minority (0–10%), medium minority (11%–36%), and high minority (36% +). Minority individuals were defined as nonwhite persons according to the U.S. Bureau of the Census and include blacks, Asians, American Indians, Eskimos, Aleuts, and other races. Alternative specifications of this variable (e.g., nonwhites and white Hispanics) tested in multiple regression analysis were not found to significantly affect the results.

9. The estimated percentage of insured homes is biased downward because it excludes homes insured through commercial dwelling fire policies. Use of these policies could be more prevalent in the inner city if there is proportionately more rental property.

10. Note that these are the coverage definitions used by the Missouri Department of Insurance and vary slightly from the definitions used in the earlier tables. The Missouri Department of Insurance defines, for the purposes of its data collection, limited coverage as dwelling fire and HO-8 policies and any other policies that offer cash value instead of replacement cost coverage. Broad coverage encompasses all other homeowners policies (except for HO-4 and HO-6).

11. Interestingly, average loss costs were lower for broad-coverage than limited-coverage policies. This is likely owing to broad-coverage policies being purchased by homeowners with a lower severity and frequency of claims, which offsets the broader amount of coverage they receive.

12. However, the standard deviations also indicate that there is a high degree of variation in these measures among the zip codes in each group. This means that the patterns seen here could be heavily influenced by random fluctuations in loss experience or other factors and may not reflect long-term or systematic patterns.

13. These figures reflect the losses and premiums paid during given calendar years, regardless of when the applicable policy was written.

14. This contrasts with a study by the Missouri Department of Insurance (1993), which indicated that some minority neighborhoods tend to have lower loss ratios than comparable white neighborhoods. The reason for the different results presented in this chapter are unclear. The two analyses aggregate data differently and use data from different time periods.

15. Incurred losses represent estimated payments on claims occurring in a given year regardless of when the applicable insurance policies were written.

16. Earned premiums represent all premiums attributable to insurance coverage in effect during the calendar year.

17. Earned premiums and the number of insured homes were compiled for the 1992 calendar year. Loss data were compiled for accidents or claims occurring in 1992.

18. As explained earlier, loss data by zip code are not currently available on a national basis. ISO homeowners territory definitions typically follow city and county boundaries, but, in a few cases, ISO territories divide a city into several parts. Zip codes were matched to the territories where they are principally located. When a zip code fell into more than one territory, the zip code was matched to the territory that contains the largest portion of the zip code.

19. Higher demand may not increase the price for a given policy if supply is relatively price-elastic, but higher demand could result in the purchase of more extensive coverage, which would raise the average premium.

20. Durbin-Watson tests suggest a possible problem with positive serial correlation with the state-effects versions of the equation (i.e., the error terms from different observations are positively correlated). Generally, the presence of serial correlation will not affect the unbiased aspect of ordinary least squares estimators, but it will affect their efficiency. In the case of positive serial correlation, this means that the standard error of the regression will be biased downward, and there will be a tendency to reject the null hypothesis when in fact it should not be rejected (Kennedy 1985).

21. The specification of the minority variable as nonwhite versus nonwhite and white Hispanics yielded similar results.

22. Previous studies on this question reached different conclusions, but these studies were subject to a number of limitations that qualify their results. See Klein (1994a) for a review of these studies.

23. A comparable study of urban Missouri automobile insurance markets by Harrington and Niehaus (1995) found that loss ratios increased with minority concentration.

24. The NAIC has recently completed a handbook that discusses various strategies to improve urban insurance market conditions (NAIC 1996).

25. A special urban insurance Neighborhood Housing Services task force (appointed by NHS) is sponsoring such a study.

26. Nationwide Mutual Insurance Company is currently developing such an approach in Baltimore, Md.

References

Doherty, Neil A., and Sharon Tennyson. 1996. "Moral Hazard, Adverse Selection, and Community Monitored Insurance Programs." University of Pennsylvania, Philadelphia. Photocopy.

Duncan, Michael P. 1995. *The Fair Housing Act and Property Insurance: The Call for Congressional Action.* Des Plaines, Ill.: National Association of Independent Insurers.

Fix, Michael, and R. J. Struyk, eds. 1993. *Clear and Convincing Evidence: Measurement of Discrimination in America.* Washington, D.C.: Urban Institute Press.

Galster, George C. 1993. "Use of Testers in Investigating Discrimination in Mortgage Lending and Insurance." In *Clear and Convincing Evidence: Measurement of Discrimination in America*, edited by M. Fix and R. J. Struyk. Washington, D.C.: Urban Institute Press.

Harrington, Scott E., and Helen I. Doerpinghaus. 1993. "The Economics and Politics of Automobile Insurance Rate Classification." *Journal of Risk and Insurance* 60: 59–84.

Harrington, Scott, and Greg Niehaus. 1992. "Dealing with Insurance Availability and Affordability Problems in Inner Cities: An Analysis of the California Proposal." *Journal of Insurance Regulation* 10: 564–84.

———. 1995. "Race and Availability/Affordability Problems in Urban Automobile Insurance Markets." University of South Carolina, Columbia. Photocopy.

Joskow, Paul L. 1973. "Cartels, Competition, and Regulation in the Property-Liability Insurance Industry." *Bell Journal of Economics* 4: 375–427.

Kennedy, Peter. 1985. *A Guide to Econometrics*. Cambridge, Mass.: MIT Press.

Klein, Robert W. 1989. *Competition in Private Passenger Automobile Insurance*. Kansas City, Mo.: National Association of Insurance Commissioners.

————. 1994a. *A Preliminary Analysis of Urban Insurance Markets*. Kansas City, Mo.: National Association of Insurance Commissioners.

————. 1994b. *The Structure and Performance of Personal Auto and Homeowners Insurance Markets*. Kansas City, Mo.: National Association of Insurance Commissioners.

————. 1995a. *The Impact of Loss Costs on Urban Homeowners Insurance Markets*. Kansas City, Mo.: National Association of Insurance Commissioners.

————. 1995b. "Insurance Regulation in Transition." *Journal of Risk and Insurance* 62: 363–404.

————. 1995c. *Structure and Performance of Homeowners Insurance Markets in St. Louis*. Kansas City, Mo.: National Association of Insurance Commissioners.

————. 1996. *Urban Homeowners Insurance Markets in Missouri*. Kansas City, Mo.: National Association of Insurance Commissioners.

Kunreuther, Howard. 1996. "The Role of Insurance in Dealing with Catastrophic Risks from Natural Disaster." University of Pennsylvania, Philadelphia. Photocopy.

Missouri Department of Insurance. 1993. *Homeowners Insurance in Missouri*. Jefferson City: Author.

NAIC. See National Association of Insurance Commissioners.

NAII. See National Association of Independent Insurers.

National Association of Independent Insurers. 1994. *An Analysis of Crime and Fire Statistics, Dwelling Characteristics, and Homeowners Insurance Losses for Selected Urban Areas*. Des Plaines, Ill.: Author.

National Association of Insurance Commissioners. 1994. *Urban Insurance Problems and Solutions: Interim Report of the NAIC Insurance Availability and Affordability Task Force*. Kansas City, Mo.: Author.

————. 1995. *Report on Profitability by Line and by State, 1994*. Kansas City, Mo.: Author.

————. 1996. *Improving Urban Insurance Markets: A Handbook on Available Options*. Kansas City, Mo.: Author.

Scherer, F. M., and David Ross. 1990. *Industrial Market Structure and Economic Performance*. Boston: Houghton Mifflin Co.

Squires, Gregory D., Ruthanne DeWolfe, and Allan S. DeWolfe. 1979. "Urban Decline or Disinvestment: Uneven Development, Redlining, and the Role of the Insurance Industry." *Social Problems* 27: 79–95.

Squires, Gregory D., and William Velez. 1988. "Insurance Redlining and the Process of Discrimination." *Review of Black Political Economy* 16: 63–75.

Squires, Gregory D., William Velez, and Karl E. Taeuber. 1991. "Insurance Redlining, Agency Location, and the Process of Urban Disinvestment." *Urban Affairs Quarterly* 26(4): 567–88.

Varian, Hal R. 1992. *Microeconomic Analysis*. New York: W. W. Norton & Co.

Chapter Four

HOMEOWNERS INSURANCE AVAILABILITY AND AGENT LOCATION

Jay D. Schultz

Accessibility to an agent is integral to whether property insurance is available or not. As early as 1968, in the report of the President's National Advisory Panel on Insurance in Riot-Affected Areas, agent placement was determined to be a major contributor to insurance availability problems in the inner city.

> The number of insurance agents and brokers selling insurance to residents and businessmen in urban core areas is relatively small. The effort to place the business may be more time-consuming and the results less lucrative than with business from other city areas and the suburbs. Agents and brokers who seek business in urban core areas find that their applications for insurance are screened carefully by the insurance company with which they deal. An agent who submits too many applications that a company considers too risky may have his agency contract terminated. (1968: 5)

The doughnut pattern of agent placement, in which agents locate in a suburban ring around a city while ignoring the inner-city core, is well documented (Illinois Public Action 1993; Massachusetts Affordable Housing Alliance 1995; Squires et al. 1991). The question is whether this pattern is related to insurability (risk) of the respective neighborhoods or whether other factors independent of insurance and economic fundamentals are involved. Squires et al. (1991) analyzed the placement of agencies in the Milwaukee, Wisconsin, metropolitan area and concluded that there is bias in the placement of agencies toward suburban areas and predominantly white areas. In a 1995 study, I expanded upon this research, with the addition of loss-cost data, and obtained similar results even after controlling for loss experience. Although agent placement is not the only factor influencing availability of homeowners insurance, it is one aspect that is easily observed. This chapter tests the hypothesis that racial composition of a community has an effect on location of personal-lines agents independent of fundamental insurance, including loss costs (a measure of insured losses, usually expressed as a loss ratio—see note 8) and economic factors.

The state of Missouri, from which this study's data are drawn, offers an exceptional opportunity to analyze insurance affordability and availability issues. The market for homeowners insurance in Missouri can be considered to be competitively driven. The patterns of exposure and of agent placement are not hindered by the Department of Insurance, the state regulatory agency. In addition, the Department of Insurance has an extensive zip code database that includes years of loss data as well as exposure and premium data. Inclusion of loss-cost data is a key factor in any analysis of availability and affordability issues.

DATA AND METHODOLOGY

This study's data were derived from four sources. Agent data (the number of agents authorized to sell homeowners insurance, per zip code by company, by agency) were obtained from the Missouri Department of Insurance Agent License database (as of October 1995). If an agent was affiliated with an agency, the agency address zip code was used. For agents not affiliated with an agency, their home address zip code is used.[1] Earned exposures[2] for the year 1994 and loss experience data for the years 1989–94 were obtained from the Department of Insurance Homeowners Insurance Zip Code database. Demographic data (average income, percentage nonwhite, percentage of homes built before 1950, percentage of houses valued at less than $35,000, percentage of houses valued at less than $50,000, and the number of owner-occupied housing units) were obtained from the U.S. Bureau of the Census, 1990 Census Summary Tape File 3 (data aggregated to the zip code level). Rating territory data, as of 1994, were acquired from the Insurance Services Office (ISO).

This study analyzes the location of agents in St. Louis City and county—collectively, the most populous area of the state. The St. Louis City/county area is divided into 61 zip codes, 58 of which were used in this research. Zip codes 63101, 63102, and 63103, which are located in the downtown business district of St. Louis City, were removed from the analysis. Since agent location in business districts is influenced more heavily by factors such as commercial insurance, and since these districts contain many fewer owner-occupied households, inclusion of these zip codes would severely bias the results.

The insurance companies used in this chapter were selected first by taking all companies with an earned-exposure market share in the St. Louis area greater than 0.5 percent. From this initial set of 36 companies, only those companies whose marketing structure (direct writer or independent agency) was known were kept, leaving 28 companies. Finally the Fair Access to Insurance Requirements (FAIR) Plan and a home service company were removed.[3] The remaining 26 companies represent 77 percent of the St. Louis market for homeowners insurance, based on earned exposures.

The unit of measure in this study for calculating agent and agency presence was agent-company combinations (agent appointments) and agency-company combinations (agency appointments). Since an agent can represent more than one company, there was a double counting of agents in the agent appointment statistic.[4] Given that the addresses of agents are less precise than agency appointment counts, they were analyzed also.

In the homeowners insurance purchasing process, consumers have a choice in three areas: (1) type of product (i.e., homeowners policy, market value policy, or fire policy; (2) company; and (3) agent. Any restriction in one of the three areas of choice will lead to restrictions in the other two areas and to availability problems. There is evidence of a strong correlation between accessibility to agents and availability problems. Agents and agency offices constitute a visible physical presence—they are easily identified by location. Accessibility to, and choice among, agents is vital to the availability of homeowners insurance. Without it, choice in the other two areas will also be limited.

It is generally accepted that personal-lines insurance (i.e., insurance such as homeowners and private passenger automobile insurance that is sold to individuals to protect them against losses not associated with commercial activity) is a localized market.[5] That is, the consumer usually prefers to purchase insurance locally. Agents who have a physical presence in a neighborhood have a definite advantage over those that do not. Evidence of this is that agents tend to sell the majority of their homeowners and automobile business locally as well (Squires et al. 1991: 569). Therefore, one can deduce that the more agents (or agencies) in an area, the more choices a consumer has.[6] With more choice comes a greater ability to shop and to obtain a better deal (i.e., there will be more competition, which leads to a more efficient market). It follows that insurance is then more available (or accessible) to the consumer.

Agents, acting in their own self-interest, will locate in the area that is most economically beneficial to them. Rational agents will locate in the area where they can earn the most money, provided they are not restricted from doing so. Many economic factors influence this decision, including the ability to sell other types of insurance (such as commercial or automobile insurance), profitability of the area, number of potential clients, and costs of operation. Another explanation for the pattern of agent location is that it is demand driven. Virtually every homeowner has a demand for homeowners insurance, albeit preferences for types and amounts of coverage will vary among homeowners. The quantity of insurance demanded in an area is determined by price (which, of course, is determined by the interaction of demand and supply).

Agents are located where they (and their companies) desire to market their products, which in turn is assumed to be determined by market forces. Therefore, the concentration of agents in an area is an indication of company (and/or agent) preference. The agent's economic incentive in choosing a location is determined primarily by the commission structure, which is generally set up as a flat percentage of premium (e.g., 15 percent of the annual premium). Agents are compensated more for obtaining a risk with a higher insured value (those risks that cost more to replace). As a result of a higher insured value, these risks also command a higher premium and are therefore generally more profitable to the company. Economic theory suggests that the potential commission of an area is important (i.e., average commission per agent). Agents will tend to move toward an area (zip code) where the average commission per agent is highest until it is equalized across all areas (zip codes). This is not to say that the ratio of houses to agents should necessarily be equal across areas. Areas where the average value of a house is higher, and where homeowners are more likely to purchase more options and endorsements, can support more agents.

When certain patterns with respect to agent location exist, there is a possibility of discrimination due to either disparate treatment or disparate impact in the placement of agents. Such discrimination may exist when a high concentration of agents coincides with a high concentration of exposures; when areas with high-minority concentrations have low agent concentrations; and when commission per agent is higher in minority areas and risk of loss is equivalent across areas. Evidence that an artificial barrier to agent location exists if risk of loss in two areas is the same but the areas are priced differently or an underwriting rule affects one area more negatively than the other.

ANALYSIS AND RESULTS

This study found that agents do locate in areas where exposures are most sought. This can be seen by correlating the agent (agency) appointment counts per owner-occupied houses with earned exposures per owner-occupied houses. The correlation, r, between agents and exposures is 0.61. Likewise, the correlation between agencies and exposures is 0.40. This is an indication of a strong positive relationship between the number of agents in an area and the number of earned exposures there.

Two ratios were used to measure market penetration: agent (agency) appointments per 1,000 exposures; and agent (agency) appointments per 1,000 owner-occupied housing units. To analyze the pattern of agent placement across neighborhoods of different racial composition, the zip codes were subdivided into quintiles from a low (quintile 1) to a high (quintile 5) percentage of nonwhite population. Table 4.1 shows the results of agent concentrations by percentage of nonwhite-defined quintiles. A much higher concentration of agent appointments was found in predominantly white areas—approximately nine times higher (r = −0.37) when measured against exposures—as opposed to in zip codes with a high nonwhite population. Similarly, as seen in table 4.1, the same pattern occurs for agency-company appointments.

As stated, economic theory suggests that, all else held constant, equilibrium is obtained when compensation per agent is equalized across market areas. If the average commission per agent in white neighborhoods is greater than or equal to that in minority neighbor-

Table 4.1 AGENT CONCENTRATION BY PERCENTAGE NONWHITE POPULATION

Quintile	Percentage Nonwhite[a]	Agents per		Agencies per	
		1,000 Exposures[b]	1,000 Owner-Occupied Houses[a]	1,000 Exposures[b]	1,000 Owner-Occupied Houses[a]
1	1.75	17.93	16.38	4.27	3.90
2	5.25	21.49	18.35	4.99	4.26
3	10.31	14.67	12.21	4.61	3.84
4	31.98	7.06	5.80	1.09	0.89
5	77.16	1.93	1.28	0.49	0.33
Correlation coefficient		−0.37	−0.39	−0.31	−0.37

a. Data from U.S. Bureau of the Census, 1990 Census.
b. Data from Missouri Department of Insurance.

hoods, there would be no incentive for agents to move from white to nonwhite areas. To test this proposition, the average commission per agent by zip code was calculated for the 26 companies studied (total premiums for all 26 companies were multiplied by 15 percent then divided by the number of agent appointments). Table 4.2 compares average commissions across minority-defined quintiles. Here the average commission per resident agent appointment was $25,891 in the areas with the greatest percentage minority population, while only $3,081 in areas with the least nonwhite representation. The correlation between percentage nonwhite and average commission was 0.50. Clearly, it is economically advantageous for agents to locate in minority neighborhoods.

If loss experience is sufficiently higher in minority areas, the agent placement just observed can be explained as a result of those areas being more risky to insure. Table 4.3 contains four indicators of loss

Table 4.2 AVERAGE COMMISSION PER AGENT

Quintile	Percentage Nonwhite[a]	Average Home Value ($)[a]	Average Commission per Agent ($)[b]
1	1.75	109,322	3,081
2	5.25	117,719	2,694
3	10.31	106,728	3,821
4	31.98	80,327	7,625
5	77.16	45,736	25,891
Correlation coefficient		−0.44	0.50

a. Data from Bureau of the Census, 1990 Census.
b. Data from Missouri Department of Insurance.

Table 4.3 FIVE-YEAR AVERAGE LOSS EXPERIENCE BY PERCENTAGE NONWHITE POPULATION

Quintile	Percentage Nonwhite[a]	Average Home Value ($)[a]	Average Loss ($)[b]	Losses per 100 Exposures[b]	Expected Loss per Exposure ($)[b]	Cash Flow Loss Ratio[b]
1	1.75	109,322	1,662	11.01	183	56.38
2	5.25	117,719	1,725	11.18	193	57.10
3	10.31	106,728	1,674	9.16	153	48.03
4	31.98	80,327	1,985	9.94	197	64.43
5	77.16	45,736	2,241	8.23	184	69.26
Correlation coefficient		−0.44	0.61	−0.50	0.03	0.53

a. Data from U.S. Bureau of the Census, 1990 Census.
b. Data from Missouri Department of Insurance.

experience. Average loss, the number of losses per 100 exposures, and expected loss per exposure indicate that risks in low-minority neighborhoods are not significantly better than those in high-minority areas.[7] The correlation between percentage nonwhite population and expected loss per exposure is 0.03 (no correlation), with expected loss per exposure $184 in areas with a large nonwhite representation and $183 in predominantly white areas. The cash flow loss ratio—the expected loss per exposure divided by the premium per exposure (average premium)—shows that low-minority areas tend to be more profitable than high-minority zip codes.[8] In the high-minority areas, these insurance companies paid out 69 cents for every dollar they received in premium, whereas in low-minority areas they paid out only 56 cents per dollar. The difference in the cash flow loss ratio, however, is explained by differences in average premium rather than differences in risk. Since the expected losses per exposure are similar between low- and high-minority areas ($183 and $184, respectively), it can be concluded that the difference in cash flow loss ratio is a product of differences in average premium.

This pattern of loss ratios is most likely the result of the apparent correlation between percentage nonwhite population and average home value ($r = -0.44$). Given the rate structure under the rating territory system, areas with lower-value houses tend to have higher loss ratios. The average amount of losses in an area is not related to the average value of the insured property in that area ($r = 0.10$). The average premium per exposure, however, is higher for the higher-valued houses (base premium is determined by the value of the property). Thus, the loss ratio is lower in those areas with higher-valued houses.

Underwriting rules which capriciously eliminate a large number of the risks in selected geographic areas may be a source of artificial restrictions to agent placement. To illustrate the disparate impact of underwriting rules, I analyzed two common guidelines: the minimum property value rule and the maximum age of home rule. As property values decrease, availability of insurance will also.

According to data from the 1990 Census (table 4.4), 44 percent of the houses in the lowest-income quintile have a value less than $35,000. Another 30 percent are valued between $35,000 and $50,000. This compares to a total of 1.67 percent of the houses in the highest-income category valued at less than $50,000. Approximately one half of the top 20 companies writing homeowners insurance (HO-3) in Missouri automatically exclude houses valued under $35,000.[9] Eight of the 20 companies will not even offer a market value policy

Table 4.4 IMPACT OF RESTRICTIVE UNDERWRITING RULES

Quintile	Average Income ($)[a]	Percentage Valued under $35,000[a]	Percentage Valued under $50,000[a]	Percentage Built before 1950[a]
1	85,880	0.60	1.67	18.13
2	47,335	1.13	3.89	12.51
3	38,423	3.62	14.85	30.37
4	29,992	13.13	44.90	47.53
5	20,583	44.15	74.26	71.39

a. Data from U.S. Bureau of the Census, 1990 Census.

(HO-8). Age limits also have a real impact, although to a somewhat lesser extent than the minimum value rule. For example, 71 percent of the houses in the low-income group would not be eligible when an underwriting rule prohibits insuring houses built before 1950. Only 18 percent of the houses in the highest-income quintile would be too old. Owners of houses built before 1950 will find it much more difficult to obtain homeowners insurance (HO-3) from 7 of the top 20 companies just because their residence is older.[10]

Comparing rates across neighborhoods can also give an indication of possible company preference. Rate and rating territory data for 11 of the 26 companies studied were obtained. The average rate for a standard homeowners policy (HO-3) for a $50,000 brick house in the lowest fire protection district was calculated. For the same house definition, the average cost per $1,000 for an additional $100,000 of insurance (from $50,000 to $150,000) was calculated. Again, these statistics were grouped by the percentage of nonwhite categories (table 4.5). Whereas the expected loss per exposure was not correlated with the percentage nonwhite variable, areas with a greater concentration of nonwhite population were systematically charged higher rates. In predominantly minority areas, the average base premium paid on a $50,000 brick home was $252, and coverage on houses valued between $50,000 and $150,000 will cost an average of $3.73 per $1,000. This compares with a rate of $191 and $3.50 per $1,000 in the areas of the lowest nonwhite representation. This translates to a correlation of 0.70 and 0.53 between percentage nonwhite population and the rate for a $50,000 home and the cost per $1,000, respectively.

The preceding analysis is a simplified look at the problem of availability of homeowners insurance, in that each factor and relationship is viewed in isolation. However, even when analyzing agent location simultaneously, through regression analysis (see table 4.6) with various insurance and demographic variables, similar results were

Table 4.5 TERRITORY BASE RATES FOR STANDARD HOMEOWNERS POLICY ON BRICK HOME

Quintile	Percentage Nonwhite[a]	Average HO-3 Rate On $50,000 Home ($)[b]	Average Cost per $1,000[b]	Expected Loss per Exposure ($)[c]
1	1.75	190.67	3.50	183
2	5.25	202.32	3.56	193
3	10.31	198.58	3.44	153
4	31.98	228.61	3.55	197
5	77.16	251.66	3.73	184
Correlation coefficient		0.70	0.53	0.03

a. Data from U.S. Bureau of the Census, 1990 Census.
b. Data from Insurance Services Office, 1994 (average cost per $1,000 based on coverage between $50,000 and $150,000).
c. Data from Missouri Department of Insurance.

Table 4.6 REGRESSION ANALYSIS RESULTS

Independent Variables	Dependent Variable Agent Appointments	
	(1)	(2)
Constant	−1.405	−0.642
	(−2.511)**	(−0.783)
Owner-occupied houses	0.438	0.466
	(−18.705)***	(−15.216)***
Average value of owner-occupied house	0.281	0.280
	(−7.6)***	(−5.513)***
Percentage houses built before 1950	0.001	0.001
	(0.907)	(1.104)
Cash flow loss ratio	−0.001	−0.002
	(−0.370)	(−1.040)
Average commission	−0.387	−0.424
	(−24.440)***	(−17.750)***
Percentage minority	−0.002	−0.004
	(−1.684)*	(−2.533)**
Cost per $1,000		−0.552
		(−1.904)*
Adjusted R^2	0.68	0.69
F-statistic	52.65***	52.84***

Note: t-statistics are in parentheses.
***Significant at .01 level. **Significant at .05 level. *Significant at .10 level.

produced. This technique estimates linear equations by minimizing the variance between the actual and predicted values of the dependent variable (the number of agent appointments per zip code). Demographic and insurance-related variables were used in the equation to estimate the predicted value. Dummy variables were also added, but not displayed in the table, to account for the difference between companies in the number of agent appointments located in a particular zip code.[11] Log-log forms of the equation are displayed in table 4.6.[12] The rationale for specifying the equations as log-log is that the expected impact of any one variable may be different at various levels of that variable. The log-log specification allows for this nonlinear relationship between independent and dependent variables.[13] Two equations were estimated. The first equation includes all 26 companies in the sample. The second equation includes the variable for the average cost per $1,000 of coverage between $50,000 and $150,000 of insurance. Only those 11 companies with rate data were used to estimate this equation.

As expected, the coefficients for the number of owner-occupied houses and the average value of owner-occupied houses were positive and significant (see table 4.6, column [1]). This means that more agents will locate in an area where there are more owner-occupied houses and where houses are more expensive. The coefficient for age of the homes in a zip code was found to be insignificant; relative age of a neighborhood has no implication for the number of agents found there. Notably, the loss ratio was found to be insignificant in the prediction of agent placement, indicating that profitability of an area has no impact on determining how many agents will be located there. Average commission was found to be very significant and negative in sign. This supports the finding that agents are not located where their potential economic gain is greatest.

In the second equation (table 4.6, column [2]), the coefficient for cost per $1,000 was found to be negative and significant. This means that relatively more agents are located in areas where rates are lower. This is not surprising, since it has already been found that the cost per $1,000 is negatively correlated with percentage minority population. This may also be the result of competitive forces (or lack thereof) at work. Percentage of nonwhite population also had a negative sign and was significant. In other words, areas that are predominantly minority have fewer agents. Together, this indicates that agent placement is not determined by the relative loss experience of the areas studied. Instead, there appears to be a bias against placing agents in inner-city, high-minority areas. There are fewer agents in minority areas, and this relationship persists even after loss costs, commissions, and profitability are taken into consideration. This is the case even though the economic incentive, potential commission, should encourage agents to locate in these areas.

SUGGESTIONS FOR FURTHER RESEARCH AND POLICY IMPLICATIONS

The connection between the access to agents and availability of homeowners insurance has been identified and shown to be a key aspect of the insurance purchasing process. When access to agents is reduced, restrictions to quality, affordable insurance exists. In this study, existing methodologies were applied to a new, more complete, data set. A statistical relationship has been established between agent location, exposures, and racial makeup of neighborhoods.

Similar studies should be conducted on other metropolitan areas to draw broader conclusions. As more years of data are collected, trends can be identified, which will add insight. Data on refusal to appoint agents by geographic location should be incorporated in future studies. By categorizing insurance companies into various groups, such as standard versus nonstandard, insight may be gained. The analysis could be expanded to include other measures of availability, such as the number of exposures in an area or some other measure of market penetration. More research must also be conducted on the use of rating territories. The regulator must continue to analyze the market for geography-related patterns. Through analyzing the causes of affordability and availability problems with statistical methods, these patterns can be identified and subsequently addressed.

This chapter reveals that the location of agents and the impact of agent location on availability problems should not be ignored by insurance regulators. As regulators audit insurance companies for marketing, underwriting, and claims practices, they should also investigate agent location patterns. There is evidence that agent location is an important determinant of insurance accessibility, if not availability, and that racial bias influences agents' decisions regarding the location of their offices. An extreme solution to this problem is to initiate tight regulatory control over the placement of agents. A less-disruptive solution would be for insurance companies to change their compensation, rating territory, and underwriting systems, resulting in the altering of economic incentives that are now in place.

CONCLUSIONS

This study has shown that the number of agents in an area is highly correlated with the number of exposures in that area. It has also been shown that the number of agents in an area decreases as the percentage of minority residents rises. These results support the contention that a doughnut pattern exists in the placement of agents. Agents locate primarily in suburban areas, whereas inner-city, predominantly minority, neighborhoods are ignored. Even after controlling for other demographic and economic variables, there is still a negative relationship between the size of the minority population and the number of agents. The study's most striking finding is that loss costs were not a factor in the determination of agent location. Also, the potential commission for a resident agent is much higher in minority neighborhoods.

A couple of institutional characteristics in the marketing and sale of homeowners insurance were offered to explain these observations. First, some underwriting rules used by insurance companies have a disparate impact on minority neighborhoods. Neighborhoods containing a disproportionate share of older houses of lower market value are adversely affected by maximum-age and minimum-value rules. A second explanation is the rating territory structure, which, on average, has allocated higher base rates for houses of equal value to minority neighborhoods.

These findings indicate that one of the reasons minority neighborhoods tend to be underserved is that companies do not have a physical presence there. This lack of presence cannot be explained by difference in loss costs or risk. Homeowners insurance is more available, through access to agents, to white neighborhoods than to comparable areas with a large minority population.

Notes

1. Business addresses of nonagency affiliated agents are not currently available in any database. Therefore home address was used in this study and is a reasonable approximation.

2. Earned exposures equal the total number of house years insured (i.e., a house that was insured on October 1, 1991, would be counted as $3/12$ of an exposure for 1991 and $9/12$ of an exposure for 1992). The types of exposures included in the data are homeowner, dwelling fire, market value, and surcharged dwelling fire policies.

3. The FAIR Plan, a publicly administered insurance pool for applicants who do not qualify for regular policies, is the residual market in Missouri. Home service companies market to low-income and high-minority areas and thus command a much more significant share of the market there. These companies apparently do not compete on price, however. Rather, they compete by utilizing a method of marketing that involves going door to door on a weekly or monthly basis to collect premiums, usually in cash.

4. As an example: A zip code has one agency with two agents, each representing three companies (A, B, C) and (A, D, E). One of the companies (A) is in common. The agent variable will have a value of 6 (A twice, B, C, D, E) for this zip code. The agency variable will have a value of 5 (A, B, C, D, E).

5. The term "local" here does not have a precise geographic definition; rather, it is defined to take into account the costs of traveling, time, and convenience. Since it has been observed that, in general, consumers do not price shop for insurance (Cummins et al. 1974: 63), these costs weigh heavily in the decision.

6. The counter-argument to this is that the agent's physical location doesn't matter since one can shop by telephone. However, even when shopping for homeowners insurance over the telephone, all else equal, there is still a preference to shop locally.

7. The loss-experience variables are based on six years of data and the experience of all companies in the Homeowners Insurance Zip Code database (approximately 95 percent of the homeowners insurance market in Missouri). Loss is also based on all policy types in the data set. Losses include those for renters and condominiums, as well as those listed in note 2.

8. Cash flow loss ratio is the percentage of premium returned to the policyholder through the payment for losses.

9. One of the companies has another type of property-value-related rule that can have the same effect as the minimum-value rule. One company does not offer a homeowners policy (HO-3). For three of these companies, this information was unavailable.

10. This is interesting in that discriminating on the basis of age of residence can be considered an illegal practice under Missouri's Unfair Trade Practices Act (§375.936 RSMo).

11. Some companies will consistently have more (or fewer) agents than the other companies per zip code. The dummy variable for company i takes on a value of 1 when an observation is attributed to company i; otherwise, it has a value of 0.

12. The coefficients in a log-log equation are interpreted as elasticities. For example, the coefficient in the equation $Log(Y) = 1 + 5 Log(X)$ indicates that Y will increase 5 percent for every 1 percent increase in X.

13. The agent appointment variable was scaled by adding 1 to its value before the log was taken. This was done because for many zip codes, the value of this variable was 0 or 1. Since this is a scaler transformation, it had no impact on the value of the coefficient estimates.

References

Cummins, J. David, Dan M. McGill, Howard E. Winklevoss, and Robert A. Zelten. 1974. *Consumer Attitudes toward Auto and Homeowners Insurance*. Philadelphia: University of Pennsylvania.

Illinois Public Action. 1993. *An Analysis of Zip Code Distribution of State Farm and Allstate Agents and Policies in Chicago*. Chicago: Author.

Massachusetts Affordable Housing Alliance. 1995. *Insurance Company Redlining: A Study of Neighborhood Offices in Roxbury, Dorchester, and Mattapan*. Boston: Author.

President's National Advisory Panel on Insurance in Riot-Affected Areas. 1968. *Meeting the Insurance Crisis of Our Cities*. Washington, D.C.: U.S. Government Printing Office.

Schultz, Jay D. 1995. "An Analysis of Agent Location and Homeowners Insurance Availability." *Journal of Insurance Regulation* 14(1): 65–89.

Squires, Gregory D., William Velez, and Karl E. Taeuber. 1991. "Insurance Redlining, Agency-Location, and the Process of Urban Disinvestment." *Urban Affairs Quarterly* 26: 567–88.

Chapter Five

DOCUMENTING DISCRIMINATION BY HOMEOWNERS INSURANCE COMPANIES THROUGH TESTING

Shanna L. Smith and Cathy Cloud

Preapplication testing has proven to be an invaluable tool for detecting discriminatory practices and policies of homeowners insurance companies. Between 1992 and 1994, the National Fair Housing Alliance (NFHA) coordinated a nine-city preapplication testing project involving the largest homeowners insurance companies in the United States. Based upon the testing results, the NFHA filed administrative complaints with the U.S. Department of Housing and Urban Development (HUD) against Nationwide Insurance Enterprises, Allstate Insurance Company, and State Farm Insurance Companies. NFHA was joined by the Toledo (Ohio) Fair Housing Center in the complaint against State Farm. The investigation included both applicant- and neighborhood-based testing methodologies.

The NFHA's investigation found that various underwriting guidelines of the companies tested virtually excluded the majority of homes in African American and Latino neighborhoods from qualifying for the best homeowners insurance coverage. Through testing and investigation, the NFHA found evidence that marketing practices were designed to avoid doing business in racially and ethnically identifiable neighborhoods, that inferior policies were marketed in minority neighborhoods, and that premiums appeared to be priced based at least in part upon the racial makeup of the neighborhood and not on the risk presented by the property. This chapter focuses not on the discriminatory effect of certain policies but on discrimination detected by testers who posed as homeowners seeking insurance quotations on similar houses.

TESTING AND INVESTIGATION OF HOMEOWNERS INSURANCE COMPANIES

Testing of the insurance industry began in the mid-1970s and was initiated by National People's Action (NPA) in Chicago. The impetus to test the industry began when residents of the white ethnic neighborhoods comprising NPA realized that they were being denied homeowners insurance coverage because of the age and value of their homes. NPA used confrontational tactics to engage the presidents of the largest companies to write coverage for their neighborhoods. The companies responded by creating the market-value policy (which insures the house for its sale value, rather than for what the house would actually cost to replace), which temporarily satisfied the neighborhood residents.

In 1978, fair housing groups recognized that limiting residents of predominantly African American or Latino neighborhoods to market-value policies was discriminatory. A fair housing group in Dayton, Ohio, was engaged in litigation under the Federal Fair Housing Act of 1968 to require insurers to write policies based on risk rather than the race of the applicant or neighborhood.[1] Fair housing groups in Cleveland and Toledo began to investigate allegations of insurance redlining and to develop testing methodologies to ascertain whether these companies were in violation of the Fair Housing Act.

The NFHA reviewed the earlier work of the Toledo Fair Housing Center and the Metropolitan Milwaukee Fair Housing Council in developing its testing methodology for the national project. To accomplish its purposes, testing methodology must remain fluid. As industry practices are modified to attempt to identify testing, our testing methodologies are adjusted to preserve the credibility of the investigation. Testing has been expanded to cover discriminatory practices and policies that discriminate against persons with disabilities. The NFHA also conducts full-application testing, which uncovers additional forms of discriminatory treatment.

NATIONAL TESTING AND INVESTIGATION PROJECT

In 1991, the board of directors of the National Fair Housing Alliance authorized the submission of an application to HUD to conduct testing of homeowners insurance companies. This decision was based, in part, on the growing number of complaints of insurance redlining received by NFHA members. The grant application was funded by HUD, and the NFHA entered into contractual agreements with fair housing agencies to conduct the tests locally. Local staff and testers were trained by the NFHA, and the tests were conducted under the guidelines of and with the supervision of NFHA staff.

This was the first national testing project designed to develop evidence across the country about the nature of discrimination by homeowners insurance companies based on the race or national origin of homeowners and the race or ethnicity of the neighborhood where the property is located. These tests were conducted for enforcement purposes, not for research purposes. The cities involved in the initial testing project conducted between 30 and 40 matched-pair telephone tests. Participants included the following fair housing organizations:

Akron, Ohio	Fair Housing Contact Service
Atlanta	Metro Fair Housing Services
Chicago	Eighteenth Street Development Corporation[2]
Cincinnati	Housing Opportunities Made Equal (HOME)
Los Angeles	Fair Housing Congress of Southern California
Louisville	Kentucky Fair Housing Council
Memphis	Housing Opportunities Corporation
Milwaukee	Metropolitan Milwaukee Fair Housing Council
Toledo, Ohio	Toledo Fair Housing Center

Insurance testing generally requires both a tester and a test house. Like mortgage lending testing, insurance testing can involve preapplication testing (obtaining quotes and information about insurance policies) and full-application testing (filing applications and making payment for actual policies), as well as applicant testing (based on the race or other characteristic of the individual that is protected under the terms of the Fair Housing Act) and neighborhood testing (based on the racial composition in which the house to be insured is located). The NFHA's national insurance project primarily involved preapplication neighborhood-based testing, although some applicant-based testing was conducted as well.

Purpose of Testing and Investigation

The purpose of testing and investigating homeowners insurance companies is to identify policies and practices that restrict and/or deny insurance to individuals or neighborhoods protected by federal or state fair housing laws. Owing in part to the fact that much information about homeowners insurance underwriting and pricing is considered privileged by the insurance industry, policies, practices, and pricing that may be discriminatory in intent or effect are not easily detected. Matched-pair testing enhances our ability to determine whether discrimination occurs and to confirm information about discrimination obtained from other sources. Testing is an essential tool because it resembles in all discernible aspects the actual homeowners insurance marketplace and the typical consumer–agent transaction. Testing evidence is compelling because reasons for differential treatment are isolated from the testing process so that race or ethnicity remains the sole factor of difference. Test houses are matched on the characteristics relevant to obtaining homeowners insurance (e.g., structure and size of house; financial status of applicant). The primary difference remaining in the test is that of the racial composition of the neighborhoods in which the test properties are located and/or a difference in race or ethnicity between testers.

Testing cannot confirm or refute all types of discrimination in the insurance marketplace. The following policies and practices, which can be discerned through testing, can be considered to violate the fair housing laws:

- Charging a higher premium based on race rather than risk;
- Refusing to write insurance in minority and/or integrated neighborhoods;
- Refusing to write standard or guaranteed replacement-cost coverage in minority and/or integrated neighborhoods;
- Establishing minimum insurance amounts in minority or integrated neighborhoods;
- Limiting protection or benefits because of age/location of property to protected groups and not to others;
- Using credit reports to restrict or deny insurance;
- Requiring inspections of homes in minority/integrated neighborhoods or selectively inspecting homes built before 1950 based on the racial composition of the neighborhood;
- Refusing to renew policies because of age/location of property for protected persons or neighborhoods; and
- Canceling policies because of age/location of property for protected persons or neighborhoods.

Testing can provide evidence supporting allegations of all of these practices, and may be the best way, outside of a legal or administrative forum, to reliably identify and document such discrimination by homeowners insurance companies. A later section of this chapter provides examples of types of discriminatory practices and policies that have been detected through testing.

SELECTION OF INSURANCE COMPANIES FOR TESTING

Although the NFHA had received allegations of discrimination against more than the three companies tested, the alliance was limited by resources and time in both the number of companies it could select as targets and the number of tests it could conduct. Nationwide, Allstate, and State Farm were thus targeted based on bona fide insurance discrimination complaints filed with private fair housing agencies; allegations from neighborhood organizations of unfair treatment from residents who received notifications of nonrenewal or cancellation; and research conducted by academics. The NFHA further took into account two primary factors in targeting these companies: (1) the egregious nature of the existing complaints; and (2) the preponderance of captive agents in the participant cities (a sufficient number of agents was necessary to allow multiple tests of a company in each city). The use of captive agents was important to ensure consistency, because captive agents generally write policies for only one insurance company. The continuing investigation of these companies by the NFHA and other fair housing agencies is based upon new bona fide complaints, review of their underwriting guidelines, information from documents disclosed in pending litigation, and information from current or former agents.

To select cities for inclusion in the project, the NFHA circulated a request for proposals to its members and to selected members of the National Council of La Raza. Participants were selected based on the following criteria: presence of several captive agents of the potential target companies; presence of racially/ethnically identifiable neighborhoods; and presence of housing stock in those neighborhoods that met criteria for age and value. The NFHA selected two companies for testing in each of the nine cities. The participating organizations in all cities except Toledo tested both Nationwide and Allstate. Toledo tested Allstate and State Farm because it was engaged in its own investigation of Nationwide. Subsequent to the HUD-funded testing project, the NFHA conducted additional tests of State Farm (in cities other than Toledo), Nationwide, and Allstate.

A random selection process was used to identify specific agents/offices for testing. In smaller cities, all captive agents were put into a pool and chosen at random. In larger cities, a smaller geographic subset of agents was put into the pool, with agents selected at random from that subset. Random selection of agents, of course, would permit conclusions that could be generalized to the company. For enforcement purposes, however, random selection is not necessary or required. A single act of discrimination is a violation of the Fair Housing Act, whether or not it is representative of all company agents. A fair housing agency may target an agent or company for testing because of marketing practices, office location, or current or prior practice of restricting coverage, or because a neighborhood group or individual provides information about differential treatment. A fair housing agency may also target a company simply to measure its behavior in the marketplace.

TESTING METHODOLOGY

The following testing methodologies were used in the national testing project, and are consistent with those currently employed by the NFHA.

Insurance Testing Conducted by Telephone

Virtually all initial transactions to secure homeowners insurance were conducted over the telephone. Generally, it is not until an inspection is conducted or a policy signed that a face-to-face meeting occurs (if at all) between the applicant and agent. As a result, after an allegation of discrimination based on telephone contacts is made against the company, the agent and company's first defense is that they did not know the applicant was African American or Latino or that the home was in a minority neighborhood. Therefore, it is important for the test to be constructed so that the agent can easily identify the race or national origin of the tester and/or the test house. The NFHA's testing controlled for these factors, in that, first, the race or ethnicity of the tester was apparent by his or her telephone voice and/or surname, and, second, the test home was located in a racially/ ethnically identifiable neighborhood.

Identifying Race or National Origin of Tester by Voice

Substantial research indicates that people make assumptions about an individual's race or national origin based on voice. Dane Archer, professor of sociology at the University of California at Santa Cruz, has spent 25 years examining the assumptions people make about others from their voices. In his work, *The Human Voice: Exploring Vocal Paralanguage* (1993), Archer demonstrates that we make conscious judgments about people with whom we speak. Archer explains that other people can "read" our voices with remarkable accuracy. He has conducted studies in which a blindfolded person listens to another person count aloud to 20; simply by hearing a person count, the blindfolded person can accurately identify the race, sex, ethnicity, education level, and age (within five years) of the person who is counting. The listener uses the pitch, tone, and intonation of the person counting to make these identifications. Archer's research indicates that there is prejudice against certain accents or dialects and stereotyped assumptions about some kinds of speech.

As stated, for purposes of testing, the testers had "racially or ethnically identifiable voices," which were reinforced by the location of the properties for which they were seeking insurance. For example, the white tester might use a Polish surname and provide a property address in a neighborhood known to be predominantly white. Likewise, the Latino caller might have an accent or use a Spanish surname and provide a property address located in a known Latino neighborhood. It should be pointed out that anyone living in a minority neighborhood, regardless of race, can be a victim of insurance discrimination. Whites living in integrated and minority neighborhoods are also directly and adversely affected by discriminatory practices and policies. The U.S. Supreme Court has long recognized that whites living in segregated housing have standing to sue under the Federal Fair Housing Act.[3] In January 1996, the state court certified and defined the class in *Toledo Fair Housing Center et al. v. Nationwide Insurance Company*[4] as all homeowners residing in census tracts that are 50 percent or more African American.

Matched-Pair Testing

To eliminate differences in treatment that may be attributable to nonracial factors, the NFHA carefully matched test houses. Insurance testing differs from other testing in that it is information about the property, rather than the individual, that determines to the largest degree the substance of a test. Test homes are always matched on the type of construction and are matched as closely as possible on number of stories, age, and approximate square footage. In some cases, testers were provided information about the property that did not conform to its actual features. These were characteristics not easily discerned by agents; if an altered characteristic was discovered by the agent, that fact was taken into consideration during analysis of the test, or the test was discarded.

Houses were matched on the number of rooms, as well as the size and type of basement, and all homes had circuit breakers. The test homes in minority neighborhoods were similar or superior to the test homes in the white neighborhoods in appearance and maintenance but had newer features such as furnace, roof, and plumbing. In the national project, test homes were not located adjacent to abandoned or vacant homes or any other "hazards." Testers were matched on approximate distance to fire hydrants and fire stations and on whether they had deadbolt locks and smoke detectors. None of the testers indicated that an existing policy had been canceled or that any claims had been filed in the last five years. All of the testers had good credit, and none had filed for bankruptcy. All the homes were intended for owner occupancy. No testers were smokers or retired, and all testers were employed. Test homes were located primarily in working- and middle-class neighborhoods. Subsequent testing has incorporated a broader range of variables, but test teams have remained matched (for example, both testers might indicate to the agent that a recent claim had been filed or that they had a similar credit flaw).

Insurance companies typically offer two defenses against allegations of discrimination based on testing: first, that the test properties were not matched; and, second, that the quotation process is scientific and that differential treatment is therefore not possible. Our testing revealed that neither of these defenses is adequate. To the first defense, we respond that we have literally hundreds of tests of insurance companies in which test properties *were* matched on features key to the insurance decision and in which discrimination still existed. In response to the assertion that the quotation process does not allow for differential treatment, we provide the following information. During this project, we utilized the same test property with a number of different agents of the same company. Even for white testers, two phenomena occurred that belie the "scientific" nature of the process: (1) agents did not routinely obtain the same information from testers with which to provide an insurance quote; and (2) different agents provided different policy and pricing information for the *same* test property. This means that the insurance process allows for discretion on the part of the agent; the greater the level of discretion, the greater the potential for discrimination.

Neighborhood-Based Testing

Neighborhood-based insurance testing measures the availability of insurance products and/or the cost, benefits, perils covered, and conditions of insurance for homes located in racially identifiable neighborhoods. When developing neighborhood-based testing for insurance, the NFHA looked to the courts' definition of neighborhood-based discrimination in the mortgage lending arena. The federal district court in Toledo, Ohio, identified the elements of a prima facie case of discrimination in financing based upon the characteristics or location of the neighborhood in which the property is located (i.e., redlining). In *Old West End Association et al. v. Buckeye Federal Savings & Loan* (1987),[5] the court held that the following elements constitute a prima facie case of neighborhood discrimination:

1. The housing sought to be secured is in a minority neighborhood;
2. An application for a loan to purchase the housing located in the minority neighborhood was made;
3. An independent appraisal concluded that the value of the housing equaled the sale price;[6]
4. The buyers were creditworthy; and
5. The loan was rejected.[7]

In consideration of these elements, the NFHA selected homes in clearly identifiable African American, Latino, and white neighborhoods; visited and photographed the homes to document their insurability; and instructed testers to inquire about the availability and cost of homeowners insurance.

The NFHA controlled for racial composition by selecting neighborhoods that contain an 80 percent or more white population and matching these with neighborhoods with a 50 percent or more African American or Latino population. Generally, neighborhoods selected for inclusion in the testing project had a homeownership rate of about 50 percent. In larger cities, the homeownership rate might have been lower. No neighborhoods selected for inclusion in the project were "blighted," and none of the neighborhoods were high income.

Applicant-Based Testing

Applicant-based insurance testing measures the availability of insurance products and/or the cost, benefits, perils covered, and conditions of insurance based upon the race or national origin of the homeowner.

Generally, the test homes were both located in predominantly white census tracts and often within the same tract or neighborhood. The voice and/or surname of the testers was critical when conducting the applicant-based tests. It was important for agents to be able to readily identify the tester's race or national origin over the telephone. Test coordinators sometimes had their testers prescreened by third parties to confirm that the tester was likely to be identified by voice as belonging to a particular racial or ethnic group.

Staff and Tester Training

Training for staff of fair housing agencies includes: a review of the operations and underwriting guidelines of insurance companies; instruction on how to recruit and select test homes and testers; procedures for matching the test homes and assigning characteristics to testers; a review and explanation of the NFHA's test assignment and report forms; and instruction on how to utilize the database and spreadsheet programs in analyzing the test results.

Testers for the national project attended a four- to six-hour training session during which they learned about the various types of policies available from insurance companies and about how an ordinary person seeks homeowners insurance. They were trained to be objective fact finders and to report information they provided to and received from the agent during the test. Testers reviewed pictures of their test home and were provided the necessary information to answer questions from the insurance agent. The NFHA's assignment and test report forms were reviewed with the testers in detail. The test coordinator or NFHA instructor conducted role plays with the testers to prepare them for a practice run with an insurance agent or staff person. Following the practice run, testers completed the report form, wrote a narrative describing the event, and were debriefed by the test coordinator. This information and the tester's performance were evaluated by the test coordinator or instructor, and further instruction was provided when necessary. Throughout the training process and testing, testers were instructed and reminded about the confidentiality of their work.

Owners or residents of the test home generally were advised about the testing process and provided with all the necessary information should the insurance agent attempt to conduct a property inspection or visit the property for other purposes. Owners or residents of the test homes were instructed to contact the test coordinator if they received mail from the insurance company or were contacted by the agent by telephone or in person.

Preapplication Tests

The test coordinator is responsible for matching the test homes and providing testers with information about the home, other characteristics to assume for the test, and the company and agent(s) to be tested, as well as instructions about when to conduct the test(s). The instructions and characteristics are comprehensive and prepare testers to comply with standard requests for information by an insurance agent. This means that the tester should not be able to be detected as different from an ordinary insurance consumer.

Testers telephoned the same insurance office and requested homeowners insurance information on properties matched on major characteristics. In the majority of tests, testers spoke with the same agent. It is important to mention here that the federal district and appellate courts have not required that testers speak with the same agent to prove discrimination. The courts have consistently and repeatedly ruled that a company is liable for the acts of its agents. Differences in agents should not result in substantive differences in policies, pricing, and conditions for obtaining homeowners insurance coverage. Testers placed their calls to the agents during a specified time period. If the agent was not available, the tester would leave a name and telephone number, along with a message indicating a need for information about homeowners insurance. If a tester left messages for an agent three times over a specified period without receiving a return telephone call, the test was ended (to do otherwise would exceed the lengths to which an ordinary consumer would go to contact an agent). If the tester and agent were engaged in "telephone tag," the tester continued to try to reach the agent until instructed otherwise by the test coordinator. All telephone calls made by testers and return calls and messages left by agents were documented.

Although at times test teams were instructed to ask for specific insurance coverage, most often the teams were instructed to allow the agent to *offer* insurance coverage or to ask what the agent recommended. Testers were instructed to ask for information about insurance policies and price quotes, and for the quote(s) to be mailed or faxed to them. Testers typically responded to questions from agents and noted the information requested by agents, as well as policy and pricing information offered.

At the completion of each test, the tester filled out a detailed report form and wrote a narrative statement describing the facts of the test. The test coordinator reviewed the tester report forms and narratives for completeness and evaluated the information. All written quotes received by the tester or test home were forwarded to the test coordinator. The test coordinator (or other designated staff) then compared the information provided to each member of the test team. Because hundreds of tests were conducted in the national project, the NFHA contracted with Community Reinvestment Associates of Des Plaines, Illinois, to develop a database and spreadsheet format to assist in analyzing the tests. Data from the tests were entered into the database. (The software converts the data into a side-by-side spreadsheet format. In addition to presenting information about the two parts of a test in an easily read format, the system calculates key figures for use in comparison [e.g., cost per $1,000 of coverage or cost per square foot]).

NATIONAL TESTING PROJECT RESULTS

In the national testing project, discrimination against African American and Latino applicants and homeowners in African American and/or Latino neighborhoods occurred 53 percent of the time. The rates of discrimination were close to 50 percent for both Allstate and Nationwide. Of the tests of State Farm, the discrimination rate was 85 percent. In the cities in which testing was conducted, the discrimination rate ranged from a low of 32 percent in Memphis to a high of 83 percent in Chicago, a city in which the testing was constructed to examine discrimination against Latino neighborhoods. In the other cities African American testers/neighborhoods were matched with white testers/neighborhoods. The discrimination took many forms, but was typified by practices or policies that restricted or denied homeowners insurance coverage to minority testers/neighborhoods. When conducting the analysis of these tests, we were easily able to detect differential treatment because of the rigors of the methodology employed in the testing project.

The following levels of discrimination were found in the nine cities:

Chicago	83 percent
Atlanta	67 percent
Toledo	62 percent
Milwaukee	58 percent

Louisville   ~~56 percent~~
Cincinnati   44 percent
Los Angeles   44 percent
Akron   37 percent
Memphis   32 percent

Types of Differential Treatment

After a comprehensive analysis of the tests, we were able to classify most of the differential treatment into six basic categories. The following paragraphs describe each category as well as provide anecdotal information about discriminatory behavior or policies detected.

CATEGORY ONE—COST

We compared cost per $1,000 of coverage for market-value policies and cost per square foot for replacement-cost policies. Discrimination took the form of higher costs in both types of calculations for African American and Latino homeowners. Differences in cost occurred not only between white and predominantly minority neighborhoods but also between minority and white homeowners in the same or similar white neighborhoods. The level of difference in cost for minority homeowners was in some cases more than twice the cost for white homeowners. In Milwaukee, for example, an African American tester received a quote that was two times higher than the amount quoted to the white tester. The test homes were matched, but the home in the African American neighborhood was newer and nicer than the home in the white neighborhood.

CATEGORY TWO—TYPE OF POLICY

We considered differences in the type of coverage available on both the dwelling and personal property. Discrimination occurred when minority testers were offered only a market-value policy (insurance up to the sale value of the home), whereas the white tester was offered a replacement-cost policy; or when the minority tester was offered a standard replacement-cost policy (typically insures the homeowner for the amount estimated to actually replace the home, up to the limits of the policy), whereas the white tester was offered a guaranteed replacement-cost policy (insures the homeowner for the entire replacement cost of the home, even if the replacement cost ultimately exceeds the stated value of the policy). White testers were routinely offered a range of choices that included standard replacement-cost and guaranteed replacement-cost policies. These policies not only provide superior coverage in terms of replacing the dwelling but coverage for a wider range of perils as well. We also noted differences in whether replacement-cost coverage was offered on personal property. Since replacement-cost policies routinely contain replacement cost on contents as a feature of the policies, white testers also had a higher level of access to replacement cost for personal property. For market-value policies, the availability of replacement cost is dependent upon the agent offering that feature as an endorsement (at an additional charge) to the terms of the policy.

CATEGORY THREE—AGENT RESPONSIVENESS

Agent responsiveness relates directly to the level of access to the agent and to policy information during the tests. Differences in treatment were noted in three primary areas: agents failed to return more than three messages left by the minority tester, but responded to messages from the paired white tester; after a preliminary discussion with a tester, an agent indicated a follow-up call would be made to provide quote information, but then no follow-up call occurred; or agents referred one tester to another agent while providing service to the paired tester. For example, in the Cincinnati metropolitan area, the following tests of a Nationwide agent occurred:

In the first test, the African American tester was asked a limited number of questions about the value and location of the house. The value of the house was $135,000, and it was located in a predominantly African American census tract. The Nationwide agent referred the tester to another Nationwide office because that office would "have more knowledge about the area and replacement cost." When the white tester called, the agent provided a quote for homeowners insurance and calculated the replacement value of the house. That house was worth $124,000 and was located in a white neighborhood. The white tester's house is about the same distance from the agent as the house of the African American tester *and* is located much closer to another Nationwide office.

In the second test, the African American tester was not referred to another office. The agent took information from the tester and said he would call back with a quote. The agent never called back. When the white tester called, the agent said he would call back with a quote, and 45 minutes later, he did call back. Both houses are located 8–10 miles from the agent, are about the same age and size, are brick, and are valued only $5,000 apart.

A series of tests of an Allstate agent in Atlanta revealed similar access issues. Over the course of the investigation, three African

American persons called the agent's office to inquire about homeowners insurance for homes located in predominantly African American neighborhoods. Each tester tried three times to reach the agent; each time the tester left his or her name, telephone number, and a message that he or she was interested in homeowners insurance. The agent never returned any of the nine messages left on his answering machine by these African American testers.

During this same time period, three white persons called the agent's office. The agent took each of their calls, provided quotations for homeowners insurance to each one over the telephone, and mailed written quotes to two of these white testers.

CATEGORY FOUR—LEVEL OF SERVICE

The level-of-service category covered a wide range of behaviors but most often included the following: agents provided more comprehensive and useful explanations of policies to white testers than to minority testers; agents offered a range of options to white testers while limiting minority testers to one policy only; agents provided information more often to white testers on how to obtain discounts (e.g., dual policy or protective device discounts); agents provided more and higher-quality information in writing to white testers than to minority testers; and agents more often contacted white testers at a later date to inquire whether they had received the quote, needed answers to questions or additional information, or wanted to set up an appointment for an inspection and to complete the application. In a State Farm test in Toledo, the white tester received a quote with a 5 percent discount for the presence of protective devices (deadbolt locks, fire extinguisher, smoke alarms) even though the agent had not ascertained that the home contained those devices. The agent did find out that the African American tester's home contained protective devices but provided *no* discount of the premium quoted.

CATEGORY FIVE—DIFFERENTIAL APPLICATION OF COMPANY POLICIES AND STANDARDS

Both African American and white testers were informed of company policies that are in many cities discriminatory in effect. These policies include minimum insurance amounts as well as maximum age limits. The discriminatory effect of these and other policies is discussed in detail in subsequent chapters of this book. The testing, however, revealed that stated company policies were not applied equally to all homeowners. For instance, minority testers were told more often of a company "policy" that prevented the agent from providing a quote without an inspection of the property, yet paired white testers received a quote without a property inspection by the agent. In other tests, minority testers were told of a company policy that prevented them from obtaining insurance from that company, whereas white testers were not told of the policy. One agent said, "I don't like to insure anything over 30 years old. . . . It is too hard after all the remodeling and things like that to mess with. I am trying to eliminate them from my portfolio." Another minority tester was told by the agent, "We don't insure for less than $55,000. Well, we can't insure it. Can't do it." The policy of refusing to insure properties because of the market value of the homes was applied only to homes located in African American neighborhoods. In fact, this company offered a replacement-cost policy for a similarly priced property located in a white neighborhood.

Paired testers were also often told about a company policy such as a maximum age limit. White testers, however, were more often told about ways to circumvent the policy and therefore obtain coverage. For example, minority testers were told that a company could not write replacement-cost coverage on homes over 50 years of age, whereas white testers were routinely told that replacement-cost coverage would be available if the working features of the house, such as wiring, had been more recently updated.

Category Six—Discouragement

We considered specific questions and comments on the part of agents to be discouraging to minority applicants. For some minority testers, the first question an agent asked in response to their request for information on homeowners insurance was whether their current insurance policy had been canceled. African American and Latino applicants were more often asked if they had filed claims, if they had good credit, or if they were employed. A Latina tester was asked by an agent in suburban Chicago for the name and telephone number of her mortgage company. The agent said: "Who's your mortgage company? Do you have a number for them?. . .The reason, ma'am, is because it's like the difference between an Escort and a Cadillac. [The mortgage company] can tell us what the house is like." This agent required the Latina homeowner to provide the name and telephone number of her mortgage lender to gather information about the property *before* providing a quote. This information was never asked of the white caller who received a quote.

Differential Treatment as Discrimination

Matched-pair testing allows us to distinguish between random differential treatment and differential treatment based on race or ethnicity. Differential treatment was categorized as discriminatory when a substantive difference was detected relating to:

- *Cost,* when the cost per $1,000 of coverage or per square foot differed by at least 5 percent;
- *Type of policy,* when the minority tester was not offered access to a replacement-cost or guaranteed replacement-cost policy, whereas the white paired tester was offered one or more of the replacement-cost policies;
- *Agent responsiveness,* when a tester's calls were not returned, when an agent referred the tester to another agent or company, or when an agent failed to call back to provide quote information;
- *Level of service,* when an agent failed to send a quote in writing to the minority tester as agreed during the telephone conversation while sending a quote to the white tester;
- *Differential application of company policy,* when the minority tester was informed of a company policy or requirement (e.g., conducting an inspection before providing a quote), but this policy or requirement was not applied to the white tester; or when both testers were told of a company policy but the white tester was told the policy would not be applied or was given information on how to circumvent the policy.

In some tests, discrimination took the form of a combination of more subtle behaviors not as substantively different as those just outlined. These behaviors by agents included more timely return of phone calls from white testers than minority testers; delays in conducting an inspection or providing a quote; not providing comprehensive brochures and business cards with a written quote; requests for information about creditworthiness, claims filed, and employment; and other behaviors that discourage potential applicants. There were many tests in which discrimination took place in several *substantive* forms, including, for example, a test in which a minority tester was offered an inferior policy at a higher price and for which a discount and written quote were not provided, whereas the white tester received a superior policy for a lower premium that was discounted for protective devices and was provided in writing.

As indicated earlier, as a result of these tests, complaints were filed with HUD against Nationwide, Allstate, and State Farm. As of this writing, HUD is investigating complaints against Nationwide and Allstate. In July 1996, a major settlement was reached by NFHA, the Toledo Fair Housing Center, and HUD with State Farm, comprising significant changes in insurance underwriting standards, including:

- Elimination of minimum-coverage eligibility amounts (i.e, value of property);
- Elimination of eligibility requirements linked to construction date cutoffs (i.e., age of property); and
- Implementation of a policy to utilize appropriate physical characteristics of the house to determine eligibility, such as wiring, heating, roof, and plumbing.

In addition, State Farm will educate consumers about insurance policy options and will encourage customers to insure to full replacement cost. State Farm will also make available in Toledo at least $1 million of first mortgage financing at reduced interest rates for homeowners in African American and Latino neighborhoods and will open sales or service facilities in urban neighborhoods in several cities across the country.[8]

The testing done by the NFHA is being replicated by fair housing organizations in cities across the country, and has been expanded to include companies that conduct business through independent as well as captive agents. Preliminary findings from this testing are consistent with the results of the NFHA project; similar acts and patterns of differential treatment have been detected.

OTHER APPROACHES AND USES OF TESTING

Full-Application Testing

Although the 1992 national project did not engage in full-application testing, the NFHA's ongoing insurance testing projects include full-application testing of both captive and independent insurance agents. Such testing is a necessary civil rights enforcement tool, since not all discrimination on the part of insurance companies can be detected through a review of underwriting guidelines or through preapplication testing. Full-application testing requires the tester to attempt to purchase a policy. The tester house retains its current insurance and, if or when coverage is extended for the test home, the test coverage is canceled by the tester *after* a policy is received. The additional cost associated with this type of test is generally the prorated share of the premium from the time the targeted company offered the insurance binder until the time the policy is terminated by the tester. Some companies may retain the full premium upon cancellation. Full-application testing can determine if the company's policy of providing a refund for canceled policies is applied equally, as well as a wealth of other information about the application of underwriting guidelines. The testing also documents whether the insurance extended to the test homes is comparable. It furthermore demonstrates if the policy discussed over the telephone is the one ultimately issued by the company. Subsequently, we can learn if a difference in the policies promised and issued was caused by the agent or the underwriter.

Full-application testing is an extremely useful vehicle for testing independent agents and agents who are primarily captive agents, but who have authority to write insurance for other companies. By reviewing the actual policies received for test homes, we can determine with which company the insurance agent places the policy, the extent of the coverage, whether an inspection was required or completed or a credit report run, and the amount of the actual annual premium versus the telephone quote. This type of testing also provides information about whether the independent insurance agent is steering homeowners in minority neighborhoods to companies that do not provide the best coverage. Further investigation can determine if some companies with which the agent does business simply refuse to insure properties in minority neighborhoods, causing the agent to refer customers to other companies.

Nonpaired Testing

Although this chapter has focused on matched-pair testing, we want to emphasize that other methods of testing can be used to develop information about homeowners insurance companies' compliance with fair housing laws. We consider use of a nonpaired test acceptable for evidentiary purposes in the following situations:

- To provide information with which to make a comparison with a bona fide complainant;
- To uncover conditions for obtaining insurance (i.e., credit check, inspection);

- To confirm information from another source about a policy or practice of an insurance company;
- To ascertain or confirm descriptions of "service areas";
- To determine if underwriting guidelines as described in written materials are applied to homes in minority or integrated neighborhoods;
- To ascertain the range of policy options in minority and integrated neighborhoods;
- To measure the level of access to agents and service by agents for homes in minority and integrated neighborhoods; and/or
- To determine other differences in treatment unrelated to specific features of the property to be insured.

Testing for Sex and Disability Issues

Whereas the testing described in this chapter is designed to document availability based upon race or national origin, testing for discrimination based on sex or disability has also been conducted. These methodologies were developed in response to the increasing number of complaints from single female–headed households and persons with disabilities. In 1996, State Farm Insurance Companies signed a conciliation agreement with HUD after it was alleged that the company refused to provide coverage for a home occupied by persons with disabilities.

CONCLUSION

Discrimination in the provision of homeowners insurance is an insidious problem not easily identified by homeowners. Most information about how insurance companies do business remains outside the public domain. Matched-pair testing is a reliable method of determining, for at least part of the insurance process, whether discrimination based on the race or ethnicity of applicants or neighborhoods or other protected characteristics occurs. Since testing is recognized as a viable and important civil rights enforcement tool by HUD, the U.S. Department of Justice, and the courts, it appears that testing of homeowners insurance companies will become an important component of public and private fair housing enforcement programs.

1. See *McDiarmid v. Economy Fire & Casualty Co.*, 604 F. Supp. 105 (S.D. Ohio 1984).

2. This organization is an affiliate of the National Council of La Raza. Unlike the other project participants, it is not a fair housing enforcement agency.

3. *Trafficante v. Metropolitan Life Insurance Company*, 409 U.S. 205 (1972).

4. *Toledo Fair Housing Center v. Nationwide Mutual Insurance Co.*, No. 93-1685 (Ohio Ct. C.P. Dec. 28, 1993).

5. *Old West End Association et al. v. Buckeye Federal Savings & Loan*, 675 F. Supp. 1100, 1103 (N.D. Ohio 1987).

6. This standard was modified in the memorandum and order in a motion for summary judgment in the *Steptoe v. Savings of America* 800 F. Supp. 1542 (N.D. Ohio 1992) case (the order was filed on August 25, 1992). In brief, the court said it would waive the appraisal standard in *Buckeye* (see note 5) when the appraisal is the reason for the loan denial. This decision eliminates the opportunity for a lender to intentionally undervalue the home with the appraisal to avoid a lawsuit.

7. If the *lender* changes the applicant's original request for the terms or conditions of a loan, this can be interpreted as rejecting the loan. If the changes in the terms or conditions discriminate against the loan applicant or the neighborhood where the housing is located, a fair housing complaint can be filed.

8. HUD Conciliation Agreements 05-94-1351-8 and 05-94-1352-8.

Reference

Archer, Dane. 1993. *The Human Voice: Exploring Vocal Paralanguage.* Documentary videotape. Berkeley: University of California Extension Center for Media.

Chapter Six

THE DISCRIMINATORY EFFECTS OF HOMEOWNERS INSURANCE UNDERWRITING GUIDELINES

D. J. Powers

Underwriting guidelines commonly used by homeowners insurance companies have a disparate impact on the classes of consumers protected by the Federal Fair Housing Act of 1968 ("the protected classes"). Few insurers today have outright policies that intentionally discriminate against the protected classes. However, through the use of allegedly neutral underwriting guidelines, insurers have accomplished the same result. As former Texas Insurance Commissioner J. Robert Hunter testified in 1994 before the U.S. Senate Committee on Banking, Housing, and Urban Affairs:

> Today, we still find insurance companies making underwriting decisions based on all kinds of factors that have nothing to do with a statistically measured or measurable probability of risk. One of these factors, unfortunately, is your location on a city map that probably does not have any red boundary lines drawn on it but it might as well because the results are the same.

For the members of the protected classes who are denied homeowners insurance, the denial is the same and the discrimination just as insidious whether based on a red line around the neighborhood or an underwriting guideline that no homes in the neighborhood can satisfy.

This chapter's analysis of the disparate impact of underwriting guidelines on the protected classes is divided into four sections. The first section explains what underwriting guidelines are. The second section analyzes how underwriting guidelines are used to discriminate against consumers. The third section shows that the actual underwriting guidelines used by homeowners insurers have a disparate impact on the protected classes. Finally, the last section analyzes whether these underwriting guidelines can satisfy the business necessity/absence of a less-discriminatory alternative defense under the Fair Housing Act.

WHAT ARE UNDERWRITING GUIDELINES?

The term *redlining* originally referred to the practice by some insurers of drawing a red line around certain areas on a map to identify neighborhoods where the insurer would not sell an insurance policy. The terms *redlining* and *unfair discrimination*, however, are now used to describe any discrimination in the availability, price, benefits, or quality of insurance based on a factor that is either (1) not related to the expected costs associated with the transfer of risk or (2) inherently unfair. Inherently unfair underwriting guidelines—those that directly and intentionally discriminate against the protected classes—are rare, although some still exist. The key barriers to insurance availability are underwriting guidelines that are not related to risk and have a disparate impact on the protected classes.

Underwriting is the process by which an insurer determines whether it will accept or reject an applicant and, if acceptable, at what price. *Underwriting guidelines* are the standards on which the insurer makes the underwriting decision. The term has been defined as:

> any rule, standard, marketing decision, or practice, whether written, oral or electronic, used by an insurer or its agent to examine, bind (provide immediate coverage, as opposed to providing coverage only when the insurer accepts the application), accept, reject, renew, non-renew, cancel, charge a different rate for the same coverage, or limit the coverages made available to a consumer or a class of consumers. (Johnson and Powers 1995)

Understanding the application of these underwriting guidelines is critical in the fight against redlining, because these guidelines determine who will be able to purchase insurance and at what price.

Underwriting guidelines are provided to insurance agents in order for the agent to initially decide whether to offer coverage and at what price. If the agent determines that the applicant meets the underwriting guideline requirements, the application is then forwarded to the insurance company's underwriter for review. If the underwriter determines that the applicant does not meet the qualifications, the underwriter either denies the application or, if the agent issued a policy, sends a notice of cancellation. Underwriting guidelines are also used to determine whether the company will renew an existing policy.

Underwriting guidelines range from very detailed and objective written rules (e.g., limitations on insuring homes under a specified value) to broad and subjective forms of guidance for the agent or underwriter (e.g., limitations on insuring consumers with "bad morals"). A more detailed study of specific underwriting guidelines is contained later in this chapter.

Research on Actual Underwriting Guidelines Used by Insurers

Outside of the insurance industry, there has been little research on actual underwriting guidelines used by insurers owing to the fact that insurers claim these guidelines are confidential trade secrets. The Texas Office of Public Insurance Counsel (OPIC), an independent state agency that advocates on behalf of insurance consumers in Texas, studied the availability of underwriting guidelines in each state and found that only nine states require the filing of underwriting guidelines with the state's insurance department. More important, OPIC found that consumers have access to the guidelines in only seven states (Bordelon 1995).

OPIC was given confidential access to the underwriting guidelines used by Texas homeowners insurers and was permitted to issue a report in 1994 without identifying the underwriting guidelines of any individual company (Office of Public Insurance Counsel 1994). That study offers the first comprehensive analysis of underwriting guidelines that are used to deny insurance or charge higher rates.

Although OPIC's study was limited to underwriting guidelines used by insurers in Texas, the study is useful nationally. The largest homeowners insurance writers in Texas—State Farm Group of Insurance Companies, Farmers Group of Insurance Companies, Allstate Group of Insurance Companies, Farm Bureau Mutual Group of Insurance Companies, USAA, and Nationwide Mutual Group of Insurance Companies—are also the largest writers nationwide. It is unlikely that these companies' underwriting guidelines vary significantly from state to state.

Underwriting guidelines represent the greatest barrier to insurance availability precisely because they are the rules that determine which consumers can obtain insurance and at what price. As this chapter demonstrates, the large majority of these underwriting guidelines have a disproportionately adverse impact on the protected classes. However, the effect of the discriminatory impact cannot be understood without a thorough knowledge of how insurers and agents use underwriting guidelines to discriminate against consumers. The next section provides that analysis.

REDLINING: LET ME COUNT THE WAYS

Insurers use underwriting guidelines to discriminate in four ways against classes of consumers that do not satisfy the insurer's underwriting guidelines: discrimination in the availability of insurance, in the price of insurance, in the benefits of insurance, and in the quality of service.

Discrimination in Availability of Insurance

Of course, insurers discriminate through the outright refusal to sell an insurance policy, creating an obvious availability problem for that consumer. Insurers frequently refuse to sell any policy, at any price, to consumers who do not satisfy the insurer's underwriting guidelines.

Redlining victims, however, are often unaware they have been denied coverage by standard and preferred companies. Insurance applicants go to an agent who represents several insurers and who will usually sell them some type of policy, even if through a Fair Access to Insurance Requirements (FAIR) Plan or a surplus lines carrier. Residual market mechanisms, also known as FAIR Plans, were created to provide homeowners insurance to consumers who could not obtain it in the voluntary market, although often at higher rates and reduced benefits. Surplus lines carriers, also known as "off-shore" and "non-admitted" insurers, are not regulated by the state. These insurers present several disadvantages to the consumer, including rates that are usually much higher than admitted companies, policy forms that are not regulated, no state guaranty coverage if the company goes broke, and lack of solvency regulation, which increases the chances that the company will be unable to pay its claims. The consumer, however, knows none of this. Instead, the consumer simply knows that the agent has offered a policy and quoted a price for homeowners insurance. Thus, the consumer assumes that no insurer has turned him or her down for insurance. In many cases, the underwriting guidelines for other insurers represented by the agent required the agent to deny coverage to that consumer.

Discrimination in Price of Insurance

Although the term redlining originally referred only to refusal to sell a policy, unfair discrimination also includes the refusal to sell appropriately priced insurance—that is, insurance at a rate charged to other consumers of similar risk. For example, an insurer who sells insurance in a minority neighborhood, but charges a higher rate than in other neighborhoods with consumers of similar risk, is just as guilty of redlining.

Underwriting guidelines determine not only whether insurance will be sold to a group of consumers but also the rate to be charged to that group of consumers. For many consumers, the price charged is a de facto decision on whether they will be able to purchase insurance at all, based on their income. For the rest, redlining means that the failure to meet the insurer's underwriting guidelines resulted in higher premiums.

Discrimination in Benefits of Insurance

Redlining also exists when the insurer offers a policy, but with limited benefits. An insurer can discriminate in the benefits of insurance by using substandard policy forms (anything less than full, replacement-value coverage), eliminating specific coverages, or requiring higher deductible payments.

The most prominent form of discrimination in the benefits of homeowners insurance is the decision to offer only an actual-cash-value policy, not a replacement-value policy. The replacement-value policy pays the replacement cost of the home, whereas the actual-cash-value policy only pays the actual market value of a home. If a $100,000 home is totally destroyed, for instance, but costs $125,000 to rebuild, the replacement-value policy would pay $125,000 but the actual-cash-value policy would only pay $100,000, requiring the consumer to raise $25,000 to rebuild his or her house. For less than a total loss, the replacement-value policy pays the cost to replace the stolen or damaged property, without any deduction for depreciation of the stolen or damaged property. The actual-cash-value policy, however, only pays for the depreciated value of stolen or damaged property.

Although the replacement-value policy is clearly more beneficial for the consumer, an insurer may offer to sell only an actual-cash-value policy if the consumer does not meet the insurer's underwriting guidelines. The need for a replacement-value policy is particularly important when the replacement cost of the home is higher than the market value, which is often the case in inner-city neighborhoods.

A second form of discrimination in insurance benefits is the exclusion of coverage for specified perils. For instance, an insurer may exclude earthquake or windstorm coverage or may refuse to insure the home's contents. The consumer, therefore, is provided fewer benefits.

A third form of discrimination in the benefits of insurance is by requiring higher deductibles. As with most insurance policies, the homeowners insurance policy includes a deductible clause. The insurer is only required to pay a claim for damages in excess of the deductible. Since most claims are for small amounts (in Texas the *average* claim is only about $2,500 [Schwartz 1994]), the deductible determines the amount of benefits to be provided under the policy.

The deductible not only affects the *amount* of the benefit, but it can often eliminate *types* of coverage. The case of roof repair is an excellent example. For most homes, a roof can be replaced for under $5,000. If the insurer requires the consumer to have a $5,000 deductible, however, the insurer has effectively eliminated coverage for roof damage. This same principle applies to lower deductibles. Starting with the lowest deductible, each new level of deductible not only reduces the amount of the benefit to be received for a loss, but it eliminates coverage for some types of loss.

Requiring higher deductibles has a direct effect on the ability of a consumer to purchase a home. The Federal National Mortgage Association (Fannie Mae), for instance, requires property insurance on first mortgages with a maximum allowable deductible of the higher of $1,000 or 1 percent of the face amount of the policy. In addition, higher deductibles have a significant impact on first-time homebuyers and marginal borrowers. In comments provided to the Texas Department of Insurance regarding the ability to sell policies with deductibles for up to 5 percent of the face amount of the policy, the Independent Bankers Association of Texas (1995) stated: "The increase in the deductible is likely to have a significant impact on the most vulnerable segment of that market, namely the first time home buyer and the marginal borrower." The Independent Bankers Association (1995) went on to point out that higher deductibles will thwart efforts by some lenders to develop special lending programs. Without the ability to purchase a policy with a lower deductible, many consumers may be unable to obtain a loan with a small enough downpayment to purchase a home.

Discrimination in Quality of Service

Finally, redlining also exists when an insurer provides inferior quality of service. For instance, an insurer may not pay claims in a certain area as quickly as in other areas, may not place any agents in an area, or may not provide a toll-free telephone number to some groups of consumers. These actions unfairly discriminate against consumers who pay the same (or higher) premiums to the insurer as other consumers who receive better service.

In conclusion, there are numerous ways in which insurers use underwriting guidelines to discriminate against groups of consumers. Any efforts to eliminate redlining must address all of these forms of discriminatory treatment, not just the refusal to sell insurance. Selling the policy is only one part of treating consumers fairly; equal treatment in the price, benefits, and quality of service is equally important.

DISPARATE IMPACT OF UNDERWRITING GUIDELINES USED BY HOMEOWNERS INSURERS

This section analyzes the underwriting guidelines used by Texas insurers, as reported by OPIC (1994) and Kincaid (1995). As mentioned earlier, the results of the OPIC report are applicable to homeowners insurance nationally because the most prominent Texas companies are national writers.

For each underwriting guideline discussed here, the OPIC report (1994) provided a market-share percentage. This percentage represents the market share of the companies using the underwriting guideline, not the percentage of companies that use the underwriting guideline. For instance, assume the market consists of 100 companies and that one company, All Farm, has 20 percent of the market. If it is the only company using a particular guideline, then insurers writing 20 percent of the market are using that guideline. Although only 1 percent of the companies use the underwriting guideline, the percentage identified by OPIC is the 20 percent market share because this measure more accurately depicts the guideline's effect on the market.

OPIC, in addition to the information in its 1994 report, provided further examples of specific underwriting guidelines in its written comments regarding rule proposals by the Texas Department of Insurance relating to use of certain underwriting guidelines (in Kincaid 1995). The examples of actual underwriting guidelines provided here were included in those comments.

Value of Home

Almost every insurer (i.e., those writing 91 percent of the market) has a minimum coverage amount guideline (OPIC 1994). Many of the companies refuse to sell a policy if the house is worth $50,000 or less (Kincaid 1994). Insurers often mislead regulators and the public by denying any underwriting limitation based on the value of the home. These insurers fail to point out that they *price* their policies based on the value of the home. For instance, an insurer group of companies may be willing to write homes of any value, but it places homes valued over $50,000 in its preferred rate company and homes valued below $50,000 in its substandard rate company. The difference in rates based on value of the home is substantial.

Minimum home-value requirements have a particularly adverse impact on African Americans. Although the national median house value for all homes is $86,529 and only 24 percent of the homes are worth less than $50,000, the median value for homes owned by blacks is $58,372, and 42 percent of the homes are valued under $50,000 (U.S. Bureau of the Census 1993). Thus, the most pervasive underwriting guideline, that based on the value of the home, affects African Americans almost twice as much as the total population of homeowners.

Age of Home

Companies writing 88 percent of the Texas homeowners insurance market have underwriting guidelines based on the age of the home (OPIC 1994). Some of these companies relax their requirements for specified heating, electrical, or plumbing improvements, although complete remodeling is often required. Many insurers, however, have outright bans on insuring homes that are more than 20, 30, 40, or 50 years old.

This underwriting guideline represents one of the greatest barriers to homeowners insurance for members of protected classes who are disproportionately located in older, inner-city neighborhoods and unable to afford the required improvements. As with value-of-the-home requirements, age-of-the-home requirements have a significantly adverse impact on African Americans. Although the median year built for all homes is 1966, the median year built for homes owned by blacks is 1959 (U.S. Bureau of the Census 1993). Table 6.1 shows the percentage of overall homes excluded by an age-of-the-home underwriting guideline and the percentage of black homes excluded by the same underwriting guideline. As table 6.1 reveals, this underwriting guideline has a significantly adverse impact on African American homeowners.

Table 6.1 EFFECT OF AGE-OF-HOME UNDERWRITING GUIDELINES

Underwriting Guideline Limit	All Homes Excluded (%)	Black Homes Excluded (%)
No homes over 20 years old	66	78
No homes over 35 years old	41	51
No homes over 45 years old	26	36

Source: U.S. Bureau of the Census (1993).

Not only are the protected classes disproportionately affected by the age-of-the-home requirement, but they are also disproportionately affected by the improvement requirements. The average income level for the white, non-Hispanic, population is significantly higher than the income level of the remainder of the population. Table 6.2 outlines percentages of households by race/ethnicity and income. It is clear from the table's data that, as a class, nonwhite homeowners have lower incomes than white homeowners. Thus, underwriting guidelines that are dependent on income, like home improvement requirements, have a disproportionate impact on the protected classes.

Location of Home

Companies with 60 percent of the Texas market have "location restrictions"—vague restrictions without objective standards that are used to deny coverage to whole neighborhoods (OPIC 1994). These guidelines are broken down in the OPIC (1994) report as follows:

- Companies writing 39 percent of the market have restrictions against substandard adjacent property.
- Companies writing 16 percent of the market have restrictions against being near commercial property.

Table 6.2 INCOME LEVEL BASED ON RACE

Annual Income	White (%)	Black (%)	Hispanic (%)
$0–$14,999	22	40	31
$15,000–$24,999	17	19	21
$25,000–$34,999	16	14	16
$35,000–$49,999	19	13	16
$50,000–$74,999	16	9	11
$75,000–$99,999	5	3	3
$100,000 +	5	1	2

Source: U.S. Bureau of the Census (1993).

- Companies writing 13 percent of the market have restrictions against high-crime neighborhoods or other economic conditions (although the report noted that none of the underwriting guidelines recommend that the agent or underwriter rely on objective standards like documentation of crime rates).
- Companies writing 3 percent of the market have restrictions against rural properties.

Examples of actual guidelines on location of the home include:

- "Persons whose property is located in a high crime area are ineligible risks."
- "Dwellings located in deteriorating and/or high crime areas are not eligible."
- "Property in recognized or known theft areas is not eligible."
- "Avoid low valued rental dwelling, rental dwellings in deteriorating neighborhoods."
- "Possible arson risk: insured residing in an economically depressed area."
- "Preferred risk [is] above-average neighborhood, no high theft exposure."
- "Preferred customer is in stable or improving area [that has a] favorable impact on market value."
- "Dwelling located in commercial neighborhood is not eligible."

The subjectivity inherent in these guidelines feeds on prejudices about the protected classes and inner-city neighborhoods. Moreover, these underwriting guidelines provide an easy way for an insurer or agent to hide intentional discrimination. An agent or company who wants to discriminate against a member of one of the protected classes, for instance, can simply base the decision on a "substandard adjacent property."

These guidelines illustrate the need for reliance on objective actuarial standards to show that underwriting guidelines are cost based. Actuarial standards were developed to ensure that underwriting guidelines are based on cost, not on prejudices and preconceived notions about communities "on the other side of the tracks." Sound actuarial principles, therefore, require data and other justifications for making judgments about anticipated experience. The purpose of these principles is to avoid arbitrary and subjective estimates, however reasonable they may appear.

Assumptions about home location, especially those related to "high-crime areas," although reasonable on their face, often fail to survive critical scrutiny. First, even if a neighborhood has a high documented crime rate, those crimes may have no relation to the homeowner's coverage. For instance, there may be a higher percentage of cars stolen in the neighborhood, but stolen cars are not covered on a homeowner's policy. If the number of homes broken into is not substantially higher than in other areas, then there is no basis for discriminating against the neighborhood on a homeowner's policy.

Second, even if there are higher numbers of thefts in the neighborhood, a sound actuarial analysis must include *all types of losses*. The underwriting guideline must reflect that the insurance *policy*, not one individual coverage, will result in higher losses. If the underwriting guideline does not identify a factor associated with higher *overall* losses on the policy, then discrimination based on the home's location is not actuarially sound. A 1994 study of paid losses in 1992 and 1993 by the Texas Department of Insurance revealed that theft losses only accounted for 9.2 percent of the paid losses statewide (Texas Department of Insurance 1994). For instance, if a neighborhood has higher theft losses but lower windstorm and hail losses, which accounted for 55 percent of the total losses, then the overall losses for the "high-crime" neighborhood may be *less* than those of other neighborhoods. No data have been offered by insurers to show that overall losses are higher in inner-city neighborhoods. Moreover, insurers vigorously oppose any efforts to publicly reveal the data necessary to make such an analysis.

Subjective underwriting guidelines that cannot be shown to be actuarially sound are a pervasive redlining problem, especially because they can be easily used as a surrogate for intentional discrimination. Any regulation of other underwriting guidelines will be rendered moot if insurers and agents are permitted to use subjective judgments that are intentionally or unintentionally based on prejudices and stereotypes against the classes of consumers protected by the Fair Housing Act.

Life-style

OPIC found that companies with 29 percent of the homeowners insurance market have an underwriting guideline for life-style (OPIC 1994). These guidelines exclude any couples, families, and friends who are not married or related by blood and who decide to combine households for financial, health, or other reasons. Examples of actual guidelines include prohibitions against:

- "Two or more unrelated insureds."
- "Unrelated occupants."
- "More than one family [living] in the home."
- "Unacceptable risks: dwelling occupied by more than 2 families."
- "Premises occupied by other than the named insurer, his/her father, mother, daughter or son" (Kincaid 1995).

These guidelines have a disproportionate impact upon low-income members of the protected classes who are required financially to live with another family or relative: only 4 percent of overall households have nonrelative occupants, but 5 percent of black and Hispanic households have nonrelative occupants (Census Bureau 1993).

In addition, underwriting guidelines pertaining to life-style include subjective standards permitting agents and underwriters to deny coverage based on vague standards euphemistically termed "moral hazards." Examples of actual underwriting guidelines include:

- "The key for successful underwriting of all personal lines insurance is that the property to be insured is an above-average risk and the moral character of the insured is above reproach."
- "Known moral hazards on the part of the owner or tenant [are unacceptable risks]."
- "[Applicant must be a] stable member of the community."
- "Desired degrees of maturity, responsibility, and stability."
- "Risk may be unacceptable if doubt be cast on the personal integrity, stability, or habits of the owner. Preferred risks: total abstainers."
- "Persons with known bad morals."
- "Persons with a defect in character which increases the potential for loss."
- "[Preferred risks include] applicants whose moral character is above reproach."
- "[Preferred risks include] an honest, average person, with high moral standards" (Kincaid 1995).

As with the underwriting guidelines related to location of the home, these subjective standards can be easily used, either intentionally or unintentionally, to discriminate based on race, color, or other protected classifications. All an insurer or agent faced with a redlining accusation need say is that he or she thought the applicant had a bad moral character. Subjective underwriting guidelines represent barriers to insurance availability that cannot be controlled except through their outright elimination.

Credit History

Companies writing 22 percent of the market use underwriting guidelines based on a consumer's credit history (OPIC 1994). These guidelines range from any negative mark on a credit report to requiring a major event, such as bankruptcy. Other guidelines are more vague, including prohibitions against insuring "applicants with a poor credit history" or "a financially distressed person."

The lack of relevant studies in this area makes it difficult to show that these guidelines adversely affect the protected classes. Moreover, since many of the underwriting guidelines are subjective, it would be difficult to collect meaningful data. However, these underwriting guidelines likely have an adverse effect on low-income consumers. Since the nonwhite population has substantially lower income than the white population, these underwriting guidelines probably have a disparate impact on the protected classes.

Employment Stability

Companies writing 19 percent of the market use underwriting guidelines based on employment history (OPIC 1994). Companies deny coverage to those consumers who are unemployed, have had excessive job changes, lack stable employment, or have not been at their current employer for a specified period, usually two years. Examples of actual guidelines include:

- "We attempt to see a pattern of stability in employment history."
- "Personal and employment stability."
- "Evidence of stability and financial stability."
- "[Applicant] must be employed or retired."
- "Applicant must be employed for four years."
- "Two years at present job or current address."
- "Favorable employment record."
- "At least two years at current or previous job or continuously employed full time for at least two years."
- "Worked for the same employer for the last eighteen months or worked in a related occupation" (Kincaid 1995).

Not surprisingly, this underwriting guideline has a disparate impact on the protected classes. For instance, in 1994 the unemployment rate for white, non-Hispanics was 5.3 percent; for blacks, 11.5 percent; and for Hispanics, 9.9 percent (U.S. Department of Labor 1994). In addition, Maguire (1993) found that the median tenure with an employer for white men was 5.3 years, compared to 4.4 years for black men and 3.2 years for Hispanic men. Hispanic women had the lowest median tenure with an employer (3.2 years), but black women had a longer median tenure (4.3 years) than white women (3.8 years). The study shows similar results for tenure in an occupation. Thus, these underwriting guidelines have a disparate impact on Hispanics and African American men.

Marital Status

The OPIC report (1994) showed that companies writing 15 percent of the Texas homeowners insurance market have underwriting guidelines based on marital status and discriminate against single and divorced consumers. Examples of actual guidelines include:

- "Moral hazards to avoid: recent divorce or marital problems."
- "Applicant must be married."
- "[Consider only consumers not] in the midst of separation or divorces."
- "Married couples living together in apartment with deadbolt lock on all exterior doors are exempted from meeting the daily occupancy requirement."
- "All persons over 25 must be individual members unless husband and wife living together."
- "[Preferred customers:] Married and own their own residence" (Kincaid 1995).

These underwriting guidelines have a disparate impact on African American homeowners. Table 6.3 outlines percentages of marital status by race/ethnicity for homeowners. Although the marital status underwriting guidelines do not appear to have a disparate impact on Hispanics, the underwriting guidelines have a substantially disparate impact on black homeowners.

Foreign Nationals

Companies writing 1 percent of the market have underwriting guidelines limiting coverage for non-U.S. citizens (OPIC 1994). These guidelines may constitute intentional discrimination based on national origin, in violation of the Fair Housing Act.

Two themes thus permeate this review of homeowners insurance underwriting guidelines. First, many of the most widely used underwriting guidelines have a disparate impact on classes of individuals protected by the Fair Housing Act. Second, many subjective underwriting guidelines can easily be used as surrogates for intentional discrimination. Although insurers have become more sophisticated by abandoning red lines and adopting extensive underwriting guidelines, the result for the protected classes is the same.

JUSTIFYING UNDERWRITING GUIDELINES WITH DISPARATE IMPACT

Although the most commonly used underwriting guidelines plainly have a disparate impact on the protected classes, use of these guidelines may not violate the Fair Housing Act if the guidelines are required for the safe and efficient operation of the insurer's business and there is no less-discriminatory alternative that could serve the same business objectives. This section analyzes the potential applicability of this defense to the use of underwriting guidelines with a discriminatory impact on the protected classes.

Test for Showing an Underwriting Guideline Is Justified

Three test components must be considered in determining whether an underwriting guideline with a disparate impact on the protected classes is justified: first, the underwriting guideline must be cost based and not a surrogate for a known risk factor; second, sound actuarial principles must be used to justify the underwriting guideline; and, finally, the burden of proof to justify the underwriting guide-

Table 6.3 HOMEOWNER MARITAL STATUS BASED ON RACE

Marital Status	White (%)	Black (%)	Hispanic (%)
Married	68	52	72
Separated	2	7	3
Widowed	13	16	8
Divorced	10	15	10
Never married	7	10	6

line must rest with the insurer. These components are discussed, in turn, next.

UNDERWRITING GUIDELINES SHOULD BE COST BASED, NOT SURROGATES

An underwriting guideline with a disparate impact on the protected classes is justified only if it meets a two-part test: it must identify a characteristic related to higher overall costs, and it must not be a surrogate for a known risk factor. Any justification for the use of underwriting guidelines must include showing that insuring the group of consumers being discriminated against would cause the insurer to incur higher overall costs. In other words, an underwriting guideline cannot be justified unless it is related to differences in the costs associated with the transfer of risk. *If there is no difference in the costs associated with assuming the risk between the group that meets the underwriting guideline and the group that does not, then there can be no business justification for treating the two groups differently.*

A logical corollary to this principle is that the insurer must show that *overall* costs are higher; it is not enough for one element of the insurance rate to be higher for the class of consumers. The homeowners insurance rate comprises several different costs, including elements of losses, insurer expenses, agent commission, and profit. If expenses to service a particular group defined by an underwriting guideline are higher, but their losses are lower, so that the *overall* costs to the insurer are the same, use of the underwriting guideline is not justified. In that case, the costs of the transfer of risk are the same. As illustrated earlier, this principle is best revealed in analyzing "high crime rates" underwriting guidelines, which indicated that an underwriting guideline is justified only if the *overall* costs associated with the transfer of risk are higher. If the other types of losses insured by the policy are less for the group being redlined by the underwriting guideline, such that the overall losses are the same, then the underwriting guideline would not be justified.

The second part of the justification test is that the underwriting guideline must identify the true risk factor and be not merely a surrogate for that factor. The underwriting guideline is justified only if the analysis of overall costs controls for all other known risk factors and identifies the unique contribution of the underwriting guideline to any explanation of differences in the expected costs associated with the transfer of risk. This should be shown through a multivariate statistical technique.

~~Surrogate underwriting guidelines, those that do not identify a cost~~
difference but are a mere surrogate for a real risk factor, fail this test. For example, some insurers require homeownership as an underwriting guideline for automobile insurance. Due to the costs of purchasing a home, most home owners are over 25 years old. Thus, the overall costs associated with the transfer of risk for homeowners will likely be less than those for renters. However, the difference in losses is due to the age of the driver, a known risk factor, not homeownership. Homeownership is merely a surrogate for age. To justify the use of homeownership as an underwriting guideline for automobile insurance, therefore, the insurer would need to show a relationship to overall costs, holding all other risk factors, including age, constant. Use of the surrogate results is unfair discrimination against renters over the age of 25.

The age-of-the-home underwriting guideline for homeowners insurance is another surrogate underwriting guideline. Although age of the home itself has not been shown to be related to risk, it is used as a surrogate for plumbing, heating, and electrical systems. Rather than discriminate against all owners of older homes, however, insurers should underwrite based on known risk factors. To justify the age-of-the-home requirement, the insurer must show that older homes with the *same plumbing, heating, and electrical systems as newer homes* have higher overall losses.

At least one court has addressed the use of surrogate underwriting guidelines, upholding a rule prohibiting underwriting guidelines for automobile insurance based on the number of cars insured: "[The rule] does not prevent insurers from accepting and rejecting risks; it merely prohibits the use of inaccurate substitutes . . . for real risk factors. . . . [The rule] prohibits the use of proxies for real risk factors" (*National Assoc. of Independent Insurers v. Texas Dept. of Ins.*, 888 S.W.2d 198 [Tex. App., Austin 1994]). The Texas Court of Appeals thus recognized that antidiscrimination laws were intended to prevent the unfair use of surrogates like race, religion, color, and nationality in making judgments about a person. Insurers should not be permitted to thwart that intent by using underwriting guidelines that are race based—either intentionally or through disparate impact.

JUSTIFICATION BASED ON SOUND ACTUARIAL PRINCIPLES

Actuaries and others have developed principles to determine when underwriting guidelines and rating factors are justified. The term *sound actuarial principles* is used to describe both the standard for justifying underwriting guidelines and the methodology to test for the standard. As a standard, sound actuarial principles means that the underwriting guideline or rating factor in question accurately distinguishes consumers on the basis of differences in expected costs associated with the transfer of risk. As a methodology, sound actuarial principles means an analysis consistent with the actuarial standards of practice and compliance guidelines promulgated by the Actuarial Standards Board of the American Academy of Actuaries.

Sound actuarial principles prohibit the use of surrogate underwriting guidelines. Procedures to hold other factors constant or to statistically control for other variables are standard actuarial, statistical, and econometric practices. Underwriting guidelines should be shown to be related to overall costs at the 95 percent confidence level by employing a statistical procedure that controls for all other known underwriting guidelines and rating factors.

Sound actuarial principles, rather than alternative standards, should be used to determine whether an underwriting guideline with a disparate impact on the protected classes is justified. Two other standards often supported by insurers are *sound underwriting* and *reasonably anticipated loss experience*. Whereas sound actuarial principles require objective standards to justify an underwriting guideline with a disparate impact on the protected classes, these other standards are completely subjective. They permit the type of arbitrary and capricious discrimination that is intended to be eliminated through antidiscrimination laws like the Fair Housing Act.

Insurer Should Bear Burden of Proof

Because insurers collect and control the relevant data regarding a particular underwriting guideline, it is extremely difficult for anyone other than the insurer to determine whether an underwriting guideline is cost based. This also makes it easy for insurers to simply adopt underwriting guidelines based on prejudices and stereotypes without any actuarial basis. Insurers have mounted large campaigns to resist public release of the data necessary to verify their claims that underwriting guidelines are actuarially sound and that inner-city neighborhoods have higher losses than other areas.

Thus, even though noncost-based underwriting guidelines with a disparate impact on the protected classes violate the Fair Housing Act, consumers have little way of knowing which underwriting guidelines are cost based. This situation is ripe for a transfer of the burden of proof—underwriting guidelines that have a disparate impact on the protected classes should be presumed to be unfair unless the insurer can show that they are cost based. Underwriting guidelines like credit history, age of the home, and value of the home have a tremendous impact on the ability of protected classes to obtain insurance in standard markets and at standard rates. Because insurers control the data, refuse to release the data, and make the affirmative decision to use an underwriting guideline, insurers should be required to justify the use of those underwriting guidelines by showing that they are actuarially sound.

Likelihood of Proving the Defense

Underwriting guidelines are typically not the result of careful, statistical studies. Rather, they are often based on hunches and subjective stereotypes about classes of consumers and types and geographic location of property. When underwriting guidelines have been challenged, insurers rarely have had data or actuarial analyses to support their underwriting guidelines. The use of subjective justifications for underwriting guidelines adversely affects those consumers who have historically been discriminated against and who are not represented in the decision-making process at most insurance companies— namely, the protected classes.

The use of credit history as an underwriting guideline offers an excellent example of how even the largest insurers use underwriting guidelines with little or no justification. Insurers claim that an insurer would not want to turn down profitable business and, therefore, would not use an underwriting guideline unless it is cost based. However, the credit history example shows that insurers do indeed use underwriting guidelines for which they have no justification or actuarial support.

Some insurers rationalize that consumers with poor credit histories cannot be relied on to pay their premium. This argument fails in two respects. First, homeowners insurance premiums are paid annually, *in advance*. Unlike automobile insurance, there is no risk that the premium will not be paid. Either the entire premium is paid or the policy is not sold. Second, in most cases the mortgagee, not the consumer, pays the premiums. Lenders will typically pay the premium even if the consumer is in default on the loan because the policy also protects the lender's interest. Thus, it is highly unlikely that the renewal premium will not be paid. In those few instances in which the renewal premium is not paid, the insurer can simply refuse to issue a renewal policy and has no need for the credit-risk underwriting guideline.

Many insurers claim that actuarial data establish that bad credit is related to higher loss costs. The Texas Department of Insurance requested several large insurers to supply data supporting the correlation between credit risk and insurance risk. Two of the largest homeowners insurers in the country replied that they had no data to support use of such a guideline (Johnson and Powers 1995). Rather, they referred the department to an article in the July 1993 *Best's Review*, which reported on a study claiming such a correlation. The article, however, was written by an employee of Equifax—the very company that sells credit reports and has a tremendous financial interest in getting insurers to buy its product. Moreover, Equifax denied repeated requests by OPIC to review the study and underlying data, even with a promise of confidentiality. In an interview on National Public Radio's *Market Place* on October 18, 1994, the author admitted that the study failed to control for other known risk factors. Thus, these leading national insurers offered as justification a secret study by a company with a tremendous financial interest in the outcome, a study that failed to follow standard actuarial and statistical procedures, as the basis for denying homeowners insurance to millions of consumers across the country.

This example points to the need to fully investigate underwriting guidelines that have no apparent relationship to risk—underwriting guidelines like credit history, value of the home, age of the home, and employment stability. It is highly probable that many of these underwriting guidelines are not actuarially sound and should be prohibited. Since they also have a disparate impact on the protected classes, that task is crucial in eliminating barriers to insurance availability.

CONCLUSION

Although traditional redlining—the refusal to sell insurance in a specific neighborhood—remains a concern, the use of underwriting guidelines with a disparate impact on the protected classes represents the greatest barrier to homeowners insurance availability today. Insurers use these underwriting guidelines to discriminate in a variety of ways. Yet, there has been no evident proof that the classes of consumers affected by these underwriting guidelines actually cause higher overall costs for the insurer. The redlining and insurance availability crisis will not be solved until the public, regulators, legislators, and insurers identify the underwriting guidelines used, collect the necessary data to determine if each is cost based, and eliminate the use of those that are not.

References

Bordelon, Rod. 1995. Letter to Consumer Information Working Group, Personal Lines—Property and Casualty Committee, National Association of Insurance Commissioners. Austin: Office of Public Insurance Counsel, September 8.

Hunter, J. Robert. 1994. Statement before the Committee on Banking, Housing, and Urban Affairs, U.S. Senate, 103rd Cong., 2nd sess., May 11.

Independent Bankers Association of Texas. 1995. Letter from Karen Neeley, General Counsel of the Independent Bankers Association of Texas, to Rod Bordelon. Filed at Texas Department of Insurance, Docket Number 2170. Austin: Texas Department of Insurance.

Johnson, Amy, and D. J. Powers. 1995. *Barriers to Homeowners Insurance Availability for Minority and Low-Income Consumers.* Washington, D.C.: U.S. Department of Housing and Urban Development.

Kincaid, Mark. 1994. *Insurance Redlining in Texas: A Preliminary Report.* Austin: Office of Public Insurance Counsel.

———. 1995. Written comments on behalf of Texas Office of Public Insurance Counsel regarding proposed rules 28 Texas Administrative Code §§21.1002, 21.1004, and 21.1006. Austin: Office of Public Insurance Counsel.

Maguire, Steven R. 1993. "Employer and Occupation Tenure: 1991 Update." *Monthly Labor Review* (June): 45.

National Assoc. of Independent Insurers v. Texas Dept. of Ins., 888 S.W.2d 198 (Tex. App., Austin 1994).

Office of Public Insurance Counsel. 1994. *A Review of Homeowners Insurance Underwriting Guidelines Used in Texas.* Austin: Author.

OPIC. *See* Office of Public Insurance Counsel.

Schwartz, Allan. 1994. Testimony in the "1994 Homeowners Insurance Benchmark Rate Hearing." Austin: Texas Department of Insurance.

Texas Department of Insurance. 1994. Staff report on "Cause of Loss Reported for Homeowners Insurance." Austin: Author, June 29.

U.S. Bureau of the Census. 1993. *1993 American Housing Survey, National Report* (Tables 3-1, 3-9, 3-14). Washington, D.C.: U.S. Government Printing Office.

———. 1994. *Current Population Reports.* Pub. no. P20-477. *Household and Family Characteristics.* Washington, D.C.: U.S. Government Printing Office.

U.S. Department of Labor, Bureau of Labor Statistics. 1994. *Household Data Annual Averages.* Washington, D.C.: Author.

Chapter Seven

INSURANCE CLAIMS DISCRIMINATION

Tom Baker and Karen McElrath

Property insurance is an essential part of the financial infrastructure of the American economy. It is also a precondition to consumer and small business participation in the standardized, low-cost, high-volume financing industry that makes homeownership and entrepreneurial capitalism possible. As succinctly described in *NAACP v. American Family Mutual Insurance Company*, "No insurance, no loan; no loan, no house" (978 F.2d 287, 298, 300–01 [7th Cir. 1992]). The same can be said for small business.

Earlier chapters have explored how discrimination in the sale of property insurance creates a barrier to full participation in the American economy. This chapter explores another aspect of insurance discrimination—discrimination in the handling of insurance claims. We use both the results of research we conducted on insurance claims following Hurricane Andrew, as well as studies by others on the role of cognition in perpetuating discrimination.

Our Hurricane Andrew insurance research consisted of surveying people who filed insurance claims, as well as conducting a series of interviews and observations. We interviewed claimants and insurance adjustors; we observed mediation sessions in which claimants and adjusters attempted to resolve disputed claims; and we interviewed mediators who conducted such sessions.

The most significant survey finding was that Hispanic claimants were only half as likely as other claimants to receive prompt payment of their claims. This was the first quantitative confirmation of earlier, anecdotal reports of insurance claims discrimination (Saadi 1987).[1] The qualitative research helped us understand the discrimination observed in the survey. As expected, no adjuster reported discriminating against Hispanics as a group, and we found little evidence of such conscious discrimination. But, as described by the adjusters we interviewed, the process of insurance claims adjusting has systematically biased effects. The significance of this conclusion extends well beyond the disparity in the timing of insurance payments documented in the survey. Because the sociological and cognitive processes that produce the difference in timing affect every aspect of insurance adjuster discretion, the discrimination observed in the survey is likely to be the tip of the insurance claims discrimination iceberg.

HURRICANE ANDREW SURVEY

In August 1992, Hurrican Andrew roared through South Florida, leaving behind over $15 billion in property damage. Twenty-eight thousand homes were destroyed, over 100,000 homes were damaged, and over 636,000 property insurance claims were filed (Florida Department of Insurance 1994). In the wake of the storm, an interdisciplinary faculty committee at the University of Miami organized a written, mail-in survey to measure the effect of the hurricane on the South Florida community.

One goal of the survey was to test for discrimination in handling residential insurance claims. To that end, the survey contained two questions designed to provide an objective basis for comparing the claims treatment of respondents:

1. When did you receive your first payment from your home insurance company?
2. When did you or another member of your household first see an adjuster at your home?[2]

We are under no illusion that these questions completely capture the insurance claims experience. We selected timing questions because they are objective, because our respondents could easily answer them without detailed knowledge of the insurance claims process, and because prompt attention from the insurance company is an important aspect of good claims-handling practice. In addition, other researchers have used timing measures in other contexts as lenses on the micro-exercise of power (e.g., Schwartz 1975). The interviews conducted in the qualitative portion of our research confirmed that both claimants and adjusters place great emphasis on the prompt handling of insurance claims.

Our insurance study's 28-page Hurricane Andrew survey questionnaire was distributed to nearly 7,000 full-time employees of the University of Miami in April 1993, seven months after the hurricane. The university is the second-largest private employer in Dade County, and it operates the largest hospital in Florida. University employees are not only professors, doctors, and secretaries but also orderlies, technicians, and cafeteria and maintenance workers. Although this well-employed group was not a random sample of the South Florida population, the group contained a good cross section of hurricane-related experience. Ninety percent of the university employees lived in Dade County, and just under half of those lived in the heavily damaged southern half of the county. Given the correlation between income and the purchase of home insurance, the survey's distribution to a comparatively advantaged sample does not undercut the strength of its conclusions. Indeed, any discrimination observed in the survey is likely to be magnified in the general population.

SURVEY RESULTS

We received 3,406 responses to the survey, a response rate of 52 percent. Seventy percent of the respondents had home insurance, and an astonishing 73 percent of those had filed a Hurrican Andrew insurance claim.

We analyzed the answers to the two timing questions using a multiple-regression analysis. The analysis controlled for the respondents' race, ethnicity, income, and education; the level of damage to the respondents' home; whether the respondent lived in the "disaster zone" in which the hurricane damage was heaviest; and whether the respondent lived in a female-headed household. In addition, when we analyzed the timing of the first insurance payment, we also controlled for whether a member of the household had seen an adjuster at the home. This analysis allowed us to determine which of these factors made a significant difference in the timing of insurance payments and adjuster visits.

When we looked at the timing of the adjuster visits, we found that only one of the factors made a significant difference. The more damage to the home, the more likely an adjuster visited the home within one month after the hurricane.[3] A respondent with very severe damage was about 55 percent more likely to have a meeting with an adjuster at the home during the first month after the hurricane than a respondent with minor damage.

It was when we looked at the timing of the first insurance payment that we found evidence of insurance claims discrimination. Controlling for the other factors we examined, Hispanic respondents were only 60 percent as likely to have been paid within a month after the hurricane as other respondents. Table 7.1 reports the regression analysis results.[4] Table 7.2 shows the relationship between race/ethnicity and timing of the first payment, without considering the other variables.

Other significant factors affecting the timing of the insurance payments were the location of the home, the amount of damage to the home, and the timing of the adjuster visit. These latter, expected findings helped to confirm the validity of the timing measure. Respondents who lived in the disaster zone were over twice as likely to receive a prompt payment. Respondents with very severe damage were nearly three times as likely to receive a prompt payment as

Table 7.1 LOGISTIC REGRESSION RESULTS FOR FIRST ADJUSTER VISIT AND FIRST INSURANCE PAYMENT

	Adjuster Meeting within One Month		Payment within One Month	
	β	Odds Ratio	β	Odds Ratio
Race/Ethnicity[a]				
Black non-Hispanic	.049		−.243	
Hispanic	−.223		−.496**	.61
Other	−.137		−.518*	.60
No response	.167		.236	
Income	.017		−.001	
Education	.005		−.012	
Female-headed household	−.356		.252	
Damage	.097*	1.10	.252***	1.29
Area[b]				
Disaster zone	.179		.789***	2.20
Broward County	.435		.373	
Met with adjuster within one month	N.A.		1.681***	5.37
Constant	−.976		−2.367	

Notes: See note 4, in text, for further explanation of table data; β = beta weight;
N.A. = not applicable.
a. Omitted category is white non-Hispanic.
b. Omitted category is elsewhere in Dade County.
*p < .05; **p < .01; ***p < .001.

Table 7.2 CROSS-TABULATION OF TIMING OF FIRST INSURANCE PAYMENT AND RACE/ETHNICITY

Race/Ethnicity	Percentage of Claimants Who Received a Payment Within One Month after Hurricane
White non-Hispanic	42
Black non-Hispanic	39
Hispanic	25

met with an adjuster at the home during the first month were over five times as likely to receive a prompt payment (see table 7.1).

We then checked for what social scientists call "interaction effects" among the significant factors affecting the timing of insurance payments. We discovered two such effects: one between location and ethnicity and another between adjuster visits and ethnicity. Unpacking these interaction effects provided important insights into our results that had been obscured in the initial regression analysis.

We first unpacked the interaction between ethnicity and location by looking separately at respondents who lived in the disaster zone. Among that group, we found that ethnicity was not a significant factor in the timing of their payments. But, among respondents who lived outside the disaster zone, ethnicity was strongly significant. Outside the disaster zone, Hispanics were less than 60 percent as likely as other respondents to receive an insurance payment within the first month. This finding suggests that location in the disaster zone mitigated insurance claims discrimination, perhaps because that location provided objective evidence of the validity of the insurance claim.

We then unpacked the interaction between ethnicity and the timing of adjuster visits by looking separately at respondents who did not report meeting with an adjuster at the home during the first month after the hurricane. As we learned from our interviews, many claimants were able to receive an initial insurance payment before an adjuster visited their home. This initial payment covered immediate, emergency repairs and short-term additional living expenses. Claimants obtained these payments from their insurance agents or by presenting appropriate documentation at one of the field offices many insurance companies established after the hurricane. According to the claimants we interviewed, information about the documentation required for these interim payments was rapidly communicated among the people waiting in line at the offices. Provided the claimant presented the documentation, the field office personnel made a payment.

Accordingly, many of our respondents who did not report meeting with an adjuster at home during the first month after the hurricane nevertheless received a payment during that month. Among those respondents, ethnicity was not a significant factor in the timing of the payments. But, among respondents who did report an adjuster meeting, ethnicity was strongly significant: Hispanics were only half as likely as other respondents to receive an insurance payment within the first month after the hurricane. This finding suggests that the disparity in treatment between Hispanics and non-Hispanics relates to the exercise of discretion by adjusters. Tables 7.3 and 7.4 summarize these findings.

We performed one last analysis to see whether these ethnic differences reflected more than a difference in timing. In this analysis, instead of looking at whether the respondents were paid within a month after the hurricane, we looked at whether they had been paid within three months. With this longer time horizon, ethnicity was no longer significant. This means the Hispanic difference applied to *when*, not *if* respondents were paid.

HURRICANE ANDREW INTERVIEWS AND OBSERVATIONS

The second part of our Hurricane Andrew insurance study consisted of observations of insurance claim mediations conducted at the Florida Department of Insurance Hurricane Andrew Mediation Center and interviews with claimants, adjusters, and mediators. We selected claimants to interview through a "snowball" interview program that began with people at the university and radiated outward. We selected insurance adjusters through the mediation observations. We selected mediators by asking Mediation Center officials to identify the mediators who had handled the most disputes. We also interviewed mediators who were present during five days of observation at the Mediation Center.

Table 7.3 LOCATION AND ETHNICITY

Location of Damaged Home	Did Ethnicity Make a Difference?
Inside the disaster zone	Ethnicity was not a significant factor in the timing of the first payment.
Outside the disaster zone	Hispanics were only 60 percent as likely to receive a payment within the first month.

Table 7.4 TIMING OF ADJUSTER VISIT AND ETHNICITY

Did a Member of the Household Meet with an Adjuster at the Home during the First Month?	Did Ethnicity Make a Difference?
No	Ethnicity was not a significant factor in the timing of the first payment.
Yes	Hispanics were only 50 percent as likely to receive a payment within the first month.

The interviews with claimants, adjusters, and mediators were semi-structured, meaning that we had a series of topics to cover, but the person being interviewed controlled the direction and pace of the interview. In all, we interviewed 50 claimants, 10 mediators, and 20 adjusters, and we observed 30 mediations. These interviews and observations helped us understand our survey results.

As we learned from interviewing adjusters, the correlation between the timing measures and the damage to and location of the home reflects insurance companies' formal policy of providing assistance first to the people most readily identifiable as needing that help. There were two reasons why the timing of adjuster visits did not conform as strongly to that policy as did the timing of insurance payments: (1) the destruction made it difficult for adjusters to travel to some of the most damaged areas, and (2) adjusters used other, informal criteria to allocate their time, including the order in which claims were reported, pressure from insurance agents, and the adjuster's judgment about whether the claim could be handled quickly. In addition, enough adjusters told stories about handling claims for local celebrities and at prestigious addresses to suggest a preference for such claims.

It was only through observing the mediations and, secondarily, through interviews with adjusters, that we appreciated the degree of discretion that adjusters exercise in handling insurance claims. Adjusters decide:

- The order in which claims are paid;
- The level of documentation required to support a claim;
- The amount of depreciation deducted from claims in which the insurance company is entitled to deduct depreciation;
- Whether damaged property can be replaced or must instead be repaired;
- The quality of the existing construction, which determines the quality of the reconstruction for which payment will be made;
- Whether the damage to the home is sufficient to entitle the claimant to relocate temporarily at the insurance company's expense;
- How long the claimant is entitled to remain relocated at insurance company expense; and
- Whether to press "technical" defenses to payment based on a strict interpretation of the insurance policy.

Considered in isolation, these individual points of discretion may seem inconsequential. Together, however, they give the adjuster substantial control over who gets paid, when, and how much. Indeed, both the observers and the mediators were struck by the ability of adjusters to manipulate aspects of claims to arrive at a dollar figure that would satisfy the claimants—provided the adjuster was willing.

Whether the adjuster was willing depended in part on his or her moral assessment of the claim/claimant. In our interviews and in private caucuses with mediators in the course of mediations, adjusters stressed that many people exaggerated their losses, that some smaller number of people fabricate losses, and that the adjuster has to be on the lookout for such exaggeration and fabrication. Indeed, much of the insurance adjuster's work is driven by what Baker (1994) has called the "story of the immoral insured":

> The story of the immoral insured teaches that the role of the "adjuster at the loss" is that of the "cop on the corner . . .[,] the best deterrent to overpayment." Or to put it even more succinctly, "It's a dirty job, but somebody has to keep them honest." (p. 1412)

In handling insurance claims, insurance adjusters do not have time to conduct an extensive investigation into every aspect of every claim; their job is to close claims and to do so quickly (Ross 1970). In the process, adjusters rely on their experience and intuition to assess whether the claim fits their expectations. When asked to explain how they make that assessment, the adjusters typically relied more on examples than on rules of thumb. But, when pressed, adjusters referred to the type of claim and to the social attributes of claimants. As one adjuster said, "I look at the car they drive, the other things in the house, the way they carry themselves." Other social attributes mentioned were the character of the home or neighborhood, employment status, business or professional background, immigrant status (discussed more in next subsection), perceived wealth, and what another adjuster called "a life-style that indicates a basic honesty."

ADJUSTER DISCRETION, SOCIAL COGNITION, AND INSURANCE CLAIMS DISCRIMINATION

Race is always and already there. It is not possible to "not see it," only to be unaware of race as a window through which we look at the world.
—Jones (1994)

As described in a recent article on employment discrimination, cognitive psychologists have conducted a series of experiments that have greatly advanced our understanding of discrimination (Krieger 1995). Using the results of these experiments, psychologists have developed what is known as social cognition theory (Fiske and Taylor 1991).

Social cognition theory makes four claims that are relevant to insurance claims discrimination.

First, categorization is a basic building block of cognition. We make
sense of the world by putting people and situations into categories.
Indeed, without categories, the world would present us with an end-
less stream of unique events. Second, stereotyping is simply a form
of categorization: "stereotypes, like other categorical structures, are
cognitive mechanisms that *all* people, not just 'prejudiced' ones, use
to simplify the task of perceiving, processing and retaining information about people in memory" (Krieger 1995: 1188). Third, once in
place, stereotypes affect how an individual processes information
about members of the stereotyped group. Finally, stereotypes have
this effect without, and sometimes even in spite of, the awareness of
the individual. Thus, "cognitive bias may well be both unintentional
and unconscious" (Krieger 1995: 1188).

Social cognition theory helps to explain this study's results because
categorization is the essence of what adjusters do. Is this roof leak the
result of hurricane damage or of deferred maintenance? Is this claimant with the roof leak the kind of person who takes care of property
or the kind of person who does not? Is this water-soaked bureau the
antique the claimant says it is or simply used furniture? Is this claimant with the water-soaked bureau the kind of person who owns an-
tiques or the kind of person who buys used furniture? As these examples illustrate, handling an insurance claim involves an assessment
of the claimant. Inevitably, that assessment will take into account the
adjuster's ideas about people like the claimant.

Social psychologists call such ideas about people "social schema."
Social schema include "trait schema ('leader'), role schema ('manu-
facturing plant foreman'), identity group schema ('Hispanic men') and
person impressions ('Miguel')" (Krieger 1995: 1199). The adjusters we
interviewed, while not using terms like *role schema* or *identity group
schema*, readily agreed that they categorize people according to occupation, neighborhood, life-style, and personal impressions.

As the social psychologists' research makes clear, the adjuster's
categorization cannot stop there:

> Because gender, ethnic and racial distinctions are often perceptually
> apparent, and because these categories are made salient by our social
> and cultural context, we can expect race, ethnic and gender-based
> schema to be implicated in the processing of information about other
> people. (Krieger 1995: 1202)

When an adjuster meets a claimant who is Hispanic, black, or female,
for example, that encounter activates the adjuster's corresponding so-

cial schema. "Once activated, the content of the schema will profoundly affect how we interpret a person's subsequent behavior, what about that behavior we remember, and how we use the behavior in judging the person later" (Krieger 1995: 1202). As our survey results suggest, when adjusters met with Hispanic respondents, the adjusters' "Hispanic" schemas were activated, resulting in claim payments for this group being processed more slowly than for other claimants.

Our interviews and observations suggest a plausible explanation for this effect. First, several adjusters stated that they were more likely to regard with suspicion a claim from a recent immigrant. The largest and most visible group of recent immigrants in the Miami area is Hispanic (Portes and Stepick 1993). Second, several other adjusters (who were told of the timing disparities in our survey) suggested that Hispanics may have been paid later because they could not communicate in English with the almost universally non-Spanish-speaking adjusters. University of Miami employees work in an environment in which facility with English is essential, as evidenced by the respondents' ability to complete a 28-page survey entirely in English. Thus, difficulty with the English language cannot be a complete explanation for the disparity among survey respondents. Nevertheless, this explanation, like the statements about immigrants, provides a window on the content of the adjusters' category of "Hispanic." People perceived as belonging to a group whose members are seen as "untrustworthy" or "hard to communicate with" are unlikely to be paid as quickly as those who are not. This commonsense conclusion is supported by extensive research in social cognition (Krieger 1995).

Further analysis of the survey results supports this reasoning. The finding that ethnicity mattered only among claimants who met with their adjuster during the first month after the hurricane supports our emphasis on insurance adjuster discretion. The finding that ethnicity was significant only for claims outside the disaster zone suggests that location inside the disaster zone provided sufficient objective proof of the claim's validity to overcome the effects of the stereotype. Finally, the finding that the Hispanic difference related only to *when*, not *if*, the respondents were paid suggests that claims filed by Hispanic respondents were, eventually, determined to be equally deserving of payment.

An important question remains. If social cognition theory is accurate, and if our use of that theory to explain the Hispanic "difference" observed in the survey is also accurate, why did we not also observe a female-headed household difference or a black difference in the timing of insurance payments?

Once again, our interviews and social cognition theory provide a plausible explanation, one that turns on differences between the content of adjusters' "Hispanic" schema on the one hand and adjusters' "black" and "female" schemas on the other. Before offering that explanation, however, we want to emphasize that we are extrapolating from limited data and that we are a long way from proving gender- or race-based discrimination in the handling of Hurricane Andrew insurance claims. Thus, the explanation should be regarded as a hypothesis, not a research conclusion.

As described earlier, we attributed the delay in payments to Hispanics to the "untrustworthy" and "difficult" aspects of insurance adjusters' Hispanic schemas. Our interviews and observations suggested that adjusters' "black" and "female" schemas differed from their "Hispanic" schemas in this regard. Our sense was that adjusters tended to regard black and female claimants as both "trustworthy" and "tractable." Thus, if discrimination were to occur, it would more likely take the form of a lower payment, rather than a slower payment.

This hypothesis was corroborated by some of our informants. A black mediator who handled Hurricane Andrew mediations asserted that adjusters routinely "low-balled" black claimants, several female claimants asserted that women received less-favorable payments, and one female former adjuster asserted that some adjusters take advantage of female claimants. Clearly, these are suggestions, not conclusive proof, but they are consistent with prior anecdotal reports (Saadi 1987) and are capable of being tested, provided the necessary data are made available.

REDRESSING INSURANCE CLAIMS DISCRIMINATION

Within antidiscrimination law, there are two competing visions of what constitutes legally cognizable discrimination: the "intent" vision and the "effects" vision (Jones 1994). The weakness of the intent vision as a means to redress the systematic consequences of stereotypes and past discrimination has been explored in detail by other authors (e.g., Jones 1994; Krieger 1995). We add to their accounts two observations based on our Hurricane Andrew research.

First, an intent test would erect a prohibitively high burden to proving insurance claims discrimination. Because of the multifactor, highly discretionary nature of insurance adjusting, isolating the discrete, intentionally discriminatory decision required by an intent test would be practically impossible: something approaching an adjuster confession would be necessary (cf., in the employment context, Jones 1994: 2361–63). Second, our interviews and observations suggest that insurance claims discrimination is not the result of discrete, intentionally discriminatory decisions. As Jones (1992) has written:

> Discrimination is not a discrete event. It is a reservoir or lake in which a myriad of social institutions from slavery to Jim Crow, from literature to science, from religious practice to housing patterns . . . have all deposited their streams. It is a reservoir of not merely individual hatreds and fears, but also of institutional inertia and cultural bias built upon a myriad of myths and stereotypes. (p. 367)

For these reasons, it is extremely significant that the courts have permitted effects-based discrimination claims under the Fair Housing Act.[5]

The greatest immediate challenge to redressing insurance claims discrimination is measurement. There is no shortage of explanations as to how and why insurance claims discrimination might occur (e.g., Jones 1994; Krieger 1995). There is, however, a shortage of social-scientific demonstrations of insurance claims discrimination. One of the reasons our survey is important is because we were the first to do what we did. We readily acknowledge, however, that our measures were crude and our sample was not random. What is needed are better measures of the insurance claims process and more complete data.

Because of the centrality of insurance adjuster discretion in the homeowners insurance process, any claims-performance instruments to test discrimination should be directed at measurable aspects of the claims process that are subject to adjuster discretion. As described earlier, adjusters have discretion over many aspects of the claims process that affect the timing, amount, and characterization of payments to insureds. Using these aspects as a guide, we suggest the following potential home insurance claims discrimination measures:

1. The amount of the claim payment, analyzed separately according to the category of payment (i.e., structure, contents, and additional living expenses);
2. The time from report of the claim to:
   a. Closing the claim,
   b. The first and last additional living expense payment,
   c. The first and last structure payment, and
   d. The first and last contents payment; and
3. The amount of depreciation deducted from structure and contents payments.

In the statistical analysis of these measures, it is important to control for the type of claim, the dollar limit of the insurance policy, and the type of insurance policy. As outsiders to the insurance claims process, we are open to the suggestion that there are better claims-performance measures. Indeed, the insurance industry may already have developed some for quality management purposes. Thus, this list should be regarded as illustrative rather than exhaustive.

Insurance companies are the only realistic sources of information about insurance claims needed to test the discrimination hypothesis. As our interviews with claimants made clear, claimants do not know enough about their insurance policies or their claims to be a reliable source of the information needed for more sophisticated analysis. Based on our interviews with adjusters, we believe that insurance companies not only have all the information needed for the claims-performance measures just suggested, but they have this data in computer-readable form.

Using such claims-performance measures to test insurance claims discrimination will require obtaining some information that at least some insurance companies do not have: the ethnicity, race, and gender of their claimants. There are several ways to obtain such information. The most accurate (and expensive) way is a telephone survey of claimants identified from insurance company records. Ethnicity information could also be obtained in two less expensive (and less accurate) ways: using a marketing organization to "ethnicize" the names of claimants from insurance company records; or using address information from insurance company records in combination with census information. The census approach could also be used to test racial differences[6] and, provided that the necessary software exists, the name-matching approach could be used to test gender differences.

Because insurance companies are the only sources of the necessary data, no independent research organization can conduct this research alone. In the past, insurance companies have not voluntarily provided researchers with access to their data (e.g., Heimer 1985). We see two possible ways for an independent research organization to obtain this information: in cooperation with a state insurance department or in cooperation with a plaintiff bringing an insurance discrimination claim.

State insurance departments appear to have the legal authority to require insurance companies to provide the required information. Insurance departments routinely perform market examinations in their consumer protection role (Klein 1995), and insurance claims discrimination is a consumer protection issue. Thus, an insurance department could require an insurance company to supply the necessary data and then contract with an independent research organization to collect the additional information and conduct the analysis.

Plaintiffs bringing insurance discrimination claims also appear to have the legal authority to require insurance companies to provide the required information. As insurance industry compliance counsel have acknowledged, a pattern of discrimination in the handling of insurance claims is relevant to an insurance discrimination case (Sullivan and Sandler 1995). Thus, plaintiffs who have mounted redlining discrimination cases should be interested in conducting discovery into insurance claims discrimination. Particularly in cases supported by the U.S. Department of Justice or the U.S. Department of Housing and Urban Development, plaintiffs could obtain the information in discovery and, as with a state insurance department, contract with an independent research organization to conduct the necessary analysis.

CONCLUSION

The Hurricane Andrew insurance study is important because it confirms that insurance claims discrimination exists and that it can be measured. This chapter has provided one explanation of the process of insurance claims discrimination and has suggested a research program to test that explanation. As the insurance claims discrimination record is developed, however, it is even more important that insurance companies, regulators, and antidiscrimination advocates plan how to respond to that record. If experience is any guide, it will be much easier to prove that discrimination exists than to change the social and cognitive processes that produce it.

Notes

This chapter reports findings of a research project described more completely in Baker and McElrath (1996). Interested readers are referred to that article for a further description of the research methods and statistical analysis. This chapter adds to the prior report by focusing on claims discrimination, social cognition theory, and antidiscrimination law.

1. In the disaster literature, Bolin and Bolton (1986) noted race/ethnicity differences in insurance coverage after natural disasters, but they did not explore whether these

differences resulted from purchasing patterns or from disparate treatment in the claims process.

2. The survey specified a meeting "at the home" to screen out meetings at an insurance field office, which would not present the adjuster with an opportunity to assess damage to the home.

3. The timing variables were dichotomized and analyzed using a logistic regression analysis because the survey collected the timing information using a four-category interval scale that could not be used as the dependent variable in a linear regression analysis.

4. Logistic regression differs from the more commonly used linear regression in that the former can be used to analyze associations with a dependent variable that is yes/no in character, such as receiving a payment or not. The beta weights and odds ratios reported in table 7.1 express the strength of the association between a particular independent variable and the dependent variable under analysis. Here, the dependent variable is whether the claimant received a check within a month after the hurricane, and the independent variables are race/ethnicity, income, and so forth.

A logistic regression equation predicts the log of the odds of an observation being in one category of the dependent variable versus the other. This is the beta weight (β) reported in table 7.1. An odds ratio is the antilog of the beta weight (e^{Beta}), and it always has a positive sign (i.e., it is greater than zero). An odds ratio represents the amount by which a unit change in an independent variable multiplies the odds of an observation being in one category versus the other, holding the remaining independent variables constant (Hosmer and Lemeshow 1989: 41). This means that the farther away an odds ratio for a given independent variable is from 1.00, the more strongly associated that variable is with the dependent variable, either in a positive or negative direction. We calculated the odds ratios only for the significant variables.

In the adjuster-visit equation in table 7.1, the highest odds ratio is the 1.10 reported for damage, which tells us that the more damage to the home, the more likely the respondent received an early payment. The damage variable was a seven-point scale, ranging from 0 (no damage) to 6 (roof and/or exterior walls destroyed). Moving from 1 to 6 on the damage scale increases the odds of being paid within a month by 60 percent. In the insurance-payment equation, the highest odds ratio is the 5.37 reported for the met-with-adjuster variable, which tells us that respondents who met with adjusters were much more likely to be paid within a month. The lowest odds ratio is the .60 for the Hispanic variable, which tells us that Hispanics were only 60 percent as likely to be paid within a month as other respondents.

In comparing odds ratios among independent variables, it is important to keep in mind the difference between dummy variables (i.e, yes/no variables, such as race and ethnicity in table 7.1), interval variables (i.e., variables with categories composed of ranges, such as damage in table 7.1), and continuous variables (none in table 7.1). Because the odds ratios predict the effect of increasing or decreasing the independent variable by one unit, regardless of the kind of variable under analysis, an important dummy variable can be expected to have an odds ratio farther from 1.00 than an important interval variable, just as an important interval variable can be expected to have an odds ratio farther from 1.00 than an important continuous variable (Hosmer and Lemeshow 1989: 56). In table 7.1, income, education, and damage are interval variables, and the remainder are dummy variables. (This explanation is adapted from Baker and McElrath 1996.)

5. See *Metropolitan Housing Development Corp. v. Village of Arlington Heights* (558 F.2d 1283 [7th Cir. 1977], *cert. denied*, 434 U.S. 1025 [1978]). An effects challenge would focus on the discriminatory impact of "subconscious stereotypes and prejudices," which the U.S. Supreme Court held to be an appropriate subject of a discrimination claim in *Watson v. Forth Worth Bank & Trust Co.* (487 U.S. 977 [1988]) (concerning employment discrimination).

6. The census approach would measure claims treatment in terms of the racial composition of the neighborhood, not the race of the insured. Thus, census information is at best an imperfect proxy for the race of the insured.

References

Baker, Tom. 1994. "Constructing the Insurance Relationship: Sales Stories, Claims Stories, and Insurance Contract Damages." *Texas Law Review* 72: 1395–1433.

Baker, Tom, and Karen McElrath. 1996. "Whose Safety Net? Home Insurance and Inequality." *Journal of Law and Social Inquiry* 21: 229–64.

Bolin, Robert, and Patricia Bolton. 1986. *Race, Religion, and Ethnicity in Disaster Recovery.* Colorado: Institute of Behavioral Science, University of Colorado.

Fiske, Susan T., and Shelley E. Taylor. 1991. *Social Cognition*, 2d ed. New York: McGraw Hill.

Florida Department of Insurance. 1994. "Hurricane Andrew Fact Sheet." Tallahassee, Fla.: Author. Photocopy (on file with Tom Baker).

Jones, D. Marvin. 1992. "The Death of the Employer: Image, Text, and Title VII." *Vanderbilt Law Review* 45: 349–50.

————. 1994. "No Time for Trumpets: Title VII, Equality, and the Fin de Siecle. *Michigan Law Review* 92: 2311–69.

Heimer, Carol. 1985. *Reactive Risk and Rational Action: Managing Moral Hazard in Insurance Contracts.* Berkeley: University of California Press.

Hosmer, David W., Jr., and Stanley Lemeshow. 1989. *Applied Logistic Regression.* New York: Wiley.

Klein, Robert W. 1995. "Insurance Regulation in Transition." *Journal of Risk and Insurance* 62:363.

Krieger, Linda. 1995. "The Content of Our Categories: A Cognitive Bias Approach to Discrimination and Equal Employment Opportunity. *Stanford Law Review* 47: 1161–1248.

Portes, Alejandro, and Alexander Stepick. 1993. *City on the Edge: The Transformation of Miami.* Berkeley: University of California Press.

Ross, H. Laurence. 1970. *Settled Out of Court: The Social Process of Insurance Claims Adjustment.* Chicago: Aldene Publishing Co.

Saadi, Michele. 1987. *Claim It Yourself: The Accident Victim's Guide to Personal Injury Claims.* New York: Pharos Books.

Schwartz, Barry. 1975. *Queuing and Waiting: Studies in the Social Organization of Access and Delay.* Chicago: University of Chicago Press.

Sullivan, Robert J., and Andrew L. Sandler. 1995. "Property Insurance Discrimination: The Next Civil Rights Enforcement Frontier. *Journal of Insurance Regulation* 13: 478–85.

Chapter Eight

NAACP v. AMERICAN FAMILY

William H. Lynch

On March 30, 1995, in Milwaukee, Wisconsin, U.S. Attorney General Janet Reno joined with Earl Shinhoster, then acting executive director of the National Association for the Advancement of Colored People (NAACP), to announce the largest and most comprehensive settlement to date of a homeowner's insurance redlining case. The case, in which the U.S. Department of Justice (DOJ), the NAACP, the ACLU, and other community groups brought suit against American Family Mutual Insurance Company, resulted in a $14.5 million settlement by American Family (*United States v. American Family Mutual Insurance Company*, C.A. No. 95-C-0327 [E.D. Wisc. 1995]). The company is now aggressively pursuing urban markets: $9.5 million is being put toward community relief programs, and a $5 million fund has been created for victims of racial discrimination. Settlement of the case has heightened awareness of both racial discrimination by homeowners' insurers and the impact of such discrimination on communities. It is hoped that this case will help inform responses to insurance redlining elsewhere and will contribute to positive changes in the insurance industry—changes that will benefit insurance consumers, the neighborhoods in which they live, the insurance companies, and us all.

The goals of the NAACP's class-action suit against American Family were ambitious. The NAACP and other local and national civil rights organizations sought to establish that homeowners' insurers are covered under the Federal Fair Housing Act of 1968, which prohibits racial discrimination. They also set out to prove the nature and extent of redlining and to obtain significant and effective remedies for its victims. That is, they sought an impact not only on Milwaukee and on American Family but on insurance practices of other companies throughout the country.

This chapter traces the events leading up to the filing of the lawsuit against American Family. It describes the plaintiff's legal strategies and the challenges presented by American Family's responses to them. It also traces the development of the federal government's response to claims of racial discrimination by American Family. Finally, it examines the significance of the settlement.

THE CASE

More than two and one-half years of preparation preceded the July 27, 1990, filing of the NAACP's class-action case against American Family in the Federal District Court in Milwaukee (*NAACP v. American Family Mutual Insurance Company* (978 F.2d 287 [7th Cir. 1992]), *cert. denied*, 113 S.Ct. 2335 [1993]). The case arose out of the struggle of the black community in Milwaukee to obtain homeowner's insurance free from racial discrimination. In October 1987, three black insurance agents, Julius Joseph, Samuel Parker, and John Moore, who had more than 50 years of insurance experience among them, sought the assistance of black attorney James Hall and the Milwaukee Branch of the NAACP.

The NAACP formed a redlining committee to consider how to respond. Because I had served as local lead counsel for the NAACP in a metropolitan school desegregation lawsuit, I joined the effort. With the assistance of agents Joseph, Parker, Moore, and others, we learned how racial discrimination by insurance companies affects the availability and affordability of insurance for African Americans. We learned that resolution of individual complaints by the Wisconsin Insurance Commissioner's office and establishment of a Community Insurance Information Center to educate consumers about insurance had not led to wide-scale improvement in the affordability and availability of homeowner's insurance. Despite efforts by the Wisconsin Insurance Plan (WIP) Depopulation Program, only a relatively small percentage of homes insured by WIP under Wisconsin's Fair Access to Insurance Requirements (FAIR) Plan[1] were being insured by standard companies.

We also contacted Gregory D. Squires and William Velez, of the University of Wisconsin-Milwaukee, who supplied us with company-specific information from their analysis of comparative market-share statistics (Squires and Velez 1987) and office locations (Squires, Velez, and Taeuber 1990).

Furthermore, we asked the black community for its experience with redlining. On March 19, 1988, the NAACP sponsored a town meeting at which citizens testified about their difficulties obtaining affordable automobile and homeowner's insurance and about the methods they believed insurance companies used to avoid them as customers. We also met with local elected officials to inform them about the committee's investigation and to learn about their constituents' problems obtaining insurance.

On April 8, 1988, we learned from a *Milwaukee Journal* article that six former American Family agents had filed a lawsuit including a claim that the company practiced redlining (Enriquez 1988, citing *Ziehlsdorf et al. v. American Family Insurance Group* [Case No. 88-CV-1082, Waukesha Co. Cir. Ct.]). We learned from the text of the lawsuit that American Family District Manager Michael Shannon had written a note to long-term American Family Agent Reuben Ziehlsdorf as follows: "*Quit writing all those blacks!! They are the reason for your poor persistency!*" The note was written on a life insurance production report for September 1986. Ziehlsdorf had also tape-recorded a meeting with Shannon, who said, "Very honestly, I think you write too many blacks. . . . We cannot afford them. . . . You got to sell good, solid premium-paying white people. . . . They own their homes, the white works . . . well, they can afford the insurance. . . ." Shannon had told another agent that "the only way you are going to correct your persistency is to get away from the blacks. . . ." Shannon suggested a way to discourage blacks was to tell them an annual premium was required. He said, "Then again, very honestly, be careful about writing a large number of blacks." In reference to a black customer, Shannon said, "He does not consider himself as a so-called nigger, just a high-class black man. . . . There are good blacks and bad blacks" (in Enriquez 1988).

Years before, another American Family district manager, Bill Hart, had restricted Ziehlsdorf's sales of insurance in an area that included almost all of Milwaukee's black residents at the time. An August 31, 1972, memo from Hart to Ziehlsdorf directed that "no business will be written bound between Hampton Avenue, Lincoln Avenue, the River and 43rd Street."

RESOURCE NEEDS

An effective broad-scale challenge to redlining in Milwaukee would be countered aggressively by the insurance industry and would require substantial resources. The ACLU of Wisconsin joined the NAACP in investigating and researching property insurance redlining. Although these two organizations do not routinely collaborate on cases, we were able to arrange to share the legal costs among the ACLU of Wisconsin, the national ACLU, the national NAACP, and the Legal Aid Society of Milwaukee. In fall 1994, the NAACP Legal Defense Fund also joined the effort.

DESCRIPTION OF LAWSUIT

The NAACP's 1990 complaint on behalf of eight black homeowners and members of the NAACP's Milwaukee Branch asserted that Milwaukee was the most segregated of the 50 metropolitan areas in the country with the largest black populations. As of 1980, approximately 150,000 blacks lived in the Milwaukee metropolitan area, and 97.5 percent of them (that is, all but 3,737) lived within the city boundaries. Of the 32 zip codes in Milwaukee County, 18 had nonwhite populations of less than 2 percent, and only 7 had nonwhite populations of 25 percent or higher.

American Family's market share in predominantly black areas was dramatically smaller than its share in white areas. In zip codes with less than 25 percent nonwhite residents, American Family wrote about 33 percent of the policies written by the 18 largest companies doing business in Milwaukee County. By contrast, American Family wrote only 20 percent of the policies in zip codes that were 25 percent or more nonwhite. In the three zip codes whose population was majority nonwhite, American Family's share of the policies written by the 18 largest companies was under 8 percent.

Of more than 180 American Family agencies in the Milwaukee metropolitan area, no more than 5 were in zip codes with 25 percent or more nonwhite populations. American Family employed very few black agents. Only four were black, and during the 63-year history of the company, American Family had employed only 12.

American Family implemented a specific and intentional policy of failing and refusing to provide insurance to black individuals, as illustrated by Shannon's earlier-noted directions to Ziehlsdorf. American Family's rating zones provided for higher premiums in the cities of Milwaukee, Racine, and Kenosha than in suburban areas adjacent to those cities. The three cities are among those in Wisconsin with the highest percentage of African Americans.

The NAACP's complaint alleged, among other aspects, that American Family agents refused to offer Plaintiff Celestine Lindsey replacement-cost insurance, and that an agent failed to follow through on providing her with an estimate. One agent never returned Plaintiff Dorothy Listenbee's calls, and another told her the company would not provide replacement-cost insurance. They did not inspect her home or offer her an insurance policy. An American Family agent did not return Plaintiff Lois Wood's telephone calls. She telephoned again, and he promised to drive by her home to evaluate it for American Family coverage, but he did not appear.

In other examples of redlining alleged by the case, Plaintiff Jim Milner obtained American Family homeowner's insurance because the previous owner had it. When the agent later learned Milner was black, he indicated surprise, and Milner's homeowner's policy was not renewed by American Family. American Family also refused to insure other properties Milner purchased. When Milwaukee Alderman Marvin Pratt and his wife, Diane, moved to a black area from a predominantly white area of the city, American Family automatically provided them with an inferior repair-cost policy with limited coverage. The Pratts learned of the limitations in their coverage only after suffering a loss that was not fully paid by the company. Plaintiff Simon Williams obtained American Family insurance, but when he had a loss, employees of American Family did not believe he could afford to own the items claimed. The company refused to pay fully for his loss and refused to renew his policy.

The lawsuit claimed that American Family violated the 1866 and 1870 Federal Civil Rights Acts, the Federal Fair Housing Act, the Wisconsin Fair Housing Act, and provisions of the Wisconsin Insurance Code and Regulations. The NAACP plaintiffs sought an injunction and affirmative relief necessary to eradicate the effects of American Family's unlawful practices and to prevent their recurrence. The lawsuit also sought mandatory investment of funds by American Family in the geographic area adversely affected by its discriminatory practices, compensatory and punitive money damages, and plaintiffs' costs and attorney fees.

REACTION TO THE CASE

The lawsuit was front-page news in the *Milwaukee Journal* (Gribble 1990) and the *Madison Capital Times* (Conroy 1990) (American Family is headquartered in Madison). Brief articles appeared in the *New York Times* and other publications.

The day after the lawsuit was filed, Eric Englund, president of the Wisconsin Insurance Alliance, a trade and lobbying group, described the filing as "a cheap shot at yesterday's news, which in no way, shape or form reflects [practices] today." Englund further said that "it just smacks us right in the face" (in Sussman 1990), referring to the state insurance industry.

The case was assigned to Federal District Court Judge Joseph P. Stadtmueller, a former U.S. attorney and an appointee of President George Bush. American Family chose Wisconsin's largest law firm, Foley & Lardner, to represent it. The company filed a motion to dismiss the plaintiffs' claims under the Federal Fair Housing Act and the Wisconsin Insurance Code and Regulations. They did not seek to dismiss claims under the Reconstruction Era Civil Rights Acts protecting the right to contract and the property rights of citizens, nor claims under the Wisconsin Fair Housing Act explicitly prohibiting racial discrimination by homeowner's insurers.

FEDERAL FAIR HOUSING ACT AND HOMEOWNER'S INSURANCE

American Family claimed that homeowner's insurance companies are not covered by the provisions of the Federal Fair Housing Act prohibiting racial discrimination. (The applicability of the Act to property insurance redlining is discussed in more detail by Dane, in chapter 2 of this volume.)

The Department of Justice and the National Fair Housing Alliance (NFHA), a nationwide organization of fair housing advocacy groups, filed friend of the court (amicus curiae) briefs urging Judge Stadtmueller to rule that the Federal Fair Housing Act prohibited racial discrimination by homeowners' insurers. On December 11, 1990, however, Judge Stadtmueller ordered the plaintiffs' Federal Fair Housing Act claim dismissed.

VIOLATION OF WISCONSIN INSURANCE CODE AND REGULATIONS

The insurance industry often argues that federal laws prohibiting racial discrimination should not apply to it because state insurance

laws and regulation by state insurance commissioners are adequate
to end redlining. In the *American Family* case, we claimed that the
company engaged in unfair rate discrimination or unfair classification
of risks and unfair or deceptive marketing practices in violation of
§§ 625.11(2) and 628.34(3) of the Wisconsin Insurance Code. We also
claimed the company violated § 6.68 of the insurance regulations,
which restricts companies from discriminating because of the geo-
graphical location of the risk. This regulation would apply even if race
were not the reason for refusing to issue or renew policies or for
canceling or limiting coverage because of the location of the risk.
Judge Stadtmueller dismissed our claims under the Wisconsin Insurance Code and Regulations on the grounds that they did not create a
legal basis for an individual to sue. Only the Commissioner of Insurance could enforce the provisions.

APPEALING JUDGE STADTMUELLER'S RULINGS

The NAACP plaintiffs appealed to the Court of Appeals for the Seventh Circuit in Chicago. In support of our position, the DOJ, the
NFHA, and the city of Milwaukee filed amicus curiae briefs. The city's
brief stressed that a refusal to provide replacement-cost coverage can
compel homeowners to simply abandon a building, contributing to
urban blight. The city also claimed that such practices frustrate efforts
of the federal, state, and city governments to preserve and promote
owner-occupied homes in the city and thwart the government's attempt to renew the nation's cities.

The Court of Appeals announced its decision on October 20, 1992.
The opinion, written by Judge Frank H. Easterbrook, reversed Judge
Stadtmueller's ruling dismissing the Federal Fair Housing Act claim,
but upheld his ruling dismissing our claims under the Wisconsin
Insurance Code and Regulations (in *NAACP v. American Family*
1992).

In the district court, American Family had agreed that under the
Federal Fair Housing Act proof of disparate impact would be enough
for the plaintiffs to win their case. In a footnote to its brief to the Court
of Appeals, the DOJ suggested that this might not be the case because
the issue had not yet been decided by the U.S. Supreme Court. When
American Family's attorneys read this footnote, they tried to change
their position. However, Judge Easterbrook rejected this effort and
ruled that American Family would be bound by its earlier concession

that the plaintiffs' claim under the Federal Fair Housing Act would, if viable, be subject to proof under a disparate-impact formula. The Court stated: "We therefore assume the plaintiffs' burden under [the Federal Fair Housing Act] is lighter than their burden under the other legal theories."

The Seventh Circuit's decision made the front page of the *Chicago Tribune* (Grady and Nickerson 1992), in addition to beng covered in major newspapers nationwide. American Family sought to have the Court of Appeals reconsider its decision regarding disparate impact. When this effort failed, American Family hired a Madison law firm, LaFollette & Sinykin, to file a petition with the U.S. Supreme Court (petition for writ of certiorari, March 8, 1993, *American Family Mutual Insurance Company v. NAACP*). On May 17, 1993, the Court, without comment, declined to hear American Family's appeal. In a May 18, 1993, editorial, the *Milwaukee Journal* praised the Supreme Court's action and contended that the Court of Appeals ruled wisely that the plaintiffs need not prove intent to discriminate, but must show only discriminatory results (*Milwaukee Journal* Editorial Board 1993).

INVESTIGATION, DISCOVERY, AND TRIAL PREPARATION

Between July 27, 1990, and February 6, 1995, the date when a jury trial was to begin, parties for both sides conducted over 130 depositions. The parties exchanged over 220 requests to produce documents, resulting in over 44,000 pages of documentation. The NAACP plaintiffs had 8 experts and American Family had 10 experts ready to testify.

We knew American Family had been confronted frequently about redlining, and we sought to document these confrontations as well as the company's responses. We felt it was important to document the company's knowledge of its policies and practices and their impact on black areas. It is proper to infer an intent to discriminate when an organization knows its policies have discriminatory effects and procedures can be taken to eliminate them, but the company fails to do so.

We also sought studies done by American Family to document the impact of its underwriting criteria on its homeowner's insurance business. We had assumed, like jurors probably would assume, that the insurance industry was highly scientific in its determination of its business practices. Yet, American Family could supply almost no specific studies concerning the relationship between its underwriting

criteria and its experience paying for losses. The company had begun
a study of losses for homes with woodburning stoves, but not for losses
resulting when an insured has a bad credit history, an adjacent home
is vacant or in poor condition, the home is old or of low value, or the
property's market value is low compared to its replacement cost;
nevertheless, all were matters for which the company had underwriting guidelines.

Questioning of employees and agents also showed considerable confusion over what the company's underwriting policies were and how
they were to be applied. For example, depositions of several underwriters and underwriting supervisors had to be supplemented to correct confusion over company policy on insuring properties whose
market value was substantially lower than replacement cost. Also,
interpretations of when poor credit was to be considered in making
decisions varied greatly.

Our investigation included interviews with American Family agents
and former agents both black and white. Agents who had district
managers other than Michael Shannon confirmed that they were discouraged from selling in predominantly black neighborhoods. A Cable
News Network (CNN) newsmagazine segment on December 5, 1993,
about property insurance redlining featured NAACP's case against
American Family and included interviews with Reuben Ziehlsdorf as
well as with agent Dale Latus, who discussed with special assignment
correspondent Mark Feldstein the means by which American Family
tried to discourage him from selling in predominantly black areas.
Tapes of the CNN broadcast were a dramatic and graphic means for
communicating NAACP's case against American Family to HUD, DOJ,
congressional and state officials, and the general public.[2]

QUANTITATIVE EVIDENCE

We asked Professors Squires and Velez to apply the methods they had
developed for statistically analyzing variations in an insurance company's market share depending on the racial composition of the neighborhood. Velez obtained computer files from the Office of the Insurance Commissioner containing zip code disclosure information for
the state's 25 largest insurers for the Milwaukee area from the second
quarter of 1989 through the second quarter of 1991. In the second
quarter of 1990, the quarter that ended just before our lawsuit was
filed, American Family had the largest negative correlation between

its market share and the percentage of black residents in a zip code of all the 25 companies and the Wisconsin Insurance Plan.

To take into consideration possible nonracial reasons for differences in market share, Velez used regression analysis to control for the impact of poverty, the number and percentage of owner-occupied housing units, the percentage of housing units that are vacant, and the percentage of housing units built before 1940. Even after controlling for these factors, race remained statistically significantly associated with American Family's market share in Milwaukee neighborhoods. Velez' calculations suggested that for every percentage increase in the number of blacks, approximately 14 fewer policies were written in a zip code.

In June 1993, the *Wisconsin State Journal* (Sereno and Hall 1993) and the *Milwaukee Journal* (Norman 1993) reported results of their analyses of zip code data obtained from the Insurance Commissioner's office concerning sales of homeowner's insurance in Milwaukee. Both articles reached conclusions similar to those of Squires and Velez.

Squires and Velez furthermore applied the methodology they had developed for analyzing office locations to American Family's offices in Milwaukee (Squires, Velez, and Taeuber 1990). Data for 1960, 1970, 1980, and 1990 showed that American Family closed offices in areas that became black. In 1980 American Family had no office locations in the seven neighborhood areas of Milwaukee that were 25 percent or more nonwhite. In 1960, American Family had had three offices there, but at that time the areas around the offices were less than 1 percent black. Between 1980 and 1990, American Family increased its share of all agency locations from approximately 19 percent to 25 percent, but the company's increase was almost exclusively in the suburbs. In Milwaukee, where approximately 98 percent of Milwaukee County's blacks reside, American Family increased the number of its locations from 25 to 27. In the suburbs, however, the number of locations jumped from 36 to 55. Velez concluded that there was a strong negative correlation between the percentage minority of a neighborhood and the number of agency locations.

To control for traits other than race, Velez conducted multiple regression analysis including variables for the percentage of residents below the poverty line, the percentage of housing units that were vacant, average income, the number of owner-occupied units, the percentage of housing units built before 1940, and median value of housing. The negative impact of racial composition on agency location was substantial and significant even after controlling for such traits.

Many of Milwaukee's zip codes are highly segregated racially. The data available from the insurance commissioner did not specify whether American Family's policies were on homes in the predominantly white sections or the predominantly black sections of zip codes. Analysis by census tract would better help the jury understand that the company avoided black neighborhoods. To conduct such an analysis, we engaged Professor George Galster, an urban economist who has done analyses of racial discrimination in mortgage lending. Galster's multiple regression analysis showed that the racial composition of a census tract was a statistically significant predictor of the number of American Family homeowners' policies in force per 1,000 single-family homes, even after controlling for age, overcrowding, vacancy rate, housing value, education, and income characteristics of the tract. He also separately analyzed the policies that American Family had sold since the lawsuit was filed in 1990 and the policies sold by it earlier. This was done to determine whether filing the lawsuit had resulted in increased sales of replacement-cost policies in the black areas. He concluded that race was an even *more* significant predictor of policy sales and policy type after the case was filed.

Even after controlling for features of the dwelling and the age, value, and incomes of the tract, Galster also concluded that as the percentage black of a census tract increased, American Family sold significantly fewer guaranteed replacement-cost "Goldstar" policies and significantly more inferior repair-cost policies. (The top-of-the-line Goldstar policy guarantees that the company will pay the full cost of replacing the home even if the cost exceeds the policy amount.)

Galster's analysis of American Family's market penetration differed from Velez' analysis in that Galster did not attempt to compare American Family's market behavior to that of other companies. Rather, Galster's studies examined American Family's policies as a percentage of the owner-occupied dwellings that might have been insured. The statistical accuracy of his studies depended primarily on the accuracy of the census and the data that American Family supplied from its own records, not on how accurately other companies reported data. Such studies can be done even when there is no source of data on homeowner's insurance sales by other companies.

On the other hand, the market-share studies by Squires and Velez included only properties that the private insurance companies or the FAIR Plan have in fact decided are insurable. If one assumes that the general motivation and operations of insurance companies are similar, it is more difficult for an insurance company to explain away differences in its market share than to advance reasons for differences in market penetration. Especially if both market penetration and market-share studies show sizable and statistically significant racial differences, these data reinforce each other and contribute to an inference of intentional racial discrimination.

Based on rates filed with the Wisconsin Insurance Commissioner, American Family's premiums were as low or lower than those of its competitors. When homeowners were forced to obtain insurance from another company, they had to pay higher premiums. Galster estimated that approximately 8,990 people would have obtained American Family insurance if it had not reduced its market penetration because of race. He assumed that the distribution of insurance companies chosen when American Family was not available was the same as the distribution of the market shares of the other companies in zip codes that were 30 percent or more black. For a $50,000 frame home with a $250 deductible, the weighted average premium for other companies was $65 higher than American Family's $112 premium. This meant that the approximately 8,990 persons who had to obtain insurance from another company paid more than $580,000 more for premiums during 1992 because of American Family's practices. Using similar methodology, Galster estimated that more than 3,000 policyholders received inferior repair-cost policies from American Family rather than standard replacement-cost policies.

The minimum value that a property must be to qualify for American Family insurance varied, depending on policy type, between $20,000 and $40,000. American Family required that a home be built after 1950 to qualify for a Goldstar policy. Galster concluded that American Family's minimum value and age requirements for qualifying for a Goldstar policy had a disparate impact on black homeowners. He compared the percentage of homes with values under the minimum and the percentage of homes built before 1950 in 80 percent or more black census tracts with the overall percentage of such homes in all census tracts of Milwaukee County. He concluded that the differences in proportion were statistically significant. The percentage of homes under $20,000 in black areas was approximately four times the percentage citywide (24 percent versus 6 percent, respectively). Eighty percent of the homes in black areas had a value under $40,000 compared with 32 percent citywide. In black areas, 76 percent of homes were built before 1950 compared with 60 percent citywide.

Even though our case was brought on behalf of a class of black homeowners, we documented the impact of nonblack minorities, especially Hispanics, on American Family's market share, market penetration, and agency locations. American Family's relatively low market penetration in some areas that had few blacks was explained by a relatively high combined black and Hispanic population. If we had included nonblack minorities as whites, the contrast in market shares or market penetration would not have appeared as dramatic as when nonblack minorities are included with blacks.

EXPERT WITNESSES

Most jurors are unlikely to have the experience or expertise to undertake the complex task of determining whether a large corporation's behavior evidences an intent to racially discriminate. Expert witnesses are thus necessary to help the jury understand and analyze the facts in order to determine whether or not racial discrimination has occurred. Calvin Bradford, a consultant in housing and economic development, as well as in discrimination in housing and credit, was hired as an expert witness to review and analyze the data we received from American Family as a result of our investigation and discovery, as well as data from other studies.

We also engaged an actuary as an expert to explain insurance practices to jurors and to analyze American Family's rating structure, underwriting criteria, and homeowner's policy offerings. Alan Schwartz, who had worked for the New Jersey and North Carolina insurance commissioners, was hired to assist with evaluating the financial condition of American Family and its profitability. He was also able to analyze American Family's underwriting criteria and determine whether they were justified by adequate actuarial studies. He was prepared to explain to the jury the options insurance companies have, including adjusting their rates rather than rejecting a class of possible insureds.

We also engaged Dr. Gloria Johnson-Powell, a psychiatrist at Harvard Medical School, to provide expert testimony concerning the psychological impact of racial discrimination on blacks. An understanding of the impact of racial discrimination on homeowners seeking insurance would help the jury determine the appropriate monetary damages.

One of American Family's anticipated defenses was that high losses in predominantly black areas explained both its low market share and low market penetration, as well as its lack of offices. When American Family's economist, Hal Sider, repeated Galster's market penetration study, he included data on American Family's loss experience as an additional nonrace variable. Even after consideration of American Family's loss experience, Sider's study supported the conclusion that race was significant in explaining American Family's policy penetration.

NAACP PLAINTIFFS AND THE DEPARTMENT OF JUSTICE

In part, government civil rights policy is created in cases litigated by the Justice Department's Civil Rights Division. The DOJ's decisions in cases help define the relationship between victims of discrimination and government's willingness to enforce laws designed to protect them. The DOJ's willingness to litigate a case against one company can have a significant impact on the insurance industry as a whole.

In fall 1988, the Civil Rights Division of the Department of Justice contacted the NAACP redlining committee because DOJ was investigating American Family. On February 3, 1989, a *Milwaukee Sentinel* article reported the DOJ's bias probe (Mulvey 1989). The Department had authority to file its own case against American Family or to intervene in any case that the NAACP might bring against American Family. We began to evaluate the advantages and disadvantages of the DOJ's participation.

The NAACP, the ACLU, the Legal Aid Society, and the private plaintiffs view homeowner's insurance redlining cases from a different perspective than does the DOJ. Blacks, the poor, and people whose civil liberties are violated are the constituents of the NAACP, the Legal Aid Society, and the ACLU. However, everyone is DOJ's constituency, including both consumers of insurance and insurance companies; the department's more general and less-focused purpose is to enforce the civil rights laws.

To use the current example, when the DOJ decides that a plaintiff's civil rights have been violated by an insurance company, because the DOJ is not considered an advocate of any particular constituency, its participation can enhance the credibility of a private plaintiff's case. On the other hand, if the DOJ investigates a discrimination complaint and fails to support the position of the plaintiffs, this can be perceived as tacit approval of the insurance company's behavior. Also, interpretation of the civil rights laws by the DOJ varies from time to time and from administration to administration. For example, during the Reagan and Bush administrations, the government took the position that

Congress did not recognize the effects test when it passed the Fair Housing Act in 1968. In the *American Family* case, the Bush administration informed the Seventh Circuit that the issue was not yet decided by the U.S. Supreme Court. The administration of Bill Clinton, however, has publicly abandoned this position and supports the effects test in fair housing and fair lending cases.[3]

Another area where views of the federal government and of private plaintiffs have differed has been that of the nature and scope of remedies for civil rights violations. For the most part, the ACLU, the NAACP, and other civil rights litigators have supported remedies with specific measurable goals and timetables. The imposition of measurable goals and timetables, however, is frequently opposed as "affirmative action" and as "quotas."

Another advantage of a DOJ case can be additional resources for investigation, discovery, and presentation of a case at trial. The DOJ, however, does not share information before it files a case. An investigation by the Department may put pressure on the defendant, but it does not necessarily provide private plaintiffs with documents, evidence, or the results of expert analysis to use at trial. Private litigants, however, must share the results of discovery and their investigation with the DOJ to reduce the risk of a DOJ determination that explicitly or implicitly "clears" the defendant. Moreover, keeping the Department informed may prevent or shorten a trial delay once the DOJ decides to participate.

On February 5, 1993, the Justice Department's investigation was again front-page news (*Journal* Staff 1993). The hopes of the insurance industry that the DOJ would not sue American Family were reflected in a later *Milwaukee Journal* piece by Eric Englund (1993), who opined that "the investigation by the Justice Department will provide an objective basis to evaluate the realities of today and define how tomorrows can be even better." Englund no doubt hoped that inaction by the DOJ would infer that American Family was not violating the Federal Fair Housing Act.

In April 1994, however, shortly after President Clinton appointed Deval Patrick as Assistant Attorney General for Civil Rights, the DOJ notified American Family that it intended to sue, but would consider a settlement before filing.

American Family understood the importance of political concerns to civil rights enforcement. It thus hired the Washington, D.C., firm of Patton, Boggs & Blow to represent it in its discussions with the DOJ. Secretary of Commerce Ronald Brown had been a member of that firm before his appointment to the Cabinet. The firm was widely recognized as an effective lobbying firm with extensive experience in representation before the federal government.

Shortly after the DOJ notified American Family of its intent to sue, political pressure to cut back on aggressive enforcement of civil rights laws prohibiting redlining intensified. The business community's response to the DOJ's August 1994 mortgage redlining case settlement with Chevy Chase Federal Savings Bank (discussed briefly by Ritter in the next chapter in this volume) included harsh criticism of the DOJ and of its Civil Rights Division. The DOJ had filed its case against Chevy Chase and a settlement of it on the same day. No one who applied for a loan and was turned down was a plaintiff in the case. The DOJ based its case on facts showing that Chevy Chase avoided lending for houses in the parts of its market that were predominantly black. The DOJ's market-avoidance theories came under fire (Associated Press 1994), with critics calling the settlement "a glaring example of the shot gun approach to resolving questions of bias." The *New York Times* and other newspapers reported on the split between banking regulators and the Department on the issue of the extent to which selective marketing practices constituted unlawful discrimination. As is not uncommon in Washington, D.C., the regulators were siding with the business that they oversee against consumer and civil rights activists and their allies at HUD and the DOJ. The White House was deeply reluctant to be drawn into what may be a no-win situation; taking sides could mean offending either civil rights activists or the business community (Bradsher 1994, Associated Press 1994).

The fall 1994 congressional elections resulted in Republican Party control of both the U.S. House of Representatives and the Senate for the first time in decades. Postelection analysis included criticism of the Clinton administration's record on civil rights. For example, *Newsweek* columnist Joe Klein criticized a continued belief in race-based remedies. In his opinion, "the Justice Department had pushed what *it* calls 'affirmative action' well beyond the point of reason" (p. 56). Klein believed that it was likely that an attack on race-based remedies would be the wedge issue of choice for Republicans in 1996 (Klein 1994).

After the November elections, Senator Orrin G. Hatch, the Utah Republican in line to head the Committee on the Judiciary, announced plans to hold hearings on the DOJ's civil rights policies. Hatch characterized the Department's policies "as moving in the direction of racial quotas" (in Greenhouse 1994). At the same time, civil rights organizations were pressing the Clinton administration to continue to intensify civil rights enforcement.

Matters were much simpler for the NAACP's plaintiffs, however. We were not feeling conflicting pressures from our constituents. Rather, they were unified in urging us to obtain the most effective and extensive relief we could for the class.

THE SETTLEMENT

An advantage of settlement is certainty. A judge or jury may provide no or very limited relief. Also, courts often approve settlements, the provisions of which the judge will not impose if defendants do not agree to them. When the parties agree, the remedies can be more creative and flexible.

The NAACP plaintiffs and American Family originally began settlement talks in fall 1991 shortly after the parties presented oral arguments to the Seventh Circuit. Unfortunately, talks halted after the ACLU of Wisconsin mailed a November 1991 fundraising letter about the redlining case against American Family. American Family claimed the letter was defamatory because it contended, and falsely so in American Family's view, that the company had an intentional, officially sanctioned corporate policy of refusing to sell homeowner's insurance to black people in the Milwaukee metropolitan area, based solely on their race and with the intent thereby to destroy the neighborhoods in which they live. American Family was especially upset because they believed the letter described its actions as a base and racially motivated campaign to inflict personal shame and financial loss on black people.

On March 30, 1992, American Family thus sued the ACLU of Wisconsin and its executive director for libel. American Family's attorney, Thomas Shriner, informed the press that the ACLU's letter was "the end of the settlement negotiations" (in Silver 1992). American Family's reaction to the ACLU's fundraising letter sharpened the disagreement between the parties over corporate responsibility for the effect of American Family's business practices. They disagreed about the personal responsibility of those who instituted the company's practices and knew about them. They also disagreed about the nature of the harm done to individuals whom the company treats in a discriminatory manner because of race.

The NAACP plaintiffs considered American Family's libel lawsuit a strategic lawsuit against public participation (a SLAPP suit) (in Blum 1992). The ACLU, for its part, countersued American Family, charging it with using the courts to intimidate the ACLU in violation of provisions of the state and Federal Fair Housing Acts, which prohibit retaliation against those who pursue Fair Housing Act claims and against those who assist them (Norman 1992). Needless to say, defending against American Family's libel suit and pursuing the counterclaim added to the resources that had to be devoted to the redlining issue by the ACLU.

Although the libel case had not been finally resolved, in fall 1993 American Family decided to resume settlement discussions. Meetings were frequent and lengthy and considered by both parties to be generally productive. In April 1994, while the parties were preparing detailed proposals for each other, the DOJ announced its intent to sue American Family. American Family stopped its negotiations with the NAACP plaintiffs and began discussions with DOJ. The NAACP plaintiffs were not invited to participate in them. The NAACP plaintiffs' counsel immediately traveled to Washington, D.C., to discuss with the DOJ the status of settlement discussions and the NAACP's settlement objectives and proposals, including proposals for community relief. We also discussed coordinating a DOJ case with our case. In January 1993, Judge Rudolph Randa, to whom the case had been transferred, had scheduled a final pretrial conference for January 13, 1995, and a jury trial to begin February 6, 1995.

In fall 1994 discussions involving all three parties, the NAACP plaintiffs, DOJ, and American Family, finally began. Because I could not be chief settlement negotiator, coordinate trial preparation, and do the courtroom trial work, the NAACP plaintiffs arranged with Walter Kelly, a prominent civil rights attorney, to be lead trial counsel.

In late December 1994, progress toward settlement justified extensions of the trial date, and the pace and timing of settlement discussions intensified. For example, on a family Christmas vacation, one of the telephone conferences I had with Deputy Assistant Attorney General for Civil Rights Kerry Scanlon, Justice's chief negotiator, and John Oberdorfer, American Family's chief negotiator, occurred on a mountain, where I had skied up to an outdoor telephone.

The counsel for the NAACP plaintiffs met often with them to discuss settlement proposals and strategy. On November 1, 1994, the NAACP and the U.S. attorney in Milwaukee met with leaders of black religious, business, and civil rights groups particularly to discuss community compensation. These groups voiced strong support for programs to improve accessibility and affordability of housing and to promote economic development. The programs should, they felt, involve the community in their design, operation, and implementation in order to have a significant and lasting impact.

Elements of the Settlement

In Milwaukee on March 30, 1995, Attorney General Janet Reno announced the filing of the DOJ's case against American Family and its simultaneous settlement (United States v. American Family 1995). The settlement agreements were filed with Judge Randa. The settlement was widely covered in the news, including a front-page story in the Los Angeles Times and articles in the Wall Street Journal, U.S.A. Today, the Washington Post, and Boston Globe. Taken as a whole, the settlement provides a means for American Family to serve the predominantly black community of Milwaukee to the same extent and in the same manner it serves the rest of Milwaukee. It also provides compensation to individuals and the community underserved by American Family in the past.

MONETARY COMPENSATION

A unique feature of this civil rights settlement is that it provides monetary relief not only for homeowners affected by American Family's past policies but also community compensation to provide future benefit to low- and moderate-income persons with homes in need of improvement or repair. Table 8.1 summarizes the monetary compensation provisions of the settlement.

In table 8.1, "Persons denied insurance" includes (1) those who applied and were rejected, (2) those who the company canceled or did not renew, (3) those who inquired about homeowner's insurance but who were told by the agent that they could not obtain it from American Family or were referred to another company or to the Wisconsin Insurance Plan, and (4) those who did not complete an application because of an action or inaction on the part of an agent or an American Family employee.

Part of the funds for persons who received repair-cost policies were allocated to claimants who suffered a loss that exceeded the policy limit on the inferior policy (see table 8.1). Such compensation is for the difference between the amount of the loss that would have been covered under a standard replacement-cost policy and the amount they received from American Family in settlement of their claim.

"Persons deterred" in table 8.1 are those who had an interest in applying to American Family but were deterred because they reason-

Table 8.1 MONETARY COMPENSATION IN *NAACP V. AMERICAN FAMILY*

Individual Compensation	Amount ($)	Limit per Person ($)
Persons denied insurance	3,000,000	15,000
Persons receiving repair-cost policies	1,500,000	2,000
Persons deterred from seeking insurance	420,000	1,000
Named plaintiffs and Milwaukee Branch of NAACP	80,000	10,000
Total	5,000,000	

Community Compensation	($)
Home purchase loans: interest rate subsidy	4,000,000
Home improvement loans: interest rate subsidy	1,500,000
Financing cost assistance	1,500,000
Emergency home repair assistance	2,000,000
Homeownership counseling	500,000
Total	9,500,000

Attorneys' Fees and Costs	($)
Costs	250,000
Attorneys' fees	1,750,000
Total	2,000,000

Total Amount of Settlement	16,500,000

ably concluded based upon objective facts that it was futile to apply because the company would not offer them a policy because of their race or color or the location of their home. These claims cannot be based solely on the publicity concerning the NAACP's suit or on a general assertion that American Family discriminated on the basis of race.

Persons who owned and occupied a single-family (one- to four-unit) home in the predominantly black area, no matter what their race, are eligible to share in the fund. Blacks with homes in Milwaukee outside the predominantly black community can also submit claims if they applied and were denied or had American Family insurance that was canceled or not renewed and they submit facts showing it was because of their race or color. No person is entitled to a share of the fund if the home posed a significant hazard that would have justified denial of insurance. The claimed discrimination must have occurred between July 27, 1984, and March 30, 1995.

All of the community compensation programs are for homes in the predominantly black community (see table 8.1). Interest rate subsidies can be as much as 4 percentage points. The subsidized loans will be available both through the Wisconsin Housing and Economic Development Agency, which sells municipal bonds to finance mortgages, and other private lenders. Financing cost-assistance grants of up to $3,000 per loan transaction can be used for downpayments, closing costs, mortgage insurance premiums, and appraisal fees for any loan program, not just with the NAACP insurance settlement subsidized loans.

Emergency home repair loans and grants will help people make repairs that qualify them for insurance and assist them in circumstances in which emergencies might lead to the inability to make house payments. Grants to agencies doing homeownership counseling and counseling on home maintenance help qualified families buy and continue to own homes in the predominantly black community (see table 8.1).

INCREASING SALES

For the NAACP plaintiffs, an essential component of the settlement with American Family is the company's commitment to increase its sales in the area that includes the predominantly black community of Milwaukee. Many of the provisions of the settlement are designed to enhance American Family's ability to meet this commitment. In the consent decree, American Family agreed with the NAACP plaintiffs and with the Justice Department to an objective of substantially increasing its sales of homeowner policies in the area of Milwaukee that includes the predominantly black community. In a separate agreement with the NAACP plaintiffs in which the DOJ did not join, American Family agreed to a specific goal of a total policy increase of 1,400 to 1,800 policies over five years, with an anticipated 400-policy increase in the first year. American Family exceeded the first-year goal and agreed with the NAACP to a total increase of 1,800.

Meeting increased sales goals requires additional offices. American Family agreed to hire or designate within six months four additional sales-agent positions with offices in the predominantly black community.

To provide an incentive to reach the goal for increased sales, American Family agreed to provide an extra $35 commission to its agents for each new homeowner's insurance policy on properties in the predominantly black area of Milwaukee. The DOJ did not join in this provision.

AFFIRMATIVE ACTION

The NAACP plaintiffs and American Family recognized that elimination of racially discriminatory practices and expanding sales of insurance to blacks would be enhanced by increasing employment of blacks. American Family agreed to make reasonable efforts to appoint within three years a number of black sales agents in southeastern Wisconsin that would be reasonably consistent with the percentage of blacks in that labor market. If this goal is achieved, American Family will double its agents to more than 20. The company has also agreed with the NAACP plaintiffs to goals for employment of underwriters, claims representatives, and overall employment of blacks consistent with the percentage of blacks in southeastern Wisconsin. American Family is required to report to the NAACP plaintiffs on its efforts to achieve these goals. Like the specific goals and timetables for increasing policy amounts and the specific commission incentive, these provisions for goals and timetables for employment of blacks were not joined in by the DOJ.

UNDERWRITING

To reduce opportunities for racial bias to be reflected in underwriting decisions, American Family has agreed to revise its underwriting standards to ensure that they are objective and based upon the individual traits of the home. The company's standards are to be directly related to the risk of loss or damage, and are to be capable of uniform application. American Family will no longer consider the age of a home or the traits of homes in the surrounding area. It will consider the condition of an adjacent home only if it presents an identifiable risk to the home for which insurance is sought. The mere fact that an adjacent home is not itself insurable will not be used as a basis for declining insurance. In addition, the company will limit consideration of a person's financial and credit status to objectively defined circumstances demonstrating a likelihood that the person would take action to cause losses covered by the policy and/or present false claims. Home inspections will be performed under objective criteria to identify conditions that enhance risk of loss. Applicants will be informed of repairs necessary to qualify.

To enhance the likelihood of consistent and uniform decisions by underwriters, American Family's urban underwriter must concur with any decision to reject, cancel, or not renew insurance for properties in the predominantly black area or to condition insurance on repairs being made. Also, the urban underwriter and the underwriting manager for the area must agree before credit information is used as the basis for denying an application or canceling or not renewing a policy.

American Family is also eliminating eligibility criteria for insurance, which had a disparate effect on the black community. The com-

~~pany is eliminating its minimum value and amount of insurance re-~~
quirements and will no longer take age into consideration even for
eligibility for Goldstar policies. American Family will be able to
charge a minimum premium to cover administrative, loss, and processing costs.

American Family is furthermore eliminating the requirement that
the market value of a home must be 80 percent or more of estimated
replacement cost to obtain replacement-cost homeowner's insurance.
A homeowner may obtain a standard replacement-cost policy (HO3)
if the market value is at least 40 percent of replacement cost and must
insure the home to at least 80 percent of replacement cost. In addition,
American Family has created a new policy type, a custom-value
homeowner's insurance policy, which provides flexibility for the consumer in determining how much coverage to obtain in excess of the
property's market value. If a home's market value is between 40 and
79 percent of replacement cost, the homeowner may pick a coverage
amount up to 79 percent of replacement. If the market value is between
10 and 40 percent of replacement cost, the homeowner may pick an
amount up to one and one-half times market value. In all other respects, custom-value policies are the same as standard homeowner's
policies. Premiums for them are calculated by multiplying a factor for
the percentage the requested amount of coverage is of the home's
estimated replacement cost by the premium American Family charges
for HO3 coverage at full replacement cost. Thus, American Family's
premium charge for custom-value policies is determined based on the
loss experience on all homes, including both those with standard
replacement-cost policies and those with custom-value policies.

Under the terms of the settlement, American Family will now offer
a Goldstar policy if the home's market value is at least 50 percent of
replacement cost. The company has stopped sales of repair-cost policies (HO8s and HO9s) and stopped endorsing a standard HO3 policy
that in effect made it a repair-cost policy. American Family had
charged *higher* premiums for these policies for inferior coverage. To
eliminate the differences in the incentives for agents to sell any one
of American Family's homeowner insurance products, American
Family has agreed not to vary the commission percentage based on
policy type.

MARKETING

American Family's marketing commitments include the following:

1. Undertake mass mailings and distribute at least 2,500 brochures
   each year.

2. Create new sales materials.
3. Obtain prospects for insurance from community organizations.
4. Appear on radio and television programs.
5. Develop a comprehensive urban marketing program.
6. Regularly advertise in the *Milwaukee Black Pages*, in black community newspapers, and on African American community radio stations.
7. Offer insurance to persons insured by the Wisconsin Insurance Plan if they appear to qualify.
8. Continue to employ an urban marketing director.
9. Advertise the company's job openings in the black community.

American Family's advertising will include blacks as customers and employees.

American Family has agreed to continue a training program it began prior to settlement. American Family is training all its employees, agents, and agents' employees regarding marketing, sales, and services to a racially and culturally diverse market, not just its Milwaukee area employees. The company will also provide special training to underwriters in the use of credit information and credit bureau reports and will train all its agents and employees involved with underwriting on its revised standards, including revision of its means for conducting property inspections. American Family will notify all employees and agents regarding the consent decree and the antidiscrimination requirements of civil rights laws.

To determine how effective its changes in policies and practices have been, American Family has agreed to pay for an independent testing agency to conduct a minimum of 50 paired tests per year. American Family has arranged with the Metropolitan Milwaukee Fair Housing Council to conduct this program and will share its results with the NAACP plaintiffs and the Justice Department.

Community Involvement with Settlement Compliance and Programs

In order for the community affected by discrimination to play a major role in accomplishing the changes provided for in the settlement agreement, the consent decree established a Class Committee of seven Milwaukee black homeowners. The Class Committee is charged with analyzing and responding to the numerous reports required of American Family semiannually over the five years of the settlement agreement. The Committee reviews American Family's policy growth in

~~black areas and, with American Family, sets specific objectives for~~
each year of the agreement. The Committee is working closely with
Milwaukee's Department of City Development and the Wisconsin
Housing and Economic Development Agency, who provide administrative services, and is establishing criteria and program requirements
for the community relief programs. The Committee has also worked
with the claims administrator to establish procedures for making
claims on the individual compensation fund. To meet its responsibilities on behalf of the community, interest earned on American Family's funds for the financing cost assistance, emergency home repair,
and homeownership counseling programs, as well as the individual
compensation fund, is available to the Committee to cover costs. At
the end of the five years, any interest remaining will be added to
the community-based relief programs. The Committee has sponsored numerous town meetings to explain the settlement and the
community relief programs, now called the "Greenline" programs,
as well as the claim forms and how to complete them.

RESPONSE TO THE SETTLEMENT

The response to the settlement by the insurance industry has included
scathing criticism, especially of the government's action. Jack Ramirez, of the National Association of Independent Insurers, described
the settlement as "the mother of all affirmative-action programs" and
claimed "the Justice Department used litigation scare tactics not only
to coerce money from an insurance company, but to impose racial
quotas in hiring and sales through the most detailed affirmative-action
micromanaging of a private business ever attempted" (in Novak 1995).
DOJ officials called Ramirez' criticism "outrageous" and added that
much of the wording of the settlement was driven by concerns of the
private plaintiffs (Novak 1995).

Because the Justice Department did not join in the agreement between American Family and the NAACP plaintiffs establishing goals
and timetables for hiring of blacks, criticism of the Clinton administration for supporting "affirmative action" is misplaced. The DOJ also
did not join in establishing a specific goal for increasing the number
of policies in Milwaukee's black community nor in the procedure for
future adjustments of that goal. If the policy growth total is not
reached, American Family is required to propose additional remedial

actions, and the NAACP plaintiffs may do likewise. The burden will be on American Family to show that its proposed additional steps are sufficient to reach the annual policy growth total.

As noted, the banking industry earlier harshly criticized Justice for its mortgage redlining settlement with the Chevy Chase Bank (Associated Press 1994; Bradsher 1994). These criticisms were not justified. Several criticisms of the Chevy Chase settlement, however, cannot be applied to the American Family settlement. In *American Family* there were clearly identified specific victims. In the *Chevy Chase* case the DOJ was the only plaintiff, whereas in *American Family*, the DOJ did not stand alone in defending the settlement, but was accompanied by the other named plaintiffs. Numerous articles about the settlement with American Family included interviews with the named plaintiffs and described some of the clearest evidence of the company's racial intent. Furthermore, even after settling, Chevy Chase vigorously denied it discriminated. In contrast, although the *American Family* case, like *Chevy Chase*, did not go to trial and no finding of discrimination was issued by a judge, according to the consent decree, American Family "neither admits *nor denies* the claims of the United States or the private plaintiffs" [emphasis supplied] (*United States v. American Family* 1995).

The DOJ's complaint charged American Family with intentional conduct, but did not allege disparate impact of the company's policies on predominantly black areas. In the *American Family* case, therefore, it would be unfair to criticize the DOJ for interpreting the Federal Fair Housing Act to cover claims of a disparate impact of insurance industry practices.

Judge Randa approved a notice that was published in the local newspapers and mailed to property homeowners in the predominantly black areas. The notice summarized the settlement and afforded class members an opportunity to submit written objections and to appear at a fairness hearing. No class member objected, and Judge Randa approved the settlement on July 13, 1995.

The insurance industry did not limit its critical response to issuing press statements. In summer and fall of 1995, insurance industry lobbyists had language inserted in a funding bill for HUD that would prevent HUD from spending funds to "sign, implement, or enforce any requirement or regulation relating to the application of the Fair Housing Act to the business of property insurance." The provision passed in the House of Representatives and was approved by Senate committees. The *National Underwriter* described the provision as "a legislative end run to keep HUD from trying to rectify legitimate

insurance ~~redlining and civil rights wrongs~~" ~~(National Underwriter~~
Editorial Board 1995). Fortunately, on September 27, 1995, the Senate
adopted a floor amendment sponsored by Wisconsin Senator Russell
Feingold, which deleted the redlining funding ban from the HUD
appropriations bill (Feingold 1995).

CONCLUSION

It is too early to assess the full impact of the NAACP plaintiffs' case
against American Family and its settlement. The case has helped to
educate HUD, the Justice Department, the Congress, the insurance
industry, and the general public about racial discrimination by homeowners' insurers, its effects, and ways to remedy it. As stated at the
beginning of this chapter, it is hoped that others will build upon the
success of this case. If efforts to document and expose racial discrimination by other companies in other locations continue, the insurance
industry will be unable to dismiss the *American Family* case as
unique and unrepresentative. At the same time, there is the risk
that the case and its settlement will encourage efforts by the industry to obtain legislative exemption from laws prohibiting racial
discrimination.

To build on the *American Family* case, fair housing and civil rights
organizations and the federal government must continue to expend
the resources that litigation requires and take the risks associated
with it. Despite significant political pressures, the Justice Department,
to its credit, joined with the NAACP plaintiffs to obtain a comprehensive and effective settlement. The government, however, should not
only settle cases but should also demonstrate its commitment to civil
rights enforcement by filing cases before settlement and, if necessary,
by submitting them to juries and judges for decision. Through determined and concerted efforts such as these, racial discrimination in
homeowner's insurance can be eliminated and remedied.

Notes

1. As described in previous chapters, FAIR Plans are residual market mechanisms
instituted to provide insurance to individuals who cannot obtain it in the voluntary
market.

2. For example, Senator Russell Feingold (1994), in his remarks upon introducing the Anti-Redlining and Insurance Disclosure Act of 1994, referred to the December 5, 1993, CNN broadcast and what he had learned about the facts alleged in the NAACP case against American Family.

3. The Clinton Justice Department, however, did not allege disparate impact in its complaint against American Family (United States v. American Family 1995). See text discussion on p. 182.

References

Associated Press. 1994. "Greenspan Denies Fed-Justice Dispute." Washington Post, November 3: p. B13.

Blum, Andrew. 1992. "SLAPP Suits Continue in High Gear." National Law Journal, May 18: p. 3.

Bradsher, Keith. 1994. "Rift in Administration over Justice Dept.'s Zeal in Fighting Bank-Loan Bias." New York Times, October 3: section 1, p. 14.

Conroy, Mary. 1990. "Insurer Accused of Bias." Madison Capital Times, July 27: p. 1A.

Englund, Eric. 1993. "Cries of 'Red-lining' in Insurance Industry Have No Basis." Milwaukee Journal, February 23.

Enriquez, Darryl. 1988. "Insurance Agents Allege Sales Bias." Milwaukee Journal, April 18.

Feingold, Senator Russell. 1994. Congressional Record, March 10: 2779–93.

_____. 1995. Congressional Record 141 (152, September 27): S14355–63.

Grady, William, and Matthew Nickerson. 1992. "Insurer Redlining Banned. U.S. Appeals Court Extends Protection of Fair Housing Law." Chicago Tribune, October 22: p. 1.

Greenhouse, Linda. 1994. "At the Bar: For Clinton, the Supreme Court's Docket Is a Mine Field of Politically Sensitive Cases." New York Times, November 18.

Gribble, James. 1990. "NAACP Suit Accuses Insurer of Redlining." Milwaukee Journal, July 27: p. 1.

Journal Staff. 1993. "Homeowners' Insurance: U.S. Investigating Redlining Here." Milwaukee Journal, February 5: p. 1.

Klein, Joe. 1994. "Whither Liberalism? The Question Is No Longer Direction, but Survival." Newsweek, November 21: p. 56.

Milwaukee Journal Editorial Board. 1993. "Right Ruling against Red-Lining." Milwaukee Journal, May 18.

Mulvey, Mike. 1989. "American Family Subject of Bias Probe." Milwaukee Sentinel, February 3: p. 5.

National Underwriter Editorial Board. 1995. "Insurer Attack on HUD Could Backfire." *National Underwriter*, August 21.

Norman, Jack. 1992. "Discrimination Case: ACLU Says Insurer Wants to Silence It: American Family's Libel Suit Prompts a Counter-Suit in Redlining Case Here." *Milwaukee Journal*, June 9: p. C6.

————. 1993. "Redlining Allegations: Insurer's Record Shows Disparities: Data Show American Family's Market Share Drops Off Dramatically in Minority Neighborhoods." *Milwaukee Journal*, June 15: p. 6.

Novak, Viveca. 1995. "U.S. Redlining Suit Settled by Insurer for $16 Million." *Wall Street Journal*, March 31.

Sereno, Jennifer, and Andy Hall. 1993. "Insurer Less Likely to Cover Blacks: American Family Defends Its Practices in Milwaukee." *Wisconsin State Journal*, June 12: p. 1A.

Silver, Jonathan. 1992. "Madison Insurer, ACLU, Draw Battle Lines." *Madison Capital Times*, March 31: p. 5B.

Squires, Gregory D., and William Velez. 1987. "Insurance Redlining and the Transformation of the Urban Metropolis." *Urban Affairs Quarterly* 23(1): 63–83.

Squires, Gregory D., William Velez, and Karl E. Taeuber. 1990. "Insurance Redlining, Agency Location, and the Process of Urban Disinvestment." Madison: University of Wisconsin-Madison, Center for Democracy and Ecology.

Sussman, Lawrence. 1990. "Redlining Lawsuit Called 'Cheap Shot.' Trade Group Spokesman Says NAACP Is Targeting a Practice of the Past." *Milwaukee Journal*, July 29.

Chapter Nine

RACIAL JUSTICE AND THE ROLE OF THE U.S. DEPARTMENT OF JUSTICE IN COMBATING INSURANCE REDLINING

Richard J. Ritter

The United States Department of Justice (DOJ) plays a central and powerful role in combating racial redlining in the home insurance industry, as evidenced by its involvement in the case of *United States v. American Family Mutual Insurance Company* (C.A. No. 95-C-0327 [E.D. Wisc. 1995]), discussed in the preceding chapter. This chapter begins with an overview of the Justice Department's role in eradicating discrimination in the general housing market through "pattern or practice" lawsuits and possible explanations for its failure, until recently, to bring any major race discrimination lawsuits against either mortgage lenders or property insurers—two important segments of the housing market covered by the Federal Fair Housing Act of 1968. The section following discusses approaches to developing pattern or practice insurance redlining cases, with reference to the Justice Department's lawsuit against American Family and the way in which it was patterned on the DOJ's model lending discrimination lawsuit against Decatur Federal Savings & Loan Association in Atlanta. The final section contains suggestions for future DOJ initiatives to challenge racial discrimination in the provision of homeowners insurance.

JUSTICE DEPARTMENT'S PATTERN OR PRACTICE AUTHORITY

The Justice Department has had pattern or practice authority to combat racial discrimination in housing since the Federal Fair Housing Act was originally passed by Congress in 1968.[1] Since then, the DOJ has brought hundreds of pattern or practice lawsuits around the country, contesting various forms of housing discrimination. Some of the department's landmark cases in fair housing law have challenged blockbusting (*United States v. Bob Lawrence Realty Inc.*, 474 F.2d 115

[5th Cir.], cert. denied, 414 U.S. 826 [1973]); racial steering of minority home seekers to certain areas (United States v. Pelzer Realty Co., 484 F.2d 438 [5th Cir. 1973], cert. denied, 416 U.S. 936 [1974]); racially discriminatory advertising (United States v. Hunter, 459 F.2d 205 [4th Cir.], cert. denied, 409 U.S. 934 [1972]); and municipal zoning ordinances that perpetuated residential racial segregation (United States v. City of Black Jack, 508 F.2d 1179 [8th Cir. 1974], cert. denied, 422 U.S. 1042 [1975]).

As the national debate over racial redlining by banks and property insurers escalated during the 1970s, prompting the U.S. Congress to pass anti-redlining legislation such as the Community Reinvestment Act (CRA) and the Home Mortgage Disclosure Act (HMDA), the Justice Department took significant steps to address the problem. In 1978 it sued the country's leading association of real estate appraisers, challenging racially discriminatory appraisal theories that had been embedded in standard appraisal texts for decades, namely, that the presence of certain racial and ethnic groups in a neighborhood had negative effects on property values (United States v. the American Institute of Real Estate Appraisers, 442 F. Supp. 1072 [N.D. Ill. 1977], appeal dismissed, 590 F.2d 242 [7th Cir. 1978]). The case was settled through a landmark consent decree removing all such references from the association's appraisal texts and training materials. The department also filed friend-of-the-court (amicus curiae) briefs in several private redlining lawsuits against both mortgage lenders and property insurers to establish the legal principle that such practices, if proven, violate the Fair Housing Act.[2] In the late 1970s and early 1980s, the DOJ commenced several investigations of blatant racial discrimination by lenders against Native Americans living on reservations that resulted in consent decrees prohibiting the defendants from redlining those areas. However, until the 1990s, the department had never sued a mortgage lender or property insurer for race discrimination in African American or Hispanic neighborhoods, the very types of discrimination that sparked much of the original debate over racial redlining. Why?

Part of the answer may lie in the complicated issues frequently posed by lending and property insurance cases. By the late 1970s, classical redlining seemd to be on the wane. Most lenders and home insurers no longer openly declared minority neighborhoods off-limits because of their racial characteristics. However, at some banks and insurance companies these overtly discriminatory policies were replaced by subtle underwriting, marketing, and agent location practices whose purpose or effect was to avoid any significant business from minority areas. Although such policies accomplished the same result as the more traditional forms of redlining—that is, few, if any, loans or insurance policies in minority areas—the task of proving that those practices singly or in tandem violated the Fair Housing Act posed unique and complex questions. Today, claims of racial discrimination in lending and insurance focus on seemingly race-neutral marketing and underwriting practices that may be applied in a racially discriminatory manner or have racially discriminatory effects.

"Bottom-line" racial disparities in home loan or home insurance originations may have many causes suggestive of possible unlawful discrimination. For example, marketing systems that include locating branches or offices exclusively or primarily in white areas are contributing factors, along with advertising and commission systems that are geared to suburban or affluent neighborhoods whose residents are predominantly white. Restrictive underwriting criteria and eligibility standards may further discourage marketing in minority areas. Disparate treatment of minority applicants or of those from minority areas through subtle manipulation of processing and underwriting standards may also contribute to the "bottom-line" disparities. Finally, lenders or insurers that conduct significant business in minority areas may engage in widespread discrimination through the "creaming" of risks, in which minority applicants are held to higher qualifying standards than similarly situated white applicants or are treated differently in the processing or terms and conditions of their loans or insurance policies.

Proving that these often intertwined marketing, processing, and underwriting practices violate the Fair Housing Act may require expensive and time-consuming analyses of voluminous statistical data, along with historical and anecdotal evidence of discrimination gleaned from company files and archive records, interviews with current and former employees or agents of the defendant, and testimony from individual applicants. Yet, it is precisely these types of complicated cases that Congress intended that the Justice Department undertake in giving the attorney general pattern or practice authority under the Fair Housing Act.

In the 1980s, jurisdictional questions may have inhibited the Justice Department from suing home insurers suspected of racial redlining. The department's authority under the Fair Housing Act to investigate discrimination in the home insurance industry was called into question by a 1984 federal appeals court decision (*Mackey v. Nationwide Insurance Companies*, 724 F.2d 419 [4th Cir. 1984]). Although that decision conflicted with a prior district court decision in another circuit,[3] it was the first appellate court ruling on this issue (see discussion by Dane, in chapter 2 of this volume).

BREAKING THE ICE—BACKGROUND TO AMERICAN FAMILY CASE

In July 1988, Paul Hancock became chief of the Justice Department's Housing and Civil Enforcement Section of the Civil Rights Division. Shortly thereafter, Hancock assigned Housing Section attorneys to investigate allegations of racial discrimination by the American Family Mutual Insurance Company in Milwaukee, Wisconsin, the largest home insurer in that area. (At approximately the same time, Housing Section staff were assigned to investigate alleged redlining practices by banks in Atlanta.) The American Family investigation was triggered by allegations in a Wisconsin State court lawsuit by several former agents that they were terminated because they sold too many policies in black neighborhoods.[4] One of the agents, Reuben Ziehlsdorf, alleged that his supervisor prevented him from meeting his sales quotas by instructing him not to sell policies to black persons. These overtly racial statements were recorded in a taped conversation Ziehlsdorf had with his supervisor. The Atlanta investigation was based on a Pulitzer prize-winning series of articles in the *Atlanta Journal-Constitution* titled "The Color of Money" (Dedman 1988), suggesting possible widespread racial redlining by Atlanta-area banks. One of the lenders prominently mentioned in those articles, Decatur Federal Savings & Loan Association, became the target of the DOJ's inquiry.

In December 1988, the Justice Department notified American Family of its investigation. The company refused to cooperate, citing the Fourth Circuit's decision in *Mackey v. Nationwide* (1984) as a jurisdictional bar to the investigation. Since the DOJ has no authority under the Fair Housing Act to subpoena company records in its investigations, it had to resort to outside sources and witnesses in pursuing the inquiry.

In July 1990, the NAACP and eight individuals filed a class-action lawsuit against American Family in federal district court in Milwaukee, alleging racial discrimination in the company's home insurance practices.[5] In December 1991, the district court dismissed the plaintiff's claims under the Fair Housing Act. Citing *Mackey v. Nationwide* (1984), the court held that racial discrimination in the provision of homeowners insurance was not covered by the Fair Housing Act. This decision further delayed the department's investigation. In an amicus curiae brief before the Court of Appeals for the Seventh Circuit, the department argued in support of the plaintiffs' appeal of the district court's ruling on the Fair Housing Act claim. In October 1992, the Seventh Circuit reversed this ruling and the case was remanded to the district court for trial.[6] Shortly therafter, the company agreed to cooperate in the Justice Department investigation.

THE DECATUR FEDERAL CASE

By this time, the DOJ had completed its investigation of Decatur Federal Savings & Loan Association and had sued the institution for racial redlining and other forms of lending discrimination against African Americans.[7] The complaint, the first of its kind against a major mortgage lender, accused Decatur Federal of redlining Atlanta's African American neighborhoods through subtle, racially discriminatory marketing and loan solicitation practices. The suit also alleged that African Americans who were rejected for loans were victims of disparate treatment by the bank's loan processors and underwriters. This lawsuit and accompanying settlement were groundbreaking for the precedents they set both within the lending industry and within the Justice Department in terms of developing complex lending and insurance discrimination cases. Many of the investigative techniques and legal theories developed in *Decatur Federal* were pursued in *American Family* after the DOJ resumed its investigation following the Seventh Circuit's 1992 decision. Accordingly, a brief review of the *Decatur Federal* case is important to understand the DOJ's lawsuit against American Family and its overall approach to proving racial discrimination in pattern or practice lending and insurance discrimination cases.

Statistical Analysis

The Justice Department found that from 1985 to 1990 Decatur Federal originated over 97 percent of its loans in majority white census tracts. Computer mapping showed heavy concentrations of loans in white neighborhoods throughout the Atlanta area, but no loans or only a trickle of loans in majority black areas. Decatur Federal's share of the home loan market in majority black areas was minuscule compared to its dominant market share in majority white areas. The market-share analysis was important because it controlled for explanations often advanced by lenders that their failure to make more loans in minority neighborhoods is attributable to socioeconomic disparities rather than to race. Specifically, minority neighborhoods typically include more low-income residents who cannot afford to purchase homes, experience lower population growth, have a higher proportion of rental dwellings, and experience fewer home sales and refinancings than white neighborhoods. These alleged disparities depress the demand for mortgage loans in minority areas. A market-share analysis discounts these possible socioeconomic explanations because, by definition, it looks only at credit demand (i.e., home loans made to presumably creditworthy borrowers by the bank and its competitors). Decatur Federal's strikingly low market share of loans in black neighborhoods compared to its large share of the market in white neighborhoods appeared unexplainable except on racial grounds.

An outside expert devised a statistical model using logistic regression analysis to determine whether African Americans were denied loans because of their race. That analysis, which was based on a review of several thousand loan files, showed that after controlling for the underwriting variables used by Decatur Federal's underwriters to determine credit qualifications, such as good credit history, acceptable debt-to-income ratios, and the like, many of the bank's rejections of African American applicants could not be explained except on racial grounds. The disparate treatment was further confirmed by a review of the loan files of accepted white applicants that the regression model identified as having qualifications closely similar to those of rejected African American applicants.

Historical and Anecdotal Evidence

The DOJ analyzed Decatur Federal's lending practices from the time it opened for business in 1927. It tracked the history of the bank's business operations in white areas compared to African American areas, such as branch and office locations, market territory delineations under the Community Reinvestment Act (CRA), efforts to solicit loan applications from minority areas through sales calls on real estate agents and builders active in those areas, advertising practices, commission systems, and types of loan products offered.

The DOJ found that all but 1 of the 43 branches and all 8 mortgage offices opened by Decatur Federal since 1927 were located in predominantly white areas. The only branch that opened in an African American area was closed after only three years of operation. Another branch that was in a predominantly white area when originally opened in the 1950s was closed in the 1980s when the surrounding area became predominantly African American. In the late 1970s, Decatur Federal racially gerrymandered its loan service area under the CRA to exclude over 75 percent of the black population of the city of Atlanta and Fulton County, Georgia, from its market.

Decatur Federal relied on account executives working on commission to solicit loans business. Virtually all of the account executives were white, and virtually all of the real estate agents and builders on whom they made sales calls were located in predominantly white areas. Interviews with current and former employees suggested that this was pursuant to a conscious redlining scheme. A Decatur Federal account executive stated that she was specifically instructed not to solicit loan business "south of I-20," which included many of Atlanta's black neighborhoods.

Commission systems, advertising practices, and product offerings further insured that the bank would attract loan applicants almost exclusively from white areas. The account executives' commissions increased proportionately with loan sizes, which further discouraged executives from soliciting loans in black neighborhoods where sales prices were disproportionately lower than in white neighborhoods. Decatur Federal rarely advertised through minority-directed media and made little effort to market Federal Housing Administration (FHA) or Veterans Administration (VA) loans—which it knew were in high demand in many minority neighborhoods—in part because of the low downpayment requirements of such loans and other eligibility standards favorable to low-income borrowers.

The Justice Department approach of blending statistical, historical, and anecdotal evidence to prove a pattern or practice of intentional discrimination has been endorsed by the U.S. Supreme Court in a phalanx of decisions in related areas of civil rights enforcement, such as employment discrimination, school desegregation, voting rights, and other fair housing cases.[8]

THE AMERICAN FAMILY CASE

Similar techniques and legal analyses were employed in the Justice Department's case against American Family. The DOJ has not publicly commented on the American Family case in the detail with which it has explained its action against Decatur Federal. Thus, the following discussion is based on information publicly disclosed by the DOJ in its complaint against American Family, the consent decree (*United States v. American Family* 1995) and accompanying press release, and the public record developed in the NAACP lawsuit (*NAACP v. American Family* 1992; see note 6, this chapter). The reader is also reminded that there was no trial or any judicial findings of discrimination against the company. Accordingly, the information recited reflects only evidence that from the plaintiffs' perspective might support a claim of racial redlining.

Statistical Analysis

Statistical analysis in an insurance redlining case is hampered by the absence of federal record-keeping and reporting requirements similar to those imposed on lenders under the Home Mortgage Disclosure Act (HMDA) of 1975. Among other items, the HMDA requires that lenders report the race of their loan applicants, the disposition of each application (accept, reject, etc.), and the census tract of the property on which the loan was sought. Regulation B implementing the Equal Credit Opportunity Act (ECOA) of 1974 requires that lenders retain loan files for at least 25 months to document their underwriting decisions.

Notwithstanding the absence of publicly available data for the home insurers at the federal level, statistical analysis remains an important component of an insurance redlining case, particularly if access to the insurer's records is obtained voluntarily or through discovery in civil litigation. Also, public information on home insurance activities may be available through state insurance commissioners. Some states, such as Wisconsin, require large home insurers to report to the insurance commissioner by zip code the numbers and types of homeowners policies they originate. Information on cancellations and non-renewals also may be reported.

MARKET SHARE

In the *American Family* case, a *Decatur Federal*-type market share analysis could be performed from the insurance commissioner's zip code data for the city of Milwaukee. There are approximately 28 zip codes in the city, three of which are predominantly black. Whites constitute the majority of the residents in the remaining zip codes. From 1985 to 1991, American Family originated only 8 percent of all reported homeowners policies in predominantly black zip codes, but wrote a stunning 32 percent of all policies in predominantly white zip codes (*United States v. American Family* 1995: Complaint, par. 16).

If access is obtained to the insurer's policy database, it is possible to conduct a more refined analysis of market-share disparities at the census tract level. The number of owner-occupied houses in a census tract is a fair indication of the demand or "market" for home insurance policies in the tract, since lenders almost uniformly require home-owners insurance as a condition for obtaining a mortgage to own a home. The insurer's database of policies should identify the street address of each policyholder. Those addresses may be tied to a census tract by a process known as geo-coding, which permits a comparison of the number of policies the company has on homes in each census tract to the number of owner-occupied homes in the tract. Such analysis may show that the insurer has policies on a significantly higher percentage of owner-occupied homes in majority white census tracts than in majority black census tracts. This, indeed, was the case in *American Family*, as Lynch demonstrated in the preceding chapter.

INFERIOR POLICIES MARKETED IN BLACK NEIGHBORHOODS

It may also be important in an insurance redlining case to examine market-share disparities according to the types of policies offered by the company. In *American Family*, the DOJ alleged that residents of African American neighborhoods were much more likely to receive inferior repair-cost policies from the company than were residents of white neighborhoods. Most home insurers offer a range of home in-surance policies with varying coverages, endorsements, and premi-ums. The least-desirable policies are usually called repair-cost poli-cies, because they cover only a limited number of perils and, in the event of damage to the dwelling, the insurer is only obliged to "repair" the property rather than restore it to its original condition using the same materials. (For instance, oak cabinets in a kitchen damaged by fire could be repaired with less-expensive cabinetry, regular glass could be substituted for leaded glass, etc. Or if the house were totally destroyed, the insured might have to locate another home if the re-building costs exceeded the policy limits.) Repair-cost policies fre-quently also have less-advantageous theft coverages and higher deductibles.

By contrast, the preferred homeowners policies are "all-risk" re-placement-cost policies. These policies cover a broad range of perils to the home and its contents. In the event of loss or damage to the dwelling, the insurer is obligated to restore the home to its original condition using like materials and construction. Under standard replacement-cost policies, the insurer's obligation runs up to the policy limits. Many insurers also offer top-end policies that guarantee replacement even if the claim exceeds the policy limits. These policies are aggressively marketed because the dwelling must be insured for 100 percent of its market value, resulting in higher premiums and higher agent commissions compared to lower-grade policies. American Family's guaranteed replacement-cost policy was called the "Gold Star" (*United States v. American Family* 1995: Complaint, par. 17).

Geo-coding the insurer's types of policies by census tract permits an assessment of the extent to which inferior repair-cost policies are differentially marketed in predominantly minority tracts compared to white tracts. As noted, the Justice Department alleged in *American Family* that homeowners in Milwaukee's African American neighborhoods were much more likely to receive repair-cost policies from the company than were homeowners in white areas. In 1990, 40.7 percent of American Family's policies in majority black census tracts had repair-cost coverage compared to only 5.6 percent in majority white census tracts. In other words, over 94 percent of the homes the company insured in majority white census tracts had replacement or Gold Star policies, whereas less than 60 percent of the homes it insured in majority black census tracts had these preferred policies (*United States v. American Family* 1995: Complaint, par. 17).

Insurers often claim that repair-cost policies are more prevalent in urban neighborhoods, where minorities are disproportionately concentrated, because there is a higher incidence of older, lower-priced houses in those areas than in white areas. Many of those homes represent potential "moral hazards" because their replacement costs greatly exceed their fair market values, thus tempting their owners to commit arson to collect the insurance proceeds and buy a more expensive home elsewhere. Older homes, so the argument goes, usually have higher replacement costs than newer homes because of the types of materials found in older homes (e.g., plaster walls, expensive woodwork, and elaborate or rare crown molding). In many cities, such as Milwaukee, there are proportionately more older homes in majority black neighborhoods than in majority white neighborhoods, and the values of those homes may be depressed by the racial dynamics of the housing market (i.e., few whites wanting to buy homes in black neighborhoods).

There appears to be no publicly available data to support the "moral hazard" theory, at least as applied to homeowners, which assumes their willingness to commit a felony (arson) and destroy what in most cases is their only place of habitation. As an underwriting rule, this theory dictates that a home's fair market value reasonably approximate its replacement cost. Most insurers require that the fair market value be at least 80 percent of the replacement cost in order to receive replacement coverage.[9] Homes that fall below that benchmark are usually limited to repair-cost coverage.

It is difficult to test the validity of insurer arguments in support of the 80 percent rule because they rarely retain in any central file the fair market value or estimated replacement costs of homes they insure, or data showing higher rates of arson as the gap widens between market value and replacement cost. The determination of market value and replacement cost is usually made by the agent at the time the application is taken, and is either retained in the agent's file or discarded once the policy goes into effect. Also, the agent's assessment of market value is frequently subjective or determined without uniform procedures or guidelines. Some agents may base market value on property tax assessments, whereas others may rely on sales listings of comparable homes in the neighborhood. Some agents may simply take the applicant's word for the market value of the property. The determination of replacement costs is usually more standardized. Most insurers instruct their agents to use well-known reference books (such as the *Boeckh Residential Building Guide*), which calculate replacement cost based upon the square footage of the property, type of construction (masonry, brick, wood), and building costs in the area.

However, the absence of a reliable database of information in the insurer's records on the market values and replacement costs of homes in its portfolio may also make it more difficult for the company to defend against claims of racial redlining. If the insurer's policy statistics show significantly more repair-cost policies in minority census tracts than in white census tracts, the bare contention that these disparities are attributable to a "moral hazard" allegedly caused by low market values and high replacement costs may not be sufficient to rebut the inference from those statistics that the differences are attributable to race rather than risk. Courts or juries might minimize the probative value of the insurer's arguments, since the company could easily have instructed its agents to provide the requisite market value and replacement-cost information for inclusion in the company's general database of information on its insureds. Presumably, that information combined with losses from arson would confirm whether there was any merit to the moral hazard claim.

Moreover, regression analysis based on census information may affirmatively refute this defense. Such analysis might show, for example, that after controlling for differences in the age and value of the housing stock as reflected by census data, homes in majority black tracts are still significantly more likely to receive repair-cost policies from the company than comparable homes in majority white tracts. The NAACP plaintiffs' regression analysis found such disparities in American Family, as reported by Lynch in the preceding chapter.

ANALYSIS OF LOSS DATA

Insurers often claim that they experience proportionately higher losses on homes in minority neighborhoods than in white neighborhoods and that this explains any disparities in market share or in numbers or types of policies written on homes in those areas (see Squires, chapter 1; and Klein, chapter 3, this volume). This assumes that the insurer has analyzed its loss data and found the risk of insuring homes in minority neighborhoods so high that it had to limit the number of insured homes or "exposures" in those areas. This could also explain the absence of aggressive marketing and fewer agent offices in those areas. However, insurers may not have previously analyzed their loss experience with those objectives in mind, rendering such post hoc explanations suspect or pretextual. (See *Price Waterhouse v. Hopkins*, 490 U.S. 228, 252 [1989], holding that a defendant [in a Title VII case] may not prevail "by offering a legitimate and sufficient reason for its decision if that reason did not motivate it at the time of the decision.")

Moreover, careful analysis of the insurer's loss data may belie any factual basis for these arguments. Such analyses may require expert assistance and complicated merging of databases. An insurer's loss information may be retained in files or databases separate from policy information, and, as noted earlier, insurers rarely, if ever, identify their policyholders by race or census tract. Claims and losses, if any, experienced on each policy must be linked to a policy number or other identifier in a database containing the policyholder's street address, type of policy, deductibles, and endorsements. The street address permits the geo-coding of this information by census tract, providing the final link for assessing any differences in claims and losses by policy type between white and minority census tracts. In this way, it is possible to test whether insurance redlining is driven by negative loss experience.

It is also important to understand how home insurers analyze claims and losses. There are three principal components to such analysis:

1. *Loss frequency*: the number of claims per policy or "exposure." Loss frequency is often used as an initial screen to determine if one policy feature or type of risk is generating claims at a faster rate than others.
2. *Loss severity*: the average amount of claims per policy.
3. *Loss ratio*: the amount of claims paid divided by the amount of premiums the company has received. This is frequently the factor that most concerns insurers because of its effect on overall profitability. Insurers frequently establish benchmarks for acceptable loss ratios in a given product line.

Analysis of loss data, particularly loss ratios, by census tract permits an assessment of the extent to which losses influence the insurer's market share in a particular community. In *American Family*, the company's loss data did not explain or otherwise justify its low overall market share of policies on homes in majority black census tracts in Milwaukee County, nor the preponderance of repair-cost policies in those areas (*United States v. American Family* 1995: Complaint, par. 18).

Other Evidence of Racial Discrimination

AGENT OFFICE LOCATIONS

Office locations are a central component of a home insurer's marketing program (see Schultz, chapter 4, this volume). Interviews with former sales agents, industry studies, and other sources may show that most of an agent's insurance business comes from within a two- to three-mile radius of his or her office. Frequently, most direct mail, telemarketing, cold calls, and other solicitation practices done by or on behalf of an agent occur within these areas. In *American Family*, the Justice Department alleged that the company's agents rarely placed their offices in majority black neighborhoods in Milwaukee, thus seriously inhibiting their ability to generate business and market share in those neighborhoods (*United States v. American Family* 1995: Complaint, pars. 12, 13).[10] Moreover, the DOJ alleged that as the racial residential patterns within Milwaukee changed over the years, American Family "closed a sales office each time the predominant racial group in the area surrounding the office changed from white persons to black persons" (ibid: par. 13). Once the area became predominantly black, the company almost never located a new office in those neighborhoods (ibid: par. 13). (American Family established only one new office in an area that was predominantly African American at the time the office opened.)

Current and past years' telephone directories (available in public libraries) are an important source of information for tracking the placement and movement of an insurer's office locations in response to changing racial demographics.[11] If an office address appears in one year's directory but is missing from the next, it can be assumed the office was closed or relocated. The addresses listed in each year's directory can be geo-coded to census tracts to show the racial composition of the general area where the office was located and the appropriate decennial census to show changes in racial demographics. Computer mapping of these data may present a graphic and compelling portrait of agents closing or moving their offices away from expanding African American neighborhoods. Further analysis may show that these patterns cannot be explained on nonracial grounds, such as differences in loss costs, household income, owner-occupancy, and the condition of homes in majority black census tracts compared to majority white tracts (Squires, Velez, and Taeuber 1991; see also chapter 4, this volume).

Risk Classification and Underwriting

In *Decatur Federal*, the DOJ used logistic multiple regression analysis and comparisons of individual loan files to establish a pattern or practice of racial discrimination in loan processing and underwriting. Home insurers often do not maintain files documenting their underwriting decisions in ways that would permit a regression analysis of the type used in the *Decatur Federal* and other Justice Department lending discrimination investigations. Also, as noted earlier, insurers are under no obligation to record the race of their applicants.

Individual agents or brokers are frequently viewed as home insurers' "front line" underwriters. They are chiefly responsible for deciding whether a property meets the company's underwriting standards. Their judgments are frequently based on visual inspection of the exterior of the premises, with an interior inspection left to the agent's discretion. The agent's observations and other findings on the property's condition may not be recorded at all, or may be kept only in the agent's files, and even then not systematically.

Home insurers also rely on specially trained review underwriters. However, such underwriters may not evaluate all, or even most, of the applications approved by the agents, and they rarely review risks the agents deem unacceptable. Frequently, their work is limited to reviewing unbound applications (i.e., those the agents request to be reviewed by an underwriter before becoming effective) and applications from agents whose insureds experience unusually high losses or submit large numbers of claims. If time permits, they may review samples of agents' bound applications to monitor compliance with general underwriting standards. Credit reports may be examined by either agents or review underwriters allegedly to determine the applicant's ability to make timely premium payments and/or propensity to commit insurance fraud. However, this too is usually left to their discretion.

Whereas statistical analysis of a sample of homeowners' insurance applications for which there is complete underwriting information might yield meaningful results, there are other means of proving intentional racial discrimination in home insurance underwriting. These methods are discussed next.

Historical Evidence. The insurer's archival records and old underwriting manuals may show that in earlier years the company explicitly considered the race of the applicant or the race of the neighborhood in deciding whether, or on what terms, to offer home insurance policies. For example, the records may show a prior policy of requiring more rigorous inspections of homes in black neighborhoods or of neighborhoods experiencing racial population changes, or restrictions on the type of policies offered in those areas.[12] Such evidence of past intentional discrimination may be probative of the company's current practices if recent statistics show continuing racial patterns such as low market share and a prevalence of repair-cost policies in minority neighborhoods.[13] At a minimum, such evidence imposes a heavy burden on the insurer to explain the continuing statistical disparities on nonracial grounds.

Information from Current and Former Agents and Underwriters. Testimony and documents from the insurer's current or former agents and underwriters may also bolster claims of insurance redlining. Some might acknowledge receiving explicit or thinly disguised directions at sales or staff meetings to avoid insuring homes in minority areas because of race. The statements of several former American Family agents that they were instructed not to write insurance for "too many" African American applicants triggered the Justice Department's investigation of the company. According to the Justice Department complaint, the company's employees, including district managers and underwriters, instructed sales agents that American Family "did not desire homeowner's insurance business from the area of black population concentration in the City of Milwaukee" (*United*

States v. American Family 1995: Complaint, par. 11). This information was conveyed through the use of maps, "red flag" documents, and other means that the DOJ concluded "emphasized racial considerations" (ibid.: Complaint, par. 11).

Some agents or underwriters might acknowledge that homes in minority neighborhoods are subject to more frequent or vigorous inspections than comparable homes in white areas or that trivial defects, such as peeling paint on garages or broken panes of glass, are used as pretexts not to write policies on homes in minority neighborhoods, whereas similar defects on homes in white neighborhoods are routinely overlooked. Failure of homes in minority neighborhoods to meet vague underwriting criteria, such as "pride of ownership," may be used to mask such race-based differences in treatment.

Agents or underwriters also might acknowledge that they were instructed to reject otherwise insurable homes in minority neighborhoods because of the presence of boarded-up properties or large numbers of commercial establishments in those areas, and that such concerns were rarely, if ever, used to deny coverage on homes in white areas with similar neighborhood conditions.

Agents furthermore might admit receiving instructions from their supervisors not to follow up on telephone inquiries from home insurance applicants in minority neighborhoods, or to inform them that the company did not write replacement-cost policies in their area. In *American Family*, the Justice Department alleged that the company's agents avoided business in African American neighborhoods in Milwaukee by "refusing to return telephone calls and/or by failing to keep appointments, even when a homeowner in that community sought homeowner's insurance" (*United States v. American Family* 1995: Complaint, par. 14). Matched-pair testing may corroborate the agent's testimony as well as provide independent evidence of such racially discriminatory practices.

Testimony of Applicants for Insurance. Testimony from African Americans who sought homeowners policies from American Family was an important component of the NAACP's lawsuit against the company. The plaintiffs' experiences, as recounted in the NAACP complaint, included refusals by American Family agents to conduct drive-by inspections of their homes to determine if they qualified for replacement-cost coverage and failures by agents to keep appointments or to return telephone calls to process their requests for home insurance (*NAACP v. American Family* 1992; see note 6, this chapter).

As noted in the discussion of Decatur Federal, the Justice Department found that the bank's commission system rewarded loan originators for soliciting high-end loans, which inhibited their interest and willingness to solicit loans in many black neighborhoods where sale prices were disproportionately lower than in the more affluent white suburbs. A similar problem was uncovered in *American Family*. The company's agents received increased commissions for policies on higher-priced homes because of the higher coverages and correspondingly higher premiums associated with those properties.

However, the commission system contained a further and perhaps even more serious inhibition to marketing in minority neighborhoods. American Family agents received a lower rate of commission on repair-cost policies than on replacement-cost policies, regardless of the amount of insurance purchased by the policyholder and the individual premiums (*United States v. American Family* 1995: Complaint, par. 21). Since the agents had been indoctrinated to believe that most homes in predominantly African American neighborhoods of Milwaukee only qualified for repair-cost policies because of the 80 percent rule, there were significantly less financial incentives to solicit home insurance in those areas. Such an obvious deterrent to marketing in minority neighborhoods was another component in the DOJ's complaint alleging an overall scheme by the company to avoid doing significant home insurance business in African American neighborhoods because of race.

As in *Decatur Federal*, an analysis of American Family's advertising practices showed that they too were geared primarily to the white community. The company and its agents rarely used minority-directed advertising, and when such advertising was conducted, it was through newspapers, radio stations, and other outlets targeted to discrete segments of the white community (*United States v. American Family* 1995: Complaint, par. 19).

Legal Theories

The Justice Department alleged that American Family intentionally redlined African American neighborhoods in Milwaukee from equal access to homeowners insurance because of race. It relied on the same Supreme Court guidelines for proving intentional discrimination in pattern or practice cases that formed the basis of the department's lawsuit against Decatur Federal. As discussed previously, the evidence supporting this claim was based on an array of statistics showing unexplained racial disparities in market share, types of policies written in African American neighborhoods, and placement of offices. The statistics were buttressed by anecdotal evidence of intentional racial discrimination in the company's underwriting practices and disparate treatment of applicants for homeowners insurance from African American neighborhoods. Marketing systems, commission structures, and advertising practices geared toward developing business in the white community also supported the inference that the company intended not to attract significant home insurance business from African American neighborhoods in Milwaukee because of race.

DISPARATE-IMPACT DISCRIMINATION

The Justice Department's complaint did not allege that any of American Family's home insurance policies or practices were unlawful under the disparate-impact test. Under this legal theory, as applied to insurance redlining, policies or practices that have an adverse impact on racial minorities or residents of minority areas violate the Fair Housing Act unless the insurer proves they are required by business necessity and that there is no less-discriminatory means of accomplishing the same business objectives. Under disparate-impact analysis, the plaintiff does not have to prove that the challenged policies or practices were intended for a racially discriminatory purpose or were part of an overall scheme to redline minority neighborhoods because of race. As discussed by Dane in chapter 2, the disparate-impact test has been endorsed under the Fair Housing Act by virtually all of the federal courts of appeals. The Supreme Court has sanctioned its use under Title VII, but has yet to decide whether it applies to the Fair Housing Act.

In a recent redlining lawsuit against a mortgage lender in the Washington, D.C., area, the Justice Department alleged that the bank's marketing practices were both intentionally discriminatory and had unlawful effects under the disparate impact theory (*United States v. Chevy Chase Federal Savings Bank et al.*, C.A. No. 94-1-1842JG [D.D.C. 1994]). Much of the Justice Department's evidence against Chevy Chase Federal Savings Bank paralleled the evidence of intentional racial redlining and marketing discrimination found in *Decatur Federal*.[14] Nevertheless, the complaint against Chevy Chase also contained a specific allegation of discrimination under the disparate-impact standard.

> The totality of the policies and practices described herein amount to a redlining of African American residential neighborhoods of the Washington D.C. metropolitan area. . . . The policies and practices are intended to deny, and *have the effect of denying*, an equal opportunity to residents of African American neighborhoods, to obtain mortgage financing and other types of credit transactions. *The policies and practices causing the racial impact are not justified by business necessity.* (*United States v. Chevy Chase* 1994: Complaint, par. 31, emphasis supplied)

In light of *Chevy Chase*, it is fair to ask why the Justice Department did not allege violations under the disparate-impact theory in its complaint against American Family, since both cases involved similar forms of racial redlining. The department has traditionally emphasized probing for intentional discrimination in pattern or practice investigations under the Fair Housing Act. As noted, the Supreme Court and lower court decisions permit analysis of a wide range of direct and circumstantial evidence to prove intentional discrimination. Some cases, although amenable to disparate-impact analysis, may be more effectively presented under a theory of intentional discrimination. Evidence of a pattern of intentional discrimination often has the strongest effect on judges and juries, prompting broad injunctive relief and large compensatory and punitive damage awards in some cases. Although a disparate-impact violation was alleged in the department's complaint against Chevy Chase, it was ancillary to the allegations of a pattern or practice of intentional racial redlining.

Unlike insurance, disparate-impact analysis has long been recognized by courts in lending discrimination cases under both the Fair Housing Act and the Equal Credit Opportunity Act (ECOA).[15] It is also codified in federal banking agency regulations.[16] However, at the time of the Justice Department's investigation of American Family, no court had applied disparate-impact analysis in an insurance redlining case, and the U.S. Department of Housing and Urban Development (HUD) has yet to explicitly adopt the effects test in its regulations implementing the Fair Housing Act. There was also the issue of whether the McCarran-Ferguson Act of 1945 precludes disparate-impact analysis in insurance redlining cases, with insurers alleging such analyses inevitably clash with principles of fair discrimination and risk classification sanctioned under state insurance laws (see discussion in Dane, chapter 2). The judicial imbroglio over the disparate-impact test in insurance redlining cases may have further dissuaded the department from including such an allegation in its complaint against American Family.

Proponents of the disparate-impact test argue that it is ideally suited to many underwriting issues that often surface in the debate over racial redlining, such as minimum property values, maximum age requirements, and the 80 percent rule, each of which disproportionately excludes homes in predominantly minority urban neighborhoods from coverage under certain types of policies (see Squires, chapter 1; and Powers, chapter 6, this volume). The test may also apply to insurer marketing practices (see United States v. Chevy Chase 1994). Although disparate-impact claims were absent from the Justice Department's complaint against American Family, the consent decree requires significant changes in the company's underwriting practices, such as elimination of minimum value and maximum age requirements that are often the focus of disparate-impact analysis (see discussion upcoming). It is also noteworthy that American Family presumably did not view the underwriting changes mandated by the consent decree as conflicting with its obligations under Wisconsin insurance laws or regulations. This suggests that the McCarran-Ferguson Act may not be a serious obstacle to disparate-impact challenges under the Fair Housing Act.

Minimum Property Value Requirements. Many insurers impose minimum property value or coverage requirements for homeowners insurance.[17] Those minimums may vary depending on the type of policy. For example, the insurer may require that homes have a value of at least $40,000 for replacement-cost coverage and $60,000 for a guaranteed replacement-cost policy. Census data are customarily used to determine whether such seemingly neutral economic requirements have an adverse impact on classes protected by civil rights laws, including the Fair Housing Act (see Dane, chapter 2; and Powers, chapter 6, this volume).[18] In this instance, census data for a particular community may show that homes in minority census tracts are much more likely to fall below the $40,000 minimum for replacement-cost coverage than homes in white census tracts and that even greater disparities exist at the $60,000 threshold for guaranteed replacement-cost policies.

Maximum Age Requirements. Many insurers will not write certain types of homeowners policies (frequently guaranteed replacement cost) on homes over a certain age—for example, those more than 30 years old or built before 1960. Census data on the age of the housing stock in a community frequently show that older homes that fail to meet the insurer's minimums are disproportionately concentrated in minority census tracts, again establishing the adverse impact of such standards on protected classes.

The 80 Percent Rule. Many home insurers require, as a condition for replacement-cost coverage, that the market value of the property approximate its replacement cost to avoid creating a "moral hazard" (i.e., the incentive to commit arson) and to provide sufficient premium to cover total or catastrophic losses. The 80 percent rule previously discussed, or variants of it, is a common benchmark for determining the minimum-market-value-to-replacement-cost ratio for replacement-cost policies. Establishing the adverse impact of such requirements on homes in minority areas through census data is problematical because the census provides no information on the replacement cost of homes. However, insurers may readily admit when faced with their own policy records showing disproportionately fewer replacement-cost policies in minority areas than in white areas that the 80 percent rule is the principal cause of these disparities. Testimony from agents that the rule inhibits their ability to market such policies in minority neighborhoods bolsters the impact claim. Such evidence should be sufficient to establish the discriminatory effect of the 80 percent rule and to require the insurer to justify the policy.

Credit Histories. Many home insurers use credit bureau histories to determine whether the insured is an acceptable risk for a homeowners policy. Recently, some insurers have resorted to credit scoring systems for automobile policies and may also use them for homeowners insurance (Scism 1995). The rationale for such checks is that insureds who experience financial problems, as revealed by their credit reports, may be tempted to submit fraudulent claims or have difficulty making timely payments of their premiums. Insurers rarely obtain the applicant's or insured's consent for such checks or provide them an opportunity to explain derogatory information. Frequently, the decision whether to seek a credit report is left to the discretion of the agent or underwriter, with no written guidelines or standards for evaluating the reports or determining the bases for disqualification. The insurer may order credit bureau reports on only a small percentage of applicants or insureds, and the reports may not be retained in the company's files. Insurers also will not record the race or sex of persons subject to such checks.

The failure of insurers to maintain complete or reliable records of their use of credit histories complicates analysis of the possible adverse impact of such use on classes protected by the Fair Housing

Act. However, lack of records may permit use of surrogate data, such as HMDA reports or academic studies showing that certain racial groups are more likely to have blemished credit histories than whites. Such data could at least establish that a home insurer's use of credit bureau histories is highly likely to have an adverse impact on racial minorities.

Business Justifications. Insurers will furnish purported justifications for all of the practices just described. Minimum property values or coverages are allegedly necessary to generate sufficient premium on each policy to cover administrative expenses and possible losses. Maximum age requirements assume that older properties are likely to have more structural defects than newer homes. Older homes, particularly those built before World War II, may lack updated electrical and plumbing facilities. Roofs frequently deteriorate after 15–20 years. The presumption that older homes pose higher risks may or may not be supported by the insurer's loss data. Some companies may not retain loss records in databases that permit such an analysis, and may rely on industry or academic studies to support an underwriting rule. Whether such evidence is sufficient to justify the practice under the disparate-impact test is open to question.[19]

In addition, the 80 percent market-value-to-replacement-cost standard is allegedly necessary to minimize the risk of arson (the "moral hazard"). Insurers may also allege that the rule protects consumers from underinsuring their homes and that it is necessary to generate sufficient premium to cover losses. Credit checks, as noted, are allegedly necessary to insure against fraudulent claims or delinquent payment of premium.

Under disparate-impact analysis, the insurer must prove that these practices are required by business necessity once adverse impact is shown. To meet that standard, the insurer must provide empirical evidence based on its business experience that the practice is necessary to accomplish the purported justification. Unsubstantiated testimony and reliance on "accepted industry practice" is ordinarily not sufficient (*Mieth v. Dothard*, 418 F. Supp. 1169, 1182 [M.D. Ala. 1976], aff'd. sub nom, *Dothard v. Rawlinson*, 433 U.S. 321 [1977]) (minimum height-weight requirements for prison guards that had an adverse impact on women applicants were not required by business necessity where the justification was based on unsubstantiated testimony of prison officials that the requirements were commonly followed at other prisons and that applicants below the height-weight minimums would not have sufficient strength to control prison inmates).

Less-Discriminatory Alternatives. Even if the insurer proves a business justification for the challenged practice, it may still be unlawful if there is a less-discriminatory alternative that meets the insurer's business needs.[20] This may be an Achilles heel in the armor of insurer defenses to adverse-impact claims in redlining cases. Minimum premiums may be a less-discriminatory alternative to minimum property values. Such premiums would presumably be based on the amount needed to cover losses and administrative expenses and provide an acceptable profit for the type of policy offered. Inspections based on objective and uniformly applied criteria may be a less-discriminatory alternative to the blanket exclusion of properties solely because of their age. Also, applicants or insureds whose properties need repairs based on such inspections should still be eligible for coverage if the necessary repairs are made within a reasonable time period. These alternatives were expressly agreed to by American Family in the consent decree settling the consolidated lawsuits of the private plaintiffs and Justice Department (*United States v. American Family* 1995).

Objective and uniformly applied underwriting guidelines that are directly related to the risk of loss or damage, such as the condition of the roof, heating, wiring, or plumbing as revealed by an inspection, seem plainly preferable and more valid measures of risk than arbitrary or vague criteria that may have racially discriminatory effects. For example, these standards should be better predictors of property loss or damage claims than an agent's subjective assessment that a home does not exhibit "pride of ownership." Individualized inspections could replace other commonly used underwriting criteria that have racially discriminatory effects, such as denying insurance on otherwise insurable homes because of the poor condition of an adjacent home or homes in the surrounding neighborhood. In the consent decree, American Family agreed to eliminate all such references from its underwriting manuals and to develop objective standards for individualized assessments of property risks (*United States v. American Family* 1995: par. II D).

There are less-discriminatory alternatives to the 80 percent rule, as evidenced by the custom-value replacement-cost policy adopted in the *American Family* consent decree. That policy dramatically lowers the market-value-to-replacement-cost ratio from 80 percent to 10 percent, opening a vast new market for such policies in inner-city neighborhoods. The policy is presumably priced to ensure sufficient premium to cover losses. Objective and uniformly applied standards for evaluating credit bureau reports also appear preferable to leaving such matters to the unbridled discretion of company agents and underwriters. The development of such standards is also contemplated by the consent decree in *American Family* (*United States v. American Family* 1995: par. II D 4[f]).

FUTURE JUSTICE DEPARTMENT INITIATIVES

Racial discrimination in the provision of homeowners insurance remains a pressing national problem that demands attention and certainly no less priority than lending discrimination or other types of housing discrimination. Having developed an investigative framework and solid legal theories for combating insurance redlining, it is essential that the Justice Department sustain the initiative forged by the experience in *American Family* and pursue new insurance redlining investigations. Accordingly, the Justice Department might consider the following measures in planning future enforcement initiatives in this area.

- Actively seek new redlining investigations. This search should include reviewing academic studies or newspaper articles that identify specific companies suspected of racial redlining or other forms of discrimination prohibited by the Fair Housing Act; tracking federal and state court lawsuits against home insurers that allege possible patterns of Fair Housing Act violations and consider intervening or participating as amicus curiae in those cases; and consulting community groups and others who have conducted testing of home insurers suspected of racial redlining for possible targets of pattern or practice investigations.
- Expand the DOJ Housing Section's testing program—which is currently geared toward detecting discrimination in the home sale and rental market—to include testing of home insurers.
- Conduct joint investigations with HUD of property insurers suspected of racial redlining as a follow-up to the plan for joint lending discrimination investigations announced by HUD and DOJ several years ago.
- In consultation with HUD, research state insurance laws and regulations to determine whether the McCarran-Ferguson Act poses any legitimate impediments to disparate-impact cases, such as those involving challenges to marketing and underwriting criteria.
- Include allegations of disparate-impact discrimination in appropriate cases, perhaps in addition to intentional discrimination following the *Chevy Chase* precedent.

- Propose and support federal legislation requiring insurers to publicly report data on their home insurance activities similar to the
  reporting obligations imposed on lenders under the HMDA. Such
  information should include data by census tract on pricing and
  numbers and types of home insurance policies issued, denied, canceled, renewed, and not renewed. The reports should also identify
  the race and income level of all reported applicants and policyholders, the race of the insurer's agents, and the office locations of
  these agents by census tract.
- Include in the DOJ's legislative agenda a request to Congress to
  amend the Fair Housing Act to provide the DOJ with subpoena
  power in pattern or practice investigations. HUD has such powers
  in pursuing its investigations, and there seems little reason to de-
  prive the attorney general of such power to enforce the act. Although many banks and insurers have voluntarily cooperated in
  DOJ investigations, there is no assurance that this will occur in all
  instances, and the absence of subpoena power deprives the DOJ of
  important leverage in ensuring a full and expeditious disclosure of
  necessary information.

Whereas this may be an ambitious agenda in an era of tight federal
budgets, it is fully in keeping with the Justice Department's traditional
role of focusing its pattern or practice resources on complex and difficult cases and forging new ground in civil rights enforcement. The
department can and should continue to pursue an aggressive program
to combat racially discriminatory practices in the home insurance
industry.

Notes

The views expressed in this chapter are those of the author and do not necessarily
represent the views of the U.S. Department of Justice.

1. The pattern or practice provisions of the Fair Housing Act (42 U.S.C. 3614) provide
that "whenever the Attorney General has reasonable cause to believe that any person
or group of persons is engaged in a pattern or practice of resistance to the full enjoyment
of any of the rights guaranteed by [the Fair Housing Act], or that any group of persons
has been denied any of the rights granted by [the Act] and such denial raises an issue
of general public importance, the Attorney General may commence a civil action in
any appropriate United States district court."

2. For example, the DOJ filed amicus curiae briefs in *Laufman v. Oakley Building &
Loan Co.* (408 F. Supp. 489 [S.D. Ohio 1976]) (bank redlining); and in *Dunn v. Midwestern Indemnity Co.* (472 F. Supp. 1106 [S.D. Ohio 1979]) (insurance redlining).

3. *Dunn v. Midwestern Indemnity Co.* (1979).

4. *Ziehlsdorf et al. v. American Family Insurance Group*, Case No. 88-CV-1082 (Waukesha Co. Cir. Ct.).

5. *NAACP et al. v. American Family Mutual Insurance Co.*, Case No. 90-C-0792 (E.D. Wis.).

6. *NAACP v. American Family Mutual Insurance Company*, 978 F.2d 287 (7th Cir. 1992), cert. denied, 113 Sup. Ct. 2335 (1993).

7. *United States v. Decatur Federal Savings & Loan Association*, C.A. No. 1 92-CV-2198 (N.D. Ga. 1992).

8. See, for example, *Teamsters v. United States*, 431 U.S. 324 (1977) and *Hazelwood School District v. United States*, 433 U.S. 299 (1977), emphasizing the role of statistical and historical analysis in employment discrimination cases; and *Bazemore v. Friday*, 478 U.S. 385 (1986), sanctioning the use of regression analysis to prove disparate treatment. See also *Village of Arlington Heights v. Metropolitan Housing Development Corp.*, 429 U.S. 252, 265-266 (1977), a Fair Housing Act case holding that intentional discrimination may be established through a "sensitive inquiry into such circumstantial and direct evidence of intent as may be available" and that "smoking gun" evidence is not required. Actions that have clearly foreseeable adverse racial effects may, along with other evidence, prove intentional discrimination, such as racial gerrymandering of voting districts (*Gomillion v. Lightfoot*, 364 U.S. 339 [1960]) or school attendance zones (*Columbus Board of Education v. Penick*, 443 U.S. 449 [1979]). As the Supreme Court noted in *Washington v. Davis* (426 U.S. 229, 242 [1976]), an invidious purpose may be inferred from disproportionate impact where the disparities are so severe and longstanding that they are "very difficult to explain on nonracial grounds."

These precedents for proving intentional discrimination through statistics and other circumstantial evidence are to be distinguished from disparate-impact or so-called effects test cases that emanate from *Griggs v. Duke Power Company* (401 U.S. 424 [1971]), a job discrimination case under Title VII of the Civil Rights Act of 1964. In that case, the Supreme Court held that employment practices with adverse racial effects, even if not intended for an invidious purpose, are unlawful under Title VII if there is no business necessity for the practice or there is a less-discriminatory alternative. See also *Albemarle Paper Co. v. Moody* (422 U.S. 405 [1975]); *Dothard v. Rawlinson* (433 U.S. 321 [1977]); *Connecticut v. Teal* (457 U.S. 440 [1982]); and *Watson v. Fort Worth Bank & Trust* (487 U.S. 977 [1988]). The disparate-impact test has been adopted by virtually all of the federal appellate courts in Fair Housing Act cases, but the Supreme Court has yet to address whether or how it should be applied in such cases, as it has done in job discrimination cases. See *Town of Huntington, New York v. Huntington Branch, NAACP* (488 U.S. 15 [1988]).

9. This so-called 80 percent rule is based on the assumption that the cost of the lot and foundation, which would survive any total loss, is approximatley 20 percent of the value of the home. By requiring insurance for 80 percent of replacement cost, insurers effectively require homeowners to obtain coverage for 100 percent of any maximum loss. The rule is also premised on the purported need to ensure sufficient premium to cover total losses.

10. According to the Justice Department complaint, American Family exercised significant control over where its agents could locate their offices by requiring district manager approval of office sitings (*United States v. American Family* 1995: Complaint, par. 12).

11. Telephone directories may be the only source of such information if the insurer claims it has no records showing agent office locations in earlier years and which offices, if any, were closed or relocated.

12. It is not surprising to find such explicit references to race in an insurer's files, even after the passage of the 1968 Fair Housing Act. For most of this century, standard appraisal texts perpetuated the stereotype that the presence of racial minorities in an area had a negative effect on property values. Indeed, such explicit references to race remained in many appraisal publications until as recently as 1977 when, as noted earlier, the Justice Department instrumented their removal through its landmark lawsuit against the appraisal industry (in *United States v. American Institute of Real Estate Appraisers* 1978).

13. "Proof that an employer engaged in racial discrimination prior to the effective date of Title VII might in some circumstances support the inference that such discrimination continued, particularly where relevant aspects of the decisionmaking process had undergone little changes" (*Hazelwood School District et al. v. United States*, 433 U.S. at 309, n. 15 [1977]). See also *Teamsters v. United States*, 431 U.S. at 340, n. 20 (1976) ("Statistics showing racial and ethnic imbalance [between the employer's workforce and the relevant labor market] are probative . . . because such imbalance is often a telltale sign of purposeful discrimination").

14. Disparate-impact violations were not alleged in *Decatur Federal* because that lawsuit was brought under the Bush administration, which continued to adhere to the Reagan administration's views that Congress did not recognize the effect test when it passed the Fair Housing Act in 1968. This position was argued in the Supreme Court by the U.S. solicitor general in an amicus curiae brief in *Town of Huntington, New York v. Huntington Branch, NAACP* (1988). The Clinton administration has publicly abandoned this position and supports the effects test in fair housing and fair lending cases.

15. See *Old West End Ass'n v. Buckeye Federal Savings & Loan Ass'n*, 675 F. Supp. 1100 (N.D. Ohio 1987); *Thomas v. First Federal Savings Bank of Indiana*, 653 F. Supp. 1330 (N.D. Ind. 1987); *Hansen v. Veterans Administration*, 800 F.2d 1381 (5th Cir. 1986); *Steptoe v. Savings of America*, 800 F. Supp. 1542 (N.D. Ohio 1992).

16. See Regulation B of the Federal Reserve Board recognizing the disparate-impact test under the ECOA (12 C.F.R. 202.6[a], n. 2), and the federal Interagency Policy Statement on Fair Lending, 59 Fed. Reg. 18266, March 8, 1994.

17. The insurance eligibility requirements discussed in this and the next subsection, such as minimum value and age of housing requirements, are hypothetical and are not based on American Family's policy requirements.

18. See also *Griggs v. Duke Power Co.* (1971) (Title VII); *Smith v. Town of Clarkton, N.C.*, 682 F.2d 1055 (4th Cir. 1982) (Fair Housing Act); *Halet v. Wend Investment Co.*, 672 F.2d 1305 (9th Cir. 1982) (Fair Housing Act); *Guardians Association of New York Police Dept. v. Civil Service Comm'n*, 630 F.2d 79, cert. denied, 452 U.S. 940 (1981) (Title VII); *Uniform Guidelines on Employee Selection Procedures*, 29 C.F.R. 1607 (1991); *Hazelwood School District et al. v. United States*, 433 U.S. 299, 308 fn. 14 (1977).

19. This might depend on how courts define an insurer's burden of proof in disparate-impact cases. If the company must prove a business necessity under the strict empirical standards suggested by *Griggs v. Duke Power Co.* (1971), *Albemarle Paper Co. v. Moody* (1975), and *Dothard v. Rawlinson* (1977), conclusions from industry or academic studies may be too general or speculative to meet this burden. The insurer's inability to justify such practices from its own experience and pool of insureds, when such information could have been retained and/or analyzed, may weigh against the defendant.

20. Under Title VII, the plaintiff has the burden of proof on this issue (*Griggs v. Duke Power Co.* [1971], *Albemarle Paper Co. v. Moody* [1975], *Dothard v. Rawlinson* [1977], and the 1991 amendments to Title VII). Some courts in Fair Housing Act cases place this burden on the defendant (see, e.g., *Resident Advisory Board v. Rizzo*, 564 F.2d 126 [3rd Cir. 1977], cert. denied, 435 U.S. 908 [1978]).

References

Dedman, Bill. 1988. "The Color of Money: Home Mortgage Lending Practices Discriminate against Blacks." *Atlanta Journal-Constitution*, May 1–4.

Scism, Leslie. 1995. "A Bad Credit Record Can Get You Rejected for Auto Insurance." *Wall Street Journal*, November 1–6.

Squires, Gregory D., William Velez, and Karl Taeuber. 1991. "Insurance Redlining, Agency Location and the Process of Urban Disinvestment." *Urban Affairs Quarterly* 26(4): 567–88.

Chapter Ten

WHAT'S WORKING: INSURANCE AS A LINK TO NEIGHBORHOOD REVITALIZATION

George Knight

The right to own property is an important American value. For most individuals, that right is expressed through homeownership. However, low-income people, especially those trying to buy their first home, often find themselves wandering a maze of complex barriers. The path out of the maze frequently involves counseling on matters such as credit, the home purchase process, downpayment requirements, debt capacity, physical inspection of the home, long-term debt management, and property and casualty insurance. Gaining access to property and casualty insurance can be a particularly difficult hurdle.

The Neighborhood Reinvestment Corporation assists a network of local nonprofit organizations that serve as intermediaries between aspiring homebuyers and insurance companies, lending institutions, and neighborhood improvement. As such, they stand alongside individual homebuyers in being closer to challenges such as insurance accessibility than any of the other parties in the homebuying process. This chapter describes how these NeighborWorks® organizations facilitate access to property and casualty insurance.

A HISTORICAL PERSPECTIVE

Neighborhood Reinvestment's history began in the late 1970s, when controversy over redlining in mortgage lending had reached a new crescendo. At that time the Urban Reinvestment Task Force was building a record of bringing residents, lenders, and public officials together. Because of its effectiveness, Congress changed the task force from its original interagency structure to a unique congressionally chartered entity: an independent, public nonprofit, the Neighborhood Reinvestment Corporation.

Almost from its inception, some of the neighborhood-based non-profits aligned with Neighborhood Reinvestment reported difficulty in obtaining standard residential insurance services. Residents were being declined insurance or their insurance was being canceled without explanation. Certain areas were experiencing a shortage of agents interested in serving them. Residents were underinsured and generally unable to get adequate coverage. At Neighborhood Reinvestment's invitation, insurance-industry leaders joined in a special demonstration project with Neighborhood Housing Services (NHS) of Chicago and the property-casualty insurance industry to explore new methods to meet residential insurance needs in older urban markets. Through the partnership that emerged in Chicago, company representatives were attracted to NHS block-by-block housing inspections and to the dialogue that NHS initiated for them with residents. In this way, companies saw the need for new products tailored to urban markets.

Since the time when Neighborhood Reinvestment was created, the NeighborWorks® network of independent, affordable-housing organizations has grown to encompass about 175 NeighborWorks® organizations, most typically known locally as Neighborhood Housing Services.

PARTNERSHIP MAKING

To join at the same table two very different groups of people who at times have viewed each other as adversaries can be anything but simple. The conditions needed to create a partnership can be a long way from that starting point.

Consider this meeting-room scenario:

- A resident who is a board member of a community-based organization sits opposite an insurance representative who she knows has never wanted to come into her neighborhood, who doesn't look or talk like her, and who may assume her house is dangerous, poorly kept, and essentially not worth the company's time. She doesn't view "property and casualty insurance" as an issue important enough for her to have come to this meeting.
- An insurance agent sits opposite a board member who doesn't look or talk like him, who lives on a block with abandoned houses, in a neighborhood where he does not feel welcome, and where he would never have considered homes to be worth insuring. In addition, he

knows he could make practically the same money selling one policy on a suburban property as he could selling three or four policies in this neighborhood. The agent is an entrepreneur: he is in the business to make money, and the corporate structure in which he is operating is less defined by where you sell than by how much you sell.

This scenario illustrates the range of insurance issues typically experienced in lower-income neighborhoods, and that are of concern to both resident and insurer:

- *Crime and safety.* For insurers, crime means greater losses because of theft and vandalism. For residents, crime can lead to higher claim rates. High claim rates raise premiums. They also become a reason for the carrier to drop the insurance.
- *Deferred maintenance.* Houses in certain neighborhoods, for a variety of reasons, may not have had needed repairs and maintenance. In particular, many do not have hard-wired smoke detectors. Insurers see this as a signal of potential losses from fire and liability.
- *Replacement cost versus market value.* Many urban neighborhoods have older homes built to higher standards with difficult-to-replace special features such as parquet floors, oak woodwork, or stained-glass windows. Insurance policies that would cover restoring these homes generally would be costly. Insurers do not want to cover properties for which the market value is much lower than the replacement cost, on the reasoning that this would create an incentive for arson. A few companies now have policies to cover "repair costs to contemporary standards," which can be an affordable substitute for replacement-cost coverage. Some question whether these repair policies are adequate.
- *Accessibility of insurance services.* Customers and potential customers in lower-income neighborhoods sometimes have limited access to agents, service centers, or insurance sales offices. This creates obstacles when consumers need answers to questions about claims or insurance policies. Policyholders of many income levels find insurance policies confusing if not indecipherable. In more-affluent communities, customers usually have more ready access to service centers and agents. The unavailability of agents in some areas also limits consumers' access to home and block inspections that can identify needed improvements for homeowners and public officials, and can lead to programs to finance improvements. Agents and other insurance personnel whose offices are in the actual

neighborhoods can inform residents of fire and security precautions that can, in turn, lower their insurance costs.

- *Education of underwriters.* The attitudes revealed in the previous meeting-room scenario reflect the need, often expressed by community-based groups, to bring underwriters and agents to neighborhoods to help them understand what is real and what is misperceived about crime and other public-safety concerns. Crime and neglect, as community-based organizations often assert, occurs block by block, intermingled with safe areas. Put another way, the fact that an area is urban does not mean a company should tie it to crime, just as an urban location does not mean an area is lower income. When an underwriter is familiar with a neighborhood, that person can work through stereotypes and learn how residents value where they live. "The first thing to do is bring people in—underwriters, insurance people—to see that the neighborhoods are diverse, and that they are safe, and that people take pride in ownership—that you can't paint it all with one brush," said Yvonne Sparks, NHS of St. Louis executive director. "The first thing is to raise people's awareness of the quality of the neighborhoods we work in" (Neighborhood Reinvestment Corporation 1995).
- *Agents' and companies' need to make a profit.* Agents work on commission. Companies need to write policies in an environment where reasonable losses can be absorbed, so that their products' pricing results in a profit justifiable to their stockholders or, for mutually owned companies, their policyholders. Selling property and casualty insurance in lower-income markets may well be the right thing to do, but it also needs to be profitable. By collaborating with community-based organizations, insurers may find, as did the lending industry, ways to reduce risk and cost.

At this stage, community groups and insurers are collaborating, crafting micro-solutions from city to city. Finding strategies for insuring lower-income communities that easily translate from city to city is the next step. As the industry gains experience, systemic solutions become more and more likely. The rest of this chapter gives concrete examples of the progress that is being made.

NATIONAL INSURANCE TASK FORCE

In 1994, Neighborhood Reinvestment convened a group of Neighbor-Works® executive directors and insurers in Washington, D.C., to discuss how the insurance industry could further explore residents' and business owners' insurance needs.

Since that time the National Insurance Task Force (NITF), as that group came to be called, has doubled in size, to 65 participants, consisting of representatives of insurance companies (including the nation's top 11 property and casualty companies), insurance trade associations, the National Association of Insurance Commissioners, the Illinois Department of Insurance, and five NeighborWorks® organizations: Neighborhood Housing Services of Chicago; of Los Angeles; of New York City; of Philadelphia; and of St. Louis.

In its mission statement, the NITF outlined as its goal the development of partnerships between the insurance industry and community-based organizations "to better market the products and services of both, for the benefit of the customers and communities they serve" (Neighborhood Reinvestment Corporation National Insurance Task Force [henceforth Neighborhood Reinvestment NITF] 1995b).

Models

By working with community-based organizations that have successful insurance-company partnerships and by understanding particular strategies to revitalize neighborhoods, the NITF helps insurance companies fit into those neighborhood-revitalization strategies. With an eye toward replicability, the task force examines which models would or would not work in different cities. Insurance companies, in turn, can refer to these models in shaping policy, insurance sales practices, and corporate perceptions.

Education

The task force repeatedly discussed the need to document and pass on knowledge of partnership-making that NeighborWorks® organizations and other community-based groups have accumulated. Therefore, the group produced an in-depth guide, entitled *Pathways to Partnership* (Neighborhood Reinvestment NITF 1995b), for use in starting and evaluating partnerships with insurance companies and in educating consumers.

In addition, the Illinois Department of Insurance Homeowner Task Force published an extensive educational manual for homebuyer-education instructors and for homeowners themselves (Illinois Department of Insurance 1995). The NITF recommends the manual as a good hands-on resource for helping consumers understand risk and loss issues and the need for property and casualty insurance. Community-based organizations generally report that consumers' lack of information about insurance is a common barrier that works to their disadvantage, particularly in terms of cost.

Research

Because the perception that lower-income communities pose greater risks for insurers often keeps consumers from getting insurance they can afford, the task force enlisted the assistance of the Insurance Research Council to identify actual causes of loss. Research was launched in eight cities—Chicago, St. Louis, New York, Los Angeles, New Orleans, Philadelphia, Milwaukee, and Detroit. Each of these has:

- A NeighborWorks® organization that is actively involved with insurance companies;
- Family income levels averaging 80 percent or less of the metropolitan area's median income;
- Insurers willing to allow a review of settled claims; and
- A diverse housing stock.

The research is intended to show the extent of losses in lower-income neighborhoods and reasons for the loss. This will help to point out mitigation strategies for neighborhood groups, families, and companies to reduce losses.

WHAT'S WORKING:
NEIGHBORHOOD PARTNERSHIP PLAN, PHILADELPHIA

Neighborhood Partnership Plan (NPP)—linking Philadelphia NHS, an established neighborhood council, with Allstate Insurance Company—is an example of a successful alliance that began amid considerable skepticism. Yet it has brought to Philadelphia's Fern Rock-Ogontz-Belfield neighborhood changes in the market and altered perceptions. The process that formed the partnership is worth examining as a model.

In 1994, Allstate approached Philadelphia NHS with a plan to create a partnership to address neighborhood insurance issues. After Philadelphia NHS had gauged neighborhood interest in working with

Allstate to overcome obstacles and open a market, the NHS helped form focus groups consisting of company representatives and members of a neighborhood council. The focus groups met weekly for several months in sessions that were sometimes strained but improved in tenor and productivity over time. Residents cross-examined Allstate, and Allstate too asked questions. The two parties walked neighborhood streets together.

In a sea change from previous thinking, residents came to believe that Allstate did have a genuine interest in the neighborhood. Allstate, in turn, used relationships it had with city government to push for better police services and supported a police-sponsored athletic and tutoring program for the neighborhood. Philadelphia NHS was both a participant and an intermediary, acting as a market consultant while simultaneously shaping new NHS programs to help reduce risk.

A wealth of issues came to the table as the sessions progressed. After recognizing through the focus groups the extent to which the company's typical underwriting was limiting its neighborhood business, Allstate modified its underwriting guidelines in the following major respects:

- It changed its policy of not insuring properties valued at less than $40,000.
- It agreed to insure buildings older than those covered in Allstate's traditional underwriting.
- It changed its policy of not insuring buildings with flat roofs because of potential for water damage—a central component in the Neighborhood Partnership Plan, since many of the neighborhood's structures do have flat roofs. Residents participating in the NPP can get a water-damage rider on their policies. In conjunction with this change, Allstate began offering home-maintenance seminars.
- It changed to a block-focused approach to underwriting. This means that owners who live on a block with no vacant buildings will not be penalized because of other nearby blocks that have abandoned structures.
- It began to take into account factors that might indicate that the homeowner was a better risk than indicated by typical underwriting criteria. These included issues such as whether a homeowner acquired a property with a community-based organization's help and/or with homebuyer education.

At the end of a specified 15-month period, policyholders in the NPP area are given a dividend if they qualify as a group based on a level of loss experience predetermined as acceptable. In addition, free home inspections by Allstate are now offered under the Philadelphia NPP—not to determine whether to cover a property but to show owners what the hazards are and how to fix them. Although residents were reluctant at first to open their homes in order to get coverage, they changed their views and came to see the inspections as a service. Through the plan, residents can also get a screened list of local vendors who can make repairs.

As a way to tackle the difficult problem of building abandonment, the NPP helps neighborhood groups track down owners of abandoned buildings. In addition, Allstate considers insuring properties on a case-by-case basis, establishing the principle of not denying coverage of an individual house or block simply because it is near abandoned structures. If the company does an inspection and finds particular vacant properties to be safe from fire and other hazards, neighbors may still get coverage under the NPP. Allstate has written approximately 300 insurance policies in the neighborhood, with less than 1 percent of those policies coming back with claims in the NPP's first six months.

Through Philadelphia NHS, Allstate became connected to the neighborhood and began to build a market. The company sees Philadelphia as the first of 20 cities in which it hopes to attempt a similar process—revised to include locally determined components—by collaborating with community-based organizations.

WHAT'S WORKING: ST. LOUIS NHS

In 1994, NHS of St. Louis brought together its four insurance-company partners as well as neighborhood residents and the Missouri Insurance Coalition. They agreed to form the NHS/St. Louis Insurance Services Committee, with a mission of responding to insurance-availability concerns in St. Louis. The NHS/St. Louis venture, known as the Missouri Insurance Initiative—Voluntary All Industry Partnership, now involves 22 insurance organizations as partners.

This partnership is a local response to the nationally pervasive problems of too few agents in the city; inadequate or lapsed policies among homeowners, particularly elderly residents; and a general lack of knowledge about insurance. In attempting to alleviate these and other insurance problems, the Missouri Insurance Initiative launched a variety of special efforts:

- Recruitment and training of people of color for insurance careers:
- Scholarships and internships for minorities, offered through the Missouri Insurance Education Foundation, to expose them to insurance career opportunities;
- A Community Information Center and a statewide hotline for insurance problem-solving;
- A referral network of agents willing to write policies throughout the communities; and
- An inspection program for residents to learn how to qualify for or save on insurance by reducing potential property risks.

Writing in the *St. Louis Post-Dispatch*, St. Louis NHS Executive Director Yvonne Sparks (1995), a former Allstate insurance agent and a 20-year community activist, said:

> Everyone, including the insurance industry, acknowledges that widespread discrimination existed in the past. Problems of availability, affordability, product design and customer service continue. And yes, there are still problems with the lack of diversity in the industry and its difficulty in adapting to the changing composition of its markets. . . .[But] through [the initiative's] outreach, we have found the insurance industry receptive to joint problem-solving and responsive to the needs of the community. (p. 7b)

Sparks furthermore said that if the industry is to preserve its voluntary market, it must work to meet its obligations to all applicants and customers for equitable treatment, fair prices, and professional customer service. NHS of St. Louis reviews 300–400 homeowners insurance policies a year, she said.

The numbers of people the Missouri Insurance Initiative was able to reach in its 1994–95 year—as shown here—indicate that the program is working but that success is slow and incremental:

- 1,082 individuals assisted through group presentations, referrals, and problem-solving efforts
- 19 community and trade organizations or events involved
- 13 policies converted
- 15 policies upgraded

As part of its statewide strategy, the Missouri Insurance Initiative is now taking its work to Kansas City, St. Joseph, and Springfield, through NeighborWorks® programs in those cities.

WHAT'S WORKING: CHICAGO'S RESILIENT PARTNERSHIP

Since its founding in 1975, NHS of Chicago has maintained long and productive partnerships that have set the standard for community-based organizations' interactions with the insurance industry. In 1979, NHS of Chicago initiated the first insurance partnership in what is now the NeighborWorks® network. These alliances have been continually fostered by insurers' personal involvement in all phases of NHS's work in Chicago.

In addition to pursuing, with NHS, nearly two decades of policy discussions on accessibility, affordability, and other issues, insurers have made strong links to the revitalization of Chicago neighborhoods by funding several major initiatives, including the following:

- Creation of the NHS Redevelopment Corporation, a real-estate development entity that builds new homes and rehabilitates multifamily housing. By improving multifamily buildings in largely single-family neighborhoods, the livability and insurability of these neighborhoods is greatly improved;
- Expansion into West Humboldt Park and creation of the West Humboldt NHS; and
- Establishing the NHS of Chicago Revolving Loan Fund, to enable more families to borrow affordably for the often minor repairs that can make homes insurable.

In 1993, the state's chief insurance regulators asked NHS of Chicago to organize an event for insurance companies that were doing little or no business in the city's lower-income neighborhoods. The state-sponsored conference and neighborhood bus tour that resulted was a catalyst in expanding the NHS insurance services committee. Accessibility and education committees generated the first-ever survey of neighborhood agents; focus groups of consumers were formed; and community-based organizations became involved in insurance training.

"Overall, the partnership really built on something that existed, but created a lot more variation in the number of other companies involved," said NHS of Chicago Executive Director Bruce Gottschall (Neighborhood Reinvestment NITF 1995a). "We're continuing to work to involve companies, because the competition in having companies look at how to best service markets from our point of view is a very positive effort, and one that we're seeking to encourage."

In the course of its history NHS of Chicago has built or rehabilitated 17,000 housing units and has generated direct reinvestment of $133.5 million into communities. Its insurance partnerships are an important component of NHS's neighborhood revitalization strategies.

WHAT'S WORKING: INNER CITY UNDERWRITERS

Inner City Underwriters (ICU) was founded in Chicago in 1994, with insurance companies' assistance, to help connect independent agents with insurers. By contracting with ICU, large insurance companies gain access to markets in urban neighborhoods that these insurers normally would consider too small to serve except through community-based independent agents, according to ICU Executive Director Matt Cooper (Neighborhood Reinvestment NITF 1995a). ICU has special contracts with Kemper, Aetna, ITT Hartford, Chubb and Son, and St. Paul Companies that allow ICU to work with independent agents who, owing to their relatively small volume of business, would be unable to independently contract to work directly with large companies.

The organization provides needed training for agents already working in urban neighborhoods. "Because they have not had access to the standard markets, and because they are not in the mainstream of our industry," Cooper said, "they lack the training and development to properly serve that marketplace" (Neighborhood Reinvestment NITF 1995a). ICU's educational programs therefore become a means not only of improving customers' service and of opening career paths for agents serving urban areas but also of supporting neighborhood-based businesses.

On a more general level, the organization works to control losses, which it interprets also to mean controlling costs. Cooper asserts that inner-city claims are inflated in part because neighborhood-based construction contractors lack expertise. To try to address this problem, ICU has a construction-management service that certifies local contractors and does estimates and inspections—activities that, in turn, promote locally based business.

By training agents, operating its own community-based businesses, and working to control losses, Inner City Underwriters is concerning itself with top-priority insurance issues: the affordability of insurance and availability of agents in urban areas.

WHAT'S WORKING: NHS OF NEW YORK CITY

NHS of New York City is notable for its leadership in changing corporate perceptions of urban neighborhoods. As part of this mission, NHS of New York City formed an insurance committee that meets monthly. Through this committee, NHS has given insurers a continuing and dependable venue for discussing NHS strategy and a steady impetus to recruit other insurers in neighborhood activities.

A central goal of the committee and of NHS is to reduce the proportion of residents who are dependent on the state's FAIR Plan. FAIR (Fair Access to Insurance Requirements) is a federal initiative launched in 1968 to create state-level, industry-operated insurance pools that make property insurance more accessible to those who have trouble obtaining it in the voluntary market because of abnormal exposure to risks over which they have no control. The National Association of Insurance Commissioners recently estimated that 42.7 percent of policies applying to low-income neighborhoods are in the state FAIR Plans. Typically, FAIR Plans are more expensive than private insurance, and their coverage is not as broad. Public and nonprofit organizations across the country are working, as is NHS of New York City, to reduce homeowners' reliance on FAIR Plans. Because of insurers' financial help, NHS of New York City has an insurance coordinator who is responsible for finding voluntary market insurance for city residents to replace their FAIR Plan policies. This service is not restricted to NHS customers. In its first year of operation, the insurance-assistance program of NHS of New York City helped package and secure insurance policies totaling $3.5 million in dwelling unit value.

NHS of New York City uses bus tours regularly as a way to educate insurance underwriters and executives and break stereotypes. The tour gives insurance representatives a chance to see physical improvements in urban neighborhoods, visit residents in their homes, and hear firsthand about challenges families face daily. Dramatic changes in attitude often occur as a direct result of the tour. In one case, for example, representatives from State Farm Insurance Companies, Aetna, Metlife, and the state superintendent's office volunteered at their tour's end to serve on the NHS insurance committee. One company responded to tour participation by its executives with a $45,000 grant and an in-kind contribution of equipment.

"By working with us, the insurers have learned how to make inroads into a market that is profitable but that requires them to think differently about marketing their products and services than they do in, say, Muncie, Indiana," said NHS of New York City Executive Director Francine Justa (Smith 1995).

STATE-BASED MODEL: URGING COMPETITION THROUGH REGULATION

In its 20-year effort to develop a "competitive urban insurance market and knowledgeable consumers," the state of Illinois has enacted an antidiscrimination statute, required companies to report policy data, and promoted consumers' use of smaller-scale insurers opposite the industry giant. In Illinois, the Department's Urban Insurance Issues Task Force also recently recommended that the state's FAIR Plan offer comprehensive coverage, with the same products as insurance companies offer. These changes were made, emphasized Illinois Department of Insurance Director Mark Boozell, not to increase FAIR's reach (which would be contrary to the nationwide trend) but to serve the 1.8 percent of homeowners who currently buy FAIR Plan insurance (Boozell 1995).

In another strategy to urge competition, the Illinois task force did a market study indicating that the vast majority of Chicago homeowners buy property insurance from State Farm and Allstate. Although many other companies sell insurance in Chicago, none of them held more than a 2 percent market share, whereas Allstate and State Farm had a 60 percent combined share. The study found that consumers considered the other, less-visible companies inferior. The task force recommended insurance education programs in order to show that this is not necessarily the case.

RECOGNIZING MUTUAL SELF-INTEREST

At a press conference to offer the NITF's *Pathways to Partnership* guide to the public, Philadelphia NHS Executive Director Ceane Rabada reflected on the beginnings of the task force: "I recall lots of early discussion with other task force members about how we were different: nonprofit versus profit; community-based organization versus regional and frequently national corporations; business versus social agendas. Then it hit us. We are more alike than different [in seeking to make neighborhoods safe and to encourage reinvestment]" (Neighborhood Reinvestment NITF 1995a). Recognition of that mutual self-interest is the glue that cements many partnerships between insurance companies and community-based organizations, including Neighbor-Works® organizations. The frequency with which these self-interests coincide is striking.

If both sides exchange information honestly, community-based groups can come to acknowledge that agents are entrepreneurs, that insurance companies are businesses, and that it is acceptable for them to operate as such. Insurers seek a business environment where:

- The pricing of their products can result in a profit;
- Reasonable losses are the norm;
- Neighborhoods are healthy and safe and buildings are well-maintained;
- Residents, businesses, and nonprofits support loss-reduction activities, such as upgrading of property through special lending, rehabilitation consulting, homeownership development, home-maintenance education, and public-safety programs.

These points, of course, reflect the same goals that community-based organizations and their constituents seek: vibrant, safe, and well-maintained neighborhoods, good for businesses and residents alike. As in Philadelphia, ongoing face-to-face meetings in neighborhoods—on sidewalks and streets, and in living rooms—can be the stuff of change, on both sides of the fence.

LOSS-PREVENTION STRATEGIES

Apart from the litigation activity of many fair housing groups, community-based organizations have sought out working partnerships with insurers. And, of necessity, community organizations have used insurers' financial assistance as operating funds.

"The standpoint of community-based organizations has been problem-solving," said Allen Fishbein, of the Center for Community Change (Fishbein interview, November 16, 1995). "The [community-based organization] idea is, 'Let's get all of the actors in a room and figure out how we address those problems.' It's very pragmatic."

Perhaps because of regulatory pressures, or because of long-term reality-based exposure to communities through neighborhood partnerships, community-based organizations have led the insurance

sector in challenging decades-old assumptions. Loss prevention
strategies are a first step toward educating the institutions, and possibly changing them. How aggressively some companies want to explore urban, minority, or low- to moderate-income markets varies. And
the number of major insurance companies with special urban strategies is still relatively small.

Common barriers that block reinvestment are building abandonment; older buildings that are deteriorated or in need of rehabilitation;
crime; arson; and lack of information and/or education. As part of
problem-solving efforts, some insurance companies have joined with
community-based organizations to engage in strategic loss prevention.
Specific tactics include the following:

- *Organizing data to increase access.* The American Insurance Association, the Texas Association of Independent Insurance Agents,
  community groups, insurers, and the Texas Department of Insurance have formed a partnership to bring agents into inner-city areas
  and to expand the number of insurance products available to urban
  consumers. The resulting organization—the Urban Insurance Partnership—has developed a database of existing independent insurance agencies that serve Houston's predominantly minority areas.
  Standard property-casualty insurance companies can use information from the database to contact agencies that can offer standard
  insurance products to urban consumers. Individuals who, through
  these agencies, get access to property and casualty insurance as
  part of the home-purchase process will, as homeowners, have a
  strong interest in preventing loss or damage to their property.
- *Insurance-career training for people of color.* The Atlanta Urban
  League and the American Insurance Association collaborated, with
  broad industry support, to create an "agent–insurance partnership." The program's goal is to make insurance accessible by re-
  cruiting, training, and supporting minority insurance agents in
  Atlanta. NHS of St. Louis has a similar training program.
- *Promoting homeownership.* Homeownership in many neighborhoods is a unifying force for residents, creating stakeholders and
  maintaining a sense of permanence. The stability of many older
  neighborhoods, however, is weakening as patterns of homeownership disappear. Strategies to promote homeownership are key aspects in preserving a unifying force in neighborhoods and, in insurance terms, in reducing loss. The NeighborWorks® Campaign
  for Home Ownership, a five-year effort to help 10,000 lower-income
  people in cities across the country buy homes, constitutes far-

reaching loss reduction. Allstate and State Farm were among the original national partners in the Campaign; USAA Insurance is a new partner.

- *Creating capital for neighborhood lending, property rehabilitation, and homeownership.* Older neighborhoods generally need lending products that encourage people to buy and improve homes, thereby creating momentum for investment there. For insurers, the availability of capital is directly tied to a neighborhood's stability and to its growth as a market. In late 1995, for example, USAA committed a $7 million investment to NeighborWorks'® lending efforts in Baltimore, Fort Worth, Houston, the Colorado Springs area, the Tampa area, Sacramento, and San Antonio. The investment was arranged in concert with Neighborhood Housing Services of America, which operates a secondary market to replenish and extend the lending resources of NeighborWorks® organizations.
- *Maintenance and maintenance education.* Many community-based programs do hands-on training of basic skills, such as how to use hand tools or how to do repairs to prevent a house from aging prematurely or deteriorating. It is crucial for residents to have these skills in order to keep properties safe, to reduce accidents and property losses, and to strengthen confidence in neighborhoods. The NHSs of Jamaica and Bedford-Stuyvesant, both in New York, run extensive hands-on maintenance-training programs.
- *Fire-safety programs.* Fire is a serious, pervasive threat to residents of many low-income neighborhoods. The Southern California NHS/ Insurance Industry Full Partnership is a consortium of insurance companies that works with six NHS offices to rehabilitate affordable housing. The partnership has devoted substantial energy to fire prevention and education. Said Los Angeles NHS Executive Director Lori Gay: "Los Angeles firefighters and homeowners came together in 1994 and have reduced the number of fires in our city by 50 percent." Similarly, the Northern California NeighborWorks® Network Insurance Partnership is a collaboration of five network organizations and six insurers that do business in the region. Over a four-year period, insurance-company employees and fire departments visited more than 1,000 homes in lower-income neighborhoods to encourage physical changes in structures, to make them more insurable. To this end, volunteers installed smoke detectors.
- *Community organizing, volunteerism.* Many community-based organizations are effectively using volunteer events to break down stereotypical barriers and misperceptions. Since 1990, Sacramento NHS has organized Fire Safety Days, during which a number of

insurers join with representatives of the state insurance department, NHS, and the building, fire, and police departments to perform a variety of insurance-related tasks. They walk through homes, do free safety inspections, provide smoke detectors and batteries, assess fire hazards in homes, and recommend ways to eliminate those hazards. These one-day events serve to highlight need and have been an organizing tool replicated by other community groups. Four other northern California NeighborWorks® organizations joined with Sacramento NHS in a formal insurance partnership with two insurers. One-day painting or repair events are other means of demonstrating to insurers that neighborhood pride does exist, alongside ongoing revitalization, and that urban communities are not necessarily hopeless or depressed. While visiting the St. Louis NHS prior to its annual Block-Aid event, for example, a SAFECO Insurance claims adjustor overheard staff talking of the need for money to replace six roofs. On the morning of Block-Aid, SAFECO presented the NHS with funds to replace the roofs. These sorts of interactions also create an environment where residents learn about safety conditions and what can be insured.

- *Public-safety awareness.* In Seattle, the Washington Insurance Council, a nonprofit industry trade association, approached both the city of Seattle and the Jackson Place Community Council with a plan to do a public-safety program in a distressed neighborhood. The resulting Seattle Neighborhood Action Plan has since developed a traffic plan, improved street lighting, designed a mixed-use development, provided smoke alarms and security kits for homes and businesses, conducted a door-to-door survey, and helped the neighborhood's many family businesses install shatterproof glass and remove existing bars from windows. The group also organized to work with a community policing team to close a "crack house" and arrest alleged prostitutes.

CONCLUSION

Neighborhood revitalization is hard work. Gaining access to property and casualty insurance, as a component of revitalization, is equally difficult. Solutions play out on a scale that measures house by house, block by block.

In 1994, a study by the National Association of Insurance Commissioners concluded that the unavailability of insurance products and higher insurance prices "may be driven, at least in part, by incorrect assumptions about the risk characteristics" of neighborhoods. Findings such as these have contributed to the organizing of regulatory and law-enforcement initiatives that have helped give visibility to communities' insurance needs. Neighborhood Reinvestment and the NeighborWorks® network have for years been one grassroots approach to meeting those needs. It is an approach that evolved from constructive dialogue with insurance companies, in the days when the NeighborWorks® model itself was forming.

Scores of questions remain unanswered, preventing us from putting good solutions to work more quickly. A fundamental problem is the need for a competent individual on the ground—the insurance-services coordinator who works for the nonprofit, who understands the limitations and opportunities at hand, who is skilled at bringing partners together, and who is not only neutral but perceived as such. The trick for community-based organizations and insurers is to walk the streets not just with a bullhorn but with a program. Informed advocacy, through partnerships, is changing perceptions, breaking down stereotypes incrementally, and renewing neighborhoods, insurance markets, and families who live and work there.

References

Boozell, Mark. 1995. "Heating Up the Urban Insurance Market." *Stone Soup* (published by Neighborhood Reinvestment Corp.) 13(4, Summer): 3.

Illinois Department of Insurance. 1995. *Homeowners Insurance for Home-Purchase Counselors and Homeowners*. Springfield, Ill.: Author, May.

National Association of Insurance Commissioners. 1994. *NAIC's Urban Insurance Study*. Kansas City, Mo.: Author.

Neighborhood Reinvestment Corporation. 1995. "Forum on Insurance, Community Lending Institute." Transcript of proceedings. Washington, D.C.: Author, March 6.

Neighborhood Reinvestment Corporation National Insurance Task Force. 1995a. "Insurers and Low-Income Communities, Workshop IV." Transcript of conference. Washington, D.C.: Neighborhood Reinvestment Corp., October 20.

_____. 1995b. *Pathways to Partnership*. Washington, D.C.: Neighborhood Reinvestment Corp.

Neighborhood Reinvestment NITF. See Neighborhood Reinvestment Corporation National Insurance Task Force.

Smith, Catherine A. 1995. "Addressing Issues with New Vigor." *Stone Soup* (published by Neighborhood Reinvestment Corp.) 13(4, Summer): 6–8.

Sparks, Yvonne. 1995. "A Partnership for Insurance Solutions." *St. Louis Post-Dispatch,* June 23: 7B.

Gregory D. Squires

MODEL REGULATION CLARIFYING APPLICATION OF THE FEDERAL FAIR HOUSING ACT TO HOMEOWNERS INSURANCE

Government regulations are often promulgated to clarify the meaning of a statute and how it is to be enforced. Frequently such regulations can eliminate or reduce costly litigation among parties who disagree with, or simply do not like, the intent of the statute. In the case of the Federal Fair Housing Act as it relates to insurance, a regulation could reinforce the interpretation of the act by most courts and federal law enforcement authorities that it applies to property insurance. A regulation could also clarify what specific practices are covered and how the appropriate authorities (in this case, principally the Department of Housing and Urban Development [HUD] but also the Department of Justice) would enforce the statute. The following is a proposed draft of a regulation that HUD could promulgate to further these objectives.

Title??—Housing and Urban Development
Chapter ?—Office of the Assistant Secretary
for Fair Housing and Equal Opportunity
Department of Housing and Urban Development
Subchapter ?—Fair Housing
[?? CFR Part ???]

[Docket No. _____]
Fair Housing—Prohibitions Against Discrimination

SUBPART ?—Property Insurance Activities

Agency: U.S. Department of Housing and Urban Development

Action: Proposed Regulation

Background and Justification for Regulation

Discrimination in the provision of property insurance based on race, color, religion, sex, handicap, familial status, or national origin violates Title VIII of the Civil Rights Act of 1968, as amended by the Fair Housing Amendments Act of 1988 (the Federal Fair Housing Act, hereafter referred to as "the Act"). The U.S. Department of Housing and Urban Development (HUD) is the federal agency charged with primary responsibility for administering and enforcing this law. The purpose of this regulation is to provide more detailed guidance on the specific practices that violate the Act and the circumstances under which a violation exists.

The Act, current regulations, and case law require HUD to investigate and adjudicate matters pertaining to discrimination in the provision of property insurance. Under the Act it is unlawful to:

. . . refuse to sell or rent after the making of a bona fide offer, or to refuse to negotiate for the sale or rental of, or otherwise make unavailable or deny, a dwelling to any person because of race, color, religion, sex, handicap, familial status, or national origin. (42 U.S.C. Section 804 [a])

It is also a violation of the Act to:

. . . discriminate against any person in the terms, conditions, or privileges of sale or rental of a dwelling, or in the provision of services or facilities in connection therewith because of race, color, religion, sex, handicap, familial status, or national origin. (42 U.S.C. Section 804 [b])

In addition, under the Act:

It shall be unlawful for any person or other entity whose business includes engaging in residential real estate-related transactions to discriminate against any person because of race, color, religion, sex, handicap, familial status, or national origin.
. . . 'residential real estate-related transactions' means any of the following:
(1) The making or purchasing of loans or providing other financial assistance

(a) For purchasing, constructing, improving, repairing or maintaining a dwelling; . . . (42 U.S.C. Section 805)

Because property insurance is required to secure a mortgage loan, which is generally required to purchase a dwelling, denying insurance due to membership in a protected class effectively makes housing unavailable in violation of Section 804(a). Similarly, because insurance is a service clearly connected with purchasing a dwelling, discrimination in the provision of this service due to membership in a protected class violates Section 804 (b). Property insurance is also required to maintain a dwelling, and, therefore, to enjoy the full benefits and privileges of homeownership. Therefore, discrimination in the provision of property insurance constitutes discrimination in residential real estate-related transactions in violation of Section 805.

HUD, in its capacity as the nation's chief fair housing law enforcer, has promulgated regulations defining as prohibited conduct "Refusing to provide municipal services or property or hazard insurance for dwellings or providing such services or insurance differently because of race, color, religion, sex, handicap, familial status, or national origin" (24 C.F.R. Section 100.70 [d][4]).

Case precedents such as *Dunn v. Midwestern Indemnity Mid-American Fire & Casualty Co.* (472 F. Supp. 1106 [S.D. Ohio 1979]) and *McDiarmid v. Economy Fire & Casualty Co.* (604 F. Supp. 105 [S.D. Ohio 1984]) established the applicability of the Fair Housing Act to discriminatory insurance practices. More recent precedents (*N.A.A.C.P. v. American Family Mutual Insurance Co.*, 978 F. 2d 287 [7th Cir. 1992], *cert. denied*, 113 S. Ct. 2335 [1993]; *Strange v. Nationwide Mutual Insurance Co.*, No. 93-6586 [E.D. Pa. 9-22-94]; and *Nationwide Mutual Insurance Co. v. Cisneros*, No. 94-3296 [6th Cir. May 1, 1995], *cert. denied*, 116 S. Ct. 973 [1996]) have reaffirmed this principle, according deference to HUD's substantive regulation promulgated in 1989 under standards established in *Chevron U.S.A., Inc. v. Natural Resources Defense Council* (467 U.S. 837 [1984]). But see *Mackey v. Nationwide Insurance Co.* (724 F. 2d 419 [4th Cir. 1984]). While the Fourth Circuit held to the contrary, that decision was rendered prior to the Department's regulation stating that insurance is covered by the Act. The Seventh Circuit in the 1992 *American Family* case, in finding that insurance is covered, found the reasoning of the 1984 *Mackey v. Nationwide* decision unpersuasive, stating that "events have bypassed *Mackey*" and found the regulations to be controlling, based upon the Department's statutory authority to issue them and the weight such regulations are accorded.

The primary purpose of this regulation is to clarify the Federal Fair Housing Act as it applies to property insurance. Providing insurance is a complex undertaking. No rule can anticipate every situation, changes in the marketplace, and potential disputes. Specific cases will be dealt with on a case-by-case basis with the totality of the factual circumstances examined serving as the basis for any Departmental decision.

The principles articulated in this regulation, however, will inform insurers and others on what is permitted and prohibited, and will guide HUD as it carries out its responsibilities under the Act.

Authority

This regulation is issued under the authority of the Secretary of Housing and Urban Development to administer and enforce Title VIII of the Civil Rights

Act of 1968, as amended by the Fair
Housing Amendments Act of 1988 (the
Fair Housing Act).

Scope

It is the policy of the United States to
provide, within constitutional limitations, for fair housing throughout the
United States. No person shall be sub-
jected to discrimination because of
race, color, religion, sex, handicap,
familial status, or national origin, or
because of the representation of members of these protected classes within a
neighborhood (e.g., the racial composition of an area), in the provision of
property or hazard insurance for dwellings. "Provision" includes the availability of insurance, terms and conditions under which insurance is
available, and services associated with
property insurance. These rules apply
to all insurance companies, brokers,
agents, insurance services of other financial institutions, rating organizations, regulatory agencies, and other
entities engaged in the sale, marketing, or distribution of insurance and
insurance-related services.

Exemptions

This part does not limit the applicability of any reasonable state law or regulation pertaining to discrimination,
unfair trade practices, redlining, or related matter. It does not require any
sales, pricing, marketing, or any other
practice related to the provision of insurance or insurance-related services
that would conflict with current requirements of state insurance laws or
unfair trade practices acts. It would not
require any such practice inconsistent
with sound actuarial and underwriting
principles, including, but not limited
to, the requirement that prices not be

excessive, inadequate, or unfairly
discriminatory.

Discriminatory Practices

It shall be unlawful to:

(1) Refuse to sell insurance, cancel, or
nonrenew an insurance policy, or in
any way refuse to provide or make unavailable insurance or insurance-
related services because of race, color,
religion, sex, handicap, familial status,
or national origin (this prohibition also
applies to the race, color, religion, sex,
handicap, familial status, or national
origin of other residents in the area—
e.g., the racial composition of a
community);

(2) Vary the terms or conditions (e.g.,
premium, coverage, type of policy, ex-
clusions, terms of payment, deductible
requirements, application procedures)
under which an insurance policy or
insurance-related service is available
because of race, color, religion, sex,
handicap, familial status, or national
origin (this prohibition also applies to
the race, color, religion, sex, handicap,
familial status, or national origin of
other residents in the area—e.g., the
racial composition of a community);

(3) Establish different qualifications,
requirements, or standards (e.g., income, credit rating, inspections) for
making insurance or insurance-related
services available because of race,
color, religion, sex, handicap, familial
status, or national origin (this prohibition also applies to the race, color,
religion, sex, handicap, familial status,
or national origin of other residents in
the area—e.g., the racial composition
of a community);

(4) Offer different services, facilities,
or privileges (e.g., advice and counseling, claims processing, access to
agents) in the provision of insurance or

insurance-related services because of race, color, religion, sex, handicap, familial status, or national origin (this prohibition also applies to the race, color, religion, sex, handicap, familial status, or national origin of other residents in the area—e.g., the racial composition of a community);

(5) Utilize different sales and marketing practices (e.g., underwriting and pricing guidelines, advertising, appointment and location of agents) because of race, color, religion, sex, handicap, familial status, or national origin (this prohibition also applies to the race, color, religion, sex, handicap, familial status, or national origin of other residents in the area—e.g., the racial composition of a community); or

(6) Otherwise make insurance or insurance-related services unavailable or to make them available on different terms or conditions because of race, color, religion, sex, handicap, familial status, or national origin (this prohibition also applies to the race, color, religion, sex, handicap, familial status, or national origin of other residents in the area—e.g., the racial composition of a community).

Standards of Discrimination

A variety of underwriting, inspection, marketing, agent assignment, claims processing, and other practices are prohibited under the Act. Violations may occur due to overt discrimination where an insurer or provider of an insurance-related service openly discriminates against an individual because he or she is a member of a protected group. Violations may occur due to disparate treatment when an insurer or provider of an insurance-related service treats people differently because those people are members of a protected class. Violations may also occur due to disparate impact when an insurer or provider of an insurance-related service uses a particular practice that causes a disparate impact on the basis of race, color, religion, sex, handicap, familial status, or national origin and either:

(1) The respondent fails to demonstrate that the challenged practice is related to the risk of loss and constitutes a business necessity (which generally must be established with statistical or other empirical evidence; subjective judgment, experience, or speculation are generally insufficient); or

(2) A less-discriminatory alternative that would serve the business purpose is available and the respondent refuses to adopt such an alternative.

The industry practices listed above are meant to be illustrative, but not exhaustive, of the kinds of practices that are prohibited. The commission of one incident of a particular practice does not, in and of itself, necessarily constitute a violation of the Fair Housing Act. A violation may result from one practice or from a combination of individual or repeated occurrences of a collection of the above-cited or related practices. Each case will be addressed on a case-by-case basis with the totality of fact patterns determining whether or not a violation of the Act has occurred.

In addition, the determination that a particular practice is prohibited does not require that the practice in question was the sole reason for the action taken. If an action was taken in part because of a prohibited practice, that can be sufficient to find a violation of the Fair Housing Act. For example, if an insurer denies a policy in part because of the racial composition of a neighborhood, that denial would constitute a violation of the Fair Housing Act even if other nonprohibited practices and considerations entered into the decision.

Nothing in these rules should be interpreted as restricting affirmative efforts to eliminate unlawful discrimination or the discriminatory effects of historical and contemporary practices. Such affirmative efforts may include placing agents in minority neighborhoods underserved by the industry, incentives to agents to increase their business in underserved areas, revision of underwriting standards to increase the availability of insurance, advertisements directed to minority audiences, affirmative action to increase the number of minority agents, and related steps.

ABOUT THE EDITOR

Gregory D. Squires is professor of sociology and a member of the Urban Studies Programs faculty at the University of Wisconsin-Milwaukee. For the past two years he served as a consultant to HUD on policy issues related to discrimination by financial institutions. Prior to joining the university in 1984 he spent seven years as a research analyst with the U.S. Commission on Civil Rights. Currently he is a member of the Consumer Advisory Council of the Federal Reserve Board and the Advisory Board for the Metropolitan Milwaukee Fair Housing Council. His recent publications include *Capital and Communities in Black and White* (SUNY Press, 1994) and *From Redlining to Reinvestment*, an edited collection (Temple University Press, 1992).

Tom Baker is associate professor at the University of Miami School of Law, where he teaches insurance, contracts, and health law. His research focuses on the social and cultural context of insurance institutions. His most recent article, "On the Genealogy of Moral Hazard," will appear in volume 75 of the *Texas Law Review*. Before becoming a law professor, he practiced law with the firm of Covington & Burling in Washington, D.C., where he specialized in complex insurance coverage litigation.

Cathy Cloud is deputy director of the National Fair Housing Alliance with primary responsibility for national investigations of discrimination in the housing industry. She coordinated NFHA's eight-city mortgage lending testing project and nine-city homeowners insurance testing project. She has served as a member of the Consumer Advisory Council of the Federal Reserve Board and has co-authored articles on mortgage lending discrimination.

Stephen M. Dane practices law in the areas of fair housing, mortgage lending and insurance discrimination, and employment discrimination. He is a nationally recognized expert in the mortgage lending and insurance discrimination fields, and has litigated a number of significant lending and insurance discrimination cases. Mr. Dane has testified before both houses of Congress on financial discrimination issues, and has authored many articles and training manuals relating to these fields.

Robert W. Klein is visiting associate professor and director of the Center for Risk Management and Insurance Research in the Department of Risk Management and Insurance at Georgia State University. From 1988 to 1996 he was the director of research and chief economist for the National Association of Insurance Commissioners. He has pub-

lished numerous monographs and articles on insurance and its regulation, including urban insurance problems.

George Knight is executive director of the Neighborhood Reinvestment Corporation, a public, nonprofit organization chartered by Congress in 1978 to renew distressed communities by creating and
strengthening resident-led, public-private partnerships. Prior to joining Neighborhood Reinvestment as a field service officer, he worked
as a real estate consultant for Booz, Allen & Hamilton, Inc. in Washington, D.C. He is a contributor to *Housing America: Mobilizing Bankers, Builders and Communities to Solve the Nation's Affordable Housing Crisis*, edited by Jess Lederman (Probus Publishing Co., 1993).

William H. Lynch is a Milwaukee attorney in private practice spe-
cializing in employment, housing, desegregation, and other civil
rights and discrimination cases. He was lead counsel for the plaintiffs
in *NAACP et al. v. American Family Mutual Insurance Company*,
which was resolved in 1995 by a $16.5 million settlement requiring
significant and extensive changes to increase homeowner insurance
sales in Milwaukee's African-American neighborhoods.

Karen McElrath is a lecturer in the Department of Sociology and
Social Policy, Queen's University, Belfast. Prior to this appointment,
she was an associate professor at the University of Miami. Her research interests include illicit drug use and race/ethnicity and the
legal system.

D.J. Powers is counsel for the Center for Economic Justice in Austin,
Texas, and litigates and consults on insurance redlining issues. He is
a former general counsel for the Texas Department of Insurance and
has authored numerous administrative rules prohibiting the use of
unfair underwriting guidelines. He has written extensively on insurance redlining, including "Barriers to Homeowners Insurance Availability for Minority and Low Income Consumers," prepared for the
U.S. Department of Housing and Urban Development.

Richard J. Ritter is a private consultant and litigator on fair lending
and property insurance discrimination cases. He was a trial lawyer
in the Civil Rights Division of the U.S. Department of Justice for over
twenty years. He has written and lectured about the Justice Depart-

ment's lending discrimination and insurance redlining cases, with recent articles published in *Mortgage Lending, Racial Discrimination, and Federal Policy*, edited by John Goering and Ron Wienk (Urban Institute Press, 1996) and *Mortgage Banking* magazine.

Jay D. Schultz is an economist and former staff member of the Missouri Department of Insurance. In addition to several research monographs he prepared for the Department, recent publications include "An Analysis of Agent Location and Homeowners Insurance Availability," *Journal of Insurance Regulation* (1995). His research interests are in the areas of insurance underwriting and marketing.

Shanna L. Smith is the executive director of the National Fair Housing Alliance (NFHA) and was a founding member. Prior to establishing NFHA's office, she was the executive director of the Toledo Fair Housing Center for 15 years and was one of the pioneers of lending and homeowners insurance litigation and testing. She is the author of numerous articles on fair lending and fair housing and has been an expert witness in fair housing cases.